Henry George

Susan B. Anthony

Jas. A. McN. Whistler

Peter Cartwright

Lord Timothy Dexter

Edmund Fanning

John Ledyard

Red Jacket

H. R. Helper

George Francis Train

Edwin Forrest

UNCOMMON AMERICANS

Joseph Smith

UNCOMMON AMERICANS

*Pencil Portraits of Men and Women Who
Have Broken the Rules*

By DON C. SEITZ

Author of

Joseph Pulitzer; His Life and Letters
Artemus Ward, Braxton Bragg
The Buccaneers, Etc.

ILLUSTRATED WITH PORTRAITS

INDIANAPOLIS

THE BOBBS-MERRILL COMPANY
Publishers

Printed in the United States of America

PRINTED AND BOUND
BY BRAUNWORTH & CO., INC.
BROOKLYN, NEW YORK

To

Those Who Have Failed

FOREWORD

Henry Adams once wrote a relative that he had learned the easiest way to succeed. It was to conform! This volume is devoted to sketches of individuals who did not, and made their marks. Some of the marks were black, most white, and a few red. But they were broad and plain. In days of drabness it is well to know something of unconventional success.

D. C. S.

CONTENTS

UNCOMMON AMERICANS

CHAPTER I

JOSEPH SMITH—SEER AND STATESMAN

It is a curious fact in nature that sterile surroundings are apt to produce the most fruit. In forests where their kind are plentiful, trees and vines blossom unproductively. Yet, by barren roadsides and rocky ledges, the walnut, hickory, grape and blackberry produce abundantly. Nature is determined that life shall not vanish from the earth, and exerts herself according to the need. So, too, with families. They grow large where the fields are lean, and to their children often come surprising intellects.

Vermont, beautiful to the eye but severe in climate and poor in returns from the soil, has been rich in the numbers of its offspring remarkable in their mental attainments. It would be interesting to compile a gazetteer of the great who have come from its small towns and bleak unproductive farms. They number statesmen, lawyers, soldiers and executives by the score, but of them all, two stand out in amazing distinction—Joseph Smith, Jr., and Brigham Young.

1

It is with the former we have first to deal. He was born in Sharon, Windsor County, December 23, 1805, fourth in a family of nine children, five boys and four girls. His mother was Lucy Mack, daughter of Solomon Mack, who fought at Ticonderoga in the old French and Indian War, served in the Revolution and took a turn at privateering in Connecticut waters. On the Smith side, Joseph, Jr., dated back to Samuel Smith, born one hundred and fifty years earlier in Essex County, Massachusetts. Both of his parents were psychopathic and Solomon Mack, the old soldier, wrote a queer little book when well past threescore and ten, that told of dreams and visions from the supernal.

The family raised by Joseph Smith and Lucy Mack suffered from lack of education and the comforts of life. The father was elfish and vagabondish in his tastes. He typified the Yankee, wandering from place to place, trying many things and making none of them go. Several stopping points in Vermont knew him; one in New Hampshire. In the persistent pursuit of something better farther on, he lodged for a time in Palmyra, Seneca County, New York, with his vagrom brood, where, after a spell of petty storekeeping, he "took up" a bit of ground in the neighboring town of Manchester, across the line in Ontario County, and from this point the family began to find itself. Typical "poor whites" of the northern breed, they all possessed shrewdness and cunning, with the eerie sense of the unusual that so often accompanies adolescence. The two-room shack and lean-to in which they lodged had none of the comforts of home. They lived barely, working at odd jobs and doing some small farming. Be it noted that these were not "foreigners," but of the purest New England stock, long on the soil, run-out descendents of ecstatic Puritanism.

It is one of the concomitants of pioneering to take religion hard, the revival and the camp-meeting supplying social excitement, other forms of entertainment not being attainable in the rude surroundings. Western New York was new. Not so many years had passed since General John Sullivan had driven the Senecas from their villages and blackened their fields with fire. Methodism was the most fervid of faiths. This attracted the Smiths. Joseph joined the church at fourteen. His detractors have said it did him no good, and that he soon backslid. This is quite probable. Early conversion is much like vaccination, as it often fails to take.

Joseph soon became prominent in a way. He was strong physically. In the new country there was much well-digging and he took to this as affording the desultory employment suited to his taste. As part of this profession, he mastered the mystery of the magic twig, that somehow twists and bends in the right hands when water is near the surface of the soil, so saving much vain digging.

As he grew in body Joseph expanded in mind.

At first he was considered dull and cunning. In time he became bright and fluent of speech. "Tonguey" they called him, and "slick"—two terms of admiration in rural circles. There ran through the region a fervid flow of religious exaltation, in which the youth shared. Like his grandfather, Solomon, he had dreams which he called visions, and believed that angels were his visitors. These dreams he turned to financial account as helping him to locate buried treasure. Joseph was not alone in this. It, too, was a trait of the generation, shared in every community of the sort he dwelt in.

Here again his critics set him apart as an exceptional rogue in cultivating this deception. It was quite easy to graduate from well-digging to gold-digging, and thence to the discovery of sacred relics. In this last he was again not alone. There were many seekers after the tokens of the Senecas, who might well be suspected of having had the ten lost tribes as forebears.

Joseph sincerely sought treasure. Odd pebbles turned up in the schist dislodged by well-digging. Did not the Bible tell of Urim and Thummim, sacred symbols, that would show their possessor things beyond the ken of other mortal men, and so when a strange stone appeared in the hole that became Clark Chase's well, Smith, the digger, seized the opaque object as a thing with which to visualize the unseen. It was soon put to use. Guided by "a light from Heaven," its possessor dug in a hard hillside and gravely reported that, in a cavity lined with concrete, he found a volume of golden leaves linked together, inscribed with strange letters and with them a pair of spectacles, "Urim and Thummim," by which the finder, though unlettered in tongues, could translate their meaning. He wrapped his possessions in a cloth, locked them in a chest stored in the attic of his father's house, and then began the great illusion upon which he built his career as seer and statesman.

Three men came forward to swear that they had seen these golden leaves, Oliver Cowdrey, David Whitmer and Martin Harris, and though later, all broke away from the faith, not one ever recanted his oath, that his eyes had truly beheld them.

Smith now came into contact with Sidney Rigdon, a clergyman from Warren, Ohio, who had not got on well in the Baptist church, and between them they concocted a new religion. The "Urim and Thummim" revealed that Nephi, son of Mormon, had written upon the leaves of gold the story of the Lamanites, who were the lost ten tribes of Israel, and long before had perished in America, or been absorbed in the aborigines. Here was their story and their faith, which, restored to the world, would save it, even as the second coming of Christ was to complete the salvation denied those not saved in His first mission on earth.

Night after night Joseph sat behind a curtain reading from the leaves while Rigdon transcribed the words, words that are gibberish to the reader, but sacred sounds to those who come under their spell. That he attempted to account for the lost tribes is not noteworthy; many others had done that without founding a new faith. Nor is the unintelligibility of the book greater than that of the Koran, or other attempts at Scripture-making. Crude in style and inane in contents, with its paragraphs perpetually beginning "And it came to pass" we must look beyond this pseudo-Bible to its author's "revelations," appeals and prophecies for the true source of his strength.

Having no money of his own Smith inspired Martin Harris, one of the three witnesses, to mortgage his farm for enough cash to pay E. L. Grandin for printing three thousand copies of the "Bible" at Palmyra, in 1830. Harris' wife, deeming him victimized, sequestrated one hundred and sixteen pages of the manuscript to prevent the investment. These were never duplicated, for the simple reason that the "translator" did not dare to pit his memory against a possible comparison, and so credited the disappearance to the evil one and let it go at that. He published the "Bible" under his own name as Author and Proprietor, and as long as he lived, continued his ownership of it and its believers.

For more than sixty years it was argued by Smith's opponents that he had stolen the idea, if not the words of the book, from "The Manuscript Found," written, but never published, by Solomon Spaulding, a dissenting minister at Conneaut,

Ohio, who took an interest in the mound-builders and based his effort on a theory he built up concerning them. This manuscript turned up in Honolulu in the 'nineties and was put into print. It bears no relation whatever to the Smith effusion, which was clearly his own.

Captain Frederick Marryat, in his *Diary of Monsieur Violet,* an adventurous Frenchman not further identified, but who evidently knew Smith, declares that "Urim and Thummim" were a pair of huge spectacles bearing plainly the name of the maker, "Schneider, Zurich," silver-bowed and of the crude workmanship of the eighteenth century. The gold leaves, which the faithful three forever held that they had seen, were never viewed by other mortals. When pressed concerning them, Smith explained that they had disappeared by "levitation," implying that they had been lifted to the skies by supernatural force. Well, Cotton Mather believed in "levitation," and recited instances in his *Wonders of the Invisible World.* So Joseph had precedents.

The success of most charlatans dates from the beginning of their belief in themselves. This was the next manifestation of Smith's mental strength. Believing in himself, he could convert the credulity of others to his purposes, and did so. Communion with God on the part of a rollicking, backwoods character such as he at first was, did not seem absurd to people of the same sort, who lacked his wit and ability to turn all things to account. Soon he had followers. Posing as a prophet he rallied these at Kirtland, Ohio, in sufficient numbers to build a temple and to arouse antagonism. Cooperating closely, they out-competed the farmers and the Prophet's store undersold the traders. His bank gathered in all the Mormon money. When it broke and its notes became wildcat, it brought no discomfiture to the faithful. No more did the failure of the store. These incidents, however, caused him to leave the vicinage to avoid the sheriff, and led him, in company with the then devoted Rigdon, to depart after dark on horseback for Missouri, where some of his faith had preceded him to lay out a permanent Zion, and were in trouble with their neighbors. There he located a settlement at Far West, in Daviess County, and soon fifteen thousand followers gathered at his command. Here again the economic advantages of tithes and cooperation bred unpopularity. Prejudice against his religion was only camouflage—an excuse. The real reason for what amounted to civil war was the solidarity of the sect, and the advantages this gave them over outsiders. Smith, arrested, broke jail, and fleeing for his life, acquired a town site in which some boomers had lost their investment, in Illinois, on the Mississippi, eighty miles above Quincy. To this haven he transferred his following and named the city, automatically created, Nauvoo. In two years' time it was the best made town in the state, with wide streets, good shops and a fine temple. More than this, it was well organized and had an army of its own, called the Nauvoo Legion, commanded by Smith as lieutenant-general, in gorgeous uniform, with plenty of feathers in his chapeau. He held grand reviews, attended by women on horseback. His handsome figure and ready wit made him a favorite with the ladies. His wife, Emma Hale, was a sane woman with a strong mind. That he was faithless she was undoubtedly sure, though without proof; but she dealt with him so severely that on July 12, 1843, he tried a "revelation" to subjugate her, the Lord under its terms requiring His servant Emma to go easy— so to speak. Emma was unmoved and Joseph became meek. The "revelation," further providing plural wives for the Saints here and hereafter, did not go into effect.

Smith had married "His servant Emma," the comely and sensible daughter of Hall Hale, of South Bainbridge, Chenango County, New York, January 18, 1827. Though Joseph had a "revelation" in 1830, by which she was exalted as "The Elect Lady and Daughter of God," it did not greatly impress his helpmeet. She followed him in his wanderings but did not become deluded, nor did she mourn his loss when he died. That she viewed his antics coldly need not be a matter of surprise to the wedded. Even Socrates was unpopular at home! Remarrying out of the church she lived long as the popular landlady of the Mansion House, at the town that had been Nauvoo.

Most of the people who rallied to Smith were

dull folk who required leadership and guidance. Joseph gave it. Others were lower-grade freaks not without talent. These quarreled with him and exposed him vigorously, but to no purpose, as far as influencing his hold on the flock. Indeed, no one was able to injure Joseph but himself. He guided more by precept than example. "I do not want you to think I am very righteous," he said on one occasion, "for I am not."

But was he a seer and a statesman? He was. Let us pass to the proof. The nullification conflict of the early 'thirties had its root in slavery. The owners of chattels objected to paying a tariff for the benefit of New England. They took forceful steps in South Carolina, and would have gone far in resisting Congress, had not Andrew Jackson decreed that the "union of the states must and shall be preserved."

Now, although he had set up a people apart from others, in spite of all temptations Joseph remained an American, an autocrat at home, a Democrat in his beliefs. December 25, 1832, he uttered this prophecy, which was to become all too true:

"Verily, thus saith the Lord, concerning the wars that will shortly come to pass, beginning at the rebellion of South Carolina, which will eventually terminate in the death and misery of many souls.

"The days will come that war will be poured out upon all nations, beginning at that place;

"For behold, the Southern States shall be divided against the Northern States, and the Southern States will call on other nations, even the nation of Great Britain, as it is called, and they shall also call upon other nations, in order to defend themselves against other nations; and thus war shall be poured out upon all nations.

"And it shall come to pass, after many days, slaves shall rise up against their masters, who shall be marshalled and disciplined for war:

"And it shall come to pass also, that the remnants who are left of the land will marshal themselves, and shall become exceeding angry, and shall vex the Gentiles with a sore vexation;

"And thus with the sword, and by bloodshed, the inhabitants of the earth shall mourn; and with famine, and plague, and earthquakes, and the thunder of heaven, and the fierce and vivid lightning also, shall the inhabitants of the earth be made to feel the wrath, and indignation and chastening hand of an Almighty God, until the consumption decreed, hath made a full end of all nations;

"That the cry of the saints, and of the blood of the saints, shall cease to come up into the ears of the Lord of Sabaoth, from the earth, to be avenged of their enemies.

"Wherefore, stand ye in holy places, and be not moved, until the day of the Lord come; for behold it cometh quickly, saith the Lord. Amen."

Smith perceived more plainly than the abolitionists the evil of slavery. He saw, too, that it was an economic question for the South and a moral one for the North, with no ground for adjustment. Slavery must either expand or make war. At first he preferred the former course, but not in any territory belonging to the United States. He proposed to Van Buren in 1837 that he would raise one hundred thousand men, conquer a useless Mexico and let slavery migrate thereto, as a means of saving the nation. No attention was paid to this, yet ten years later we had conquered Mexico at the behest of the slave power and by the absorption of Texas gave it room for a vast expansion. This did not solve the problem, though postponing its acuteness. Smith saw this and knew the crisis would arise anew. He proposed that the new lands of the Louisiana Purchase be sold gradually, and the money used to recompense the owners of the serfs.

"Pray Congress," he wrote, when proclaiming his candidacy for president in 1844, provoked thereto by the attitude of Van Buren and Clay toward his people, "to pay every man a reasonable price for his slaves out of the surplus revenue arising from the sale of public lands, and from the deduction of pay of members of Congress.

"Petition also, ye godly inhabitants of the slave States, your legislators to abolish slavery by the year 1850, or now, and save the abolitionists from reproach and ruin or shame.

"Break off the shackles of the poor black men and hire him to labor like human beings; for an hour of virtuous liberty on earth is worth a whole eternity of bondage."

He wrote further on the point:

"The Southern people are noble and hospitable. They will help to rid a free country of every vestige of slavery, whenever they are assured of an equivalent of their property."

What other voice in all the madness was so sane? But he advocated higher things not for the slaves alone. "Abolish the practice in the Army and Navy," he continued, "of trying men by court-martial for desertion. If a soldier or marine runs away, send him his wages with this instruction: That his country will never trust him again; he has forfeited his honor.

"Make honor the standard with all men. Be sure that good is rendered for evil in all cases; and the whole nation, like a kingdom of kings and priests, will rise up in righteousness and be respected as wise and witty on earth, and just as holy for Heaven by Jehovah, the author of perfection."

Further than this he stoutly opposed imprisonment for debt.

He foresaw the need of a Federal Reserve banking system. That his bank had gone wild was a reproach not to its promoter, but to the methods of the day. His was not the only wreck in the land. "For the accommodation of the people in every State and Territory," he urged, "let Congress show their wisdom by granting a national bank, with branches in each State and Territory, where the capital stock shall be held by the nation for the mother bank, and by the States and Territories for the branches; and whose officers and directors shall be elected yearly by the people, with wages at the rate of two dollars per day for services; which several banks shall never issue any more bills than the amount of capital stock in her vaults and the interest.

"The net gain of the mother bank shall be applied to the national revenue, and that of the branches to the States' and Territories' revenues. And the bills shall be par throughout the nation, which will mercifully cure that fatal disorder known in cities as brokerage, and leave the people's money in their own pockets."

The pressure of persecution bound the flock together and made it a factor politically in Illinois. The vote controlled Hancock County and held the balance of power in the Congressional District in which Nauvoo was located. Its growth promised to give it a similar status in the state. Smith used it as a shuttlecock between parties. By instinct he was a Democrat and a Unionist, but he received such scant favor from President Van Buren when appealed to for protection in the Missouri troubles, that in the interest of his people, he became independent. Van Buren, in a personal interview, declared that he did not dare to interfere, as it would bring down upon him the wrath of all Missouri. Clay and Calhoun were candidates for the 1844 nomination. Smith polled them and three others prominent in the race, asking, "What would be your rule of action toward the Latter-Day Saints should you be elected president of the United States?" The three did not reply. Calhoun answered feebly that if he became president he would obey the Constitution; as for Missouri, the case did not come under Federal jurisdiction. Smith answered that his note appeared very complacent and fair on a sheet of white paper and added: "O nullifying South Carolina! O little tempestuous Rhode Island!" Then he laid down a dictum upon which Abraham Lincoln had to rest his cause— sixteen years later:

"And let me say that all men who say that Congress has no power to restore and defend the rights of her citizens have not the love of the truth abiding in them. Congress has power to protect the nation against foreign invasion and internal broil; and whenever that body passes an act to maintain right with any power, or to restore right to any portion of her citizens, it is the SUPREME LAW OF THE LAND; and should a State refuse submission, that State is guilty of *insurrection or rebellion,* and the President has as much power to repeal it as Washington had to march against the 'whisky boys' at Pittsburgh, or General Jackson had to send an armed force to suppress the rebellion of South Carolina."

Equally emphatic was his stand on constitutional rights:

"It is one of the first principles of my life and one that I have cultivated from my childhood, having been taught it by my father, to allow every one the liberty of conscience. I am the greatest advocate of the Constitution of the United States there is on the earth. In my feelings I am always ready to die in the protection of the weak and oppressed in their just rights. The only fault I find with the Constitution is, it is not broad enough to cover the whole ground."

Clay responded that he, as a candidate, could enter into no engagements, make no promises, but "thought" religious communities ought to enjoy the security and protection of the Constitution and the laws.

To this obvious equivocation Smith sent Clay a hot reply: "Can anything," he asked, "be drawn from your life, character or conduct that is worthy of being held up to the gaze of this nation as a model of virtue, charity or wisdom?" With much tart invective he led up to a description of world affairs that might well fit those of 1925, saying:

"Why, sir, the condition of the whole earth is lamentable. Texas dreads the teeth and the nails of Mexico. Oregon has the rheumatism, brought on by a horrid exposure to the heat and cold of British and American trappers. Canada has caught a bad cold from extreme fatigue in the patriot war. South America has the headache caused by bumps against the beams of Catholicity and Spanish Sovereignty. Spain has the gripes from age and inquisition. France trembles and wastes under the effects of contagious diseases. England groans with the gout, and wiggles with wine. Italy and the German States are pale with the contiguous dynasties, duchies and domains, have the mumps so severely, that the whole head is sick, and the whole heart is faint. Russia has the cramp by lineage. Turkey has the numb palsy. Africa, from the curse of God, has lost the use of her limbs. China is ruined by the queen's evil, and the rest of Asia fearfully exposed to the small-pox, the natural way, from British peddlers. The islands of the sea are almost dead with the scurvy. The Indians are blind and lame; and the United States, which ought to be the good physician with 'balm from Gilead' and an 'asylum for the oppressed,' has boosted and is boosting up into the council chamber of the Government a clique of political gamblers, to play for the old clothes and old shoes of a sick world, and 'no pledge, no promise to any particular portion of the people' that the rightful heirs will ever receive a cent of their Father's legacy."

He bade Clay farewell in these striking words: "I mourn for the depravity of the world; I despise the hypocrisy of Christendom; I hate the imbecility of American statesmen; I detest the shrinkage of candidates for office from pledges and responsibility; I long for a day of righteousness, when 'He whose right it is to reign shall judge the poor, and reprove with equity for the meek of the earth;' and I pray God, who hath given our fathers a promise of a perfect government in the last days, to purify the hearts of the people and hasten the welcome day."

Smith appreciated the wrongs of the Indians, already acute, and having conceived that they were the descendants of his Lamanites, planned to unite them in the bosom of his church in the vast domain that was unclaimed by the United States, and but hazily possessed by Mexico. There certainly existed some strange affinity between the Mormons and the aborigines, as was later shown in the great trek to Salt Lake, when thousands of helpless people tramped the plains in safety, where well-armed wagon trains and Uncle Sam's dragoons passed at their peril.

The tragedy that ended Joseph Smith's life was the result of a split with "General" J. C. Bennett, who had come to Nauvoo as an adventurer and was soon high in the councils. He developed ambitions of his own, collected a following and started a newspaper—one of the easiest ways of getting into a scrape. It was called the *Expositor* and but one number was issued—on June 7, 1844. Its contents were so vitriolic that the city council passed a resolution decreeing the "removal" of its plant as a nuisance. The city marshal and his aids were sent to enforce the decree. Finding the doors locked, the party broke them open, "pied" the type and made the plant useless.

There instantly rose an outcry that the Saints

had laid their unhallowed hands upon the sacred liberty of the press, which was quite true. The authorities sent Governor Ford a report in justification of their action, but it had set the devil loose. Surrounding communities armed themselves against Nauvoo. Smith's arrest, and that of his close associates in the matter, was demanded, as well as the disarmament of the Nauvoo Legion, which was able to muster five thousand men.

Governor Ford made Carthage his headquarters and there met a committee from Nauvoo, to which he urged that Smith submit to legal procedure. The latter took the request under advisement and at first decided to ignore it; no one dared to come to Nauvoo to take him. With the thought in mind that it might be well to keep out of range until the excitement calmed down, he crossed over to Missouri, but his sense of fatalism would not let him rest in security, so, after a few days, he returned to Nauvoo, determined to face the situation. Ford promised protection and called large numbers of militia to his support. Taking the road from Nauvoo to Carthage, Smith, with his brother Hyrum and a number of others as escort, met, when four miles from town, a company of sixty cavalry on their way to take from the Legion arms that were the property of the state. With the strange prescience that had so often served him, the Prophet said: "I am going like a lamb to the slaughter; but I am calm as a summer morning; I have a conscience void of offense toward God and towards all men. I shall die innocent and it shall yet be said of me—he was murdered in cold blood."

Captain Dunn, commandant of the troops, asked Smith to return to Nauvoo and aid in securing the delivery of the arms. This he did on the promise that he would be escorted in safety to Carthage. The arms were obtained without difficulty, but on turning toward Carthage, Smith stopped as he passed his farm, and gave it a long and lingering look. This caused comment, to which he responded with feeling: "If some of you had such a farm, and knew you would not see it any more. you would want to take a look at it for the last time."

Then he continued his fatal journey to Carthage. The party reached the town at midnight, to find it full of militiamen. Smith went to the hotel and in the morning surrendered to a constable, but later he and Hyrum were served with warrants charging them with treason. Governor Ford was still in town with the state troops, who showed signs of getting out of control. Some officers and citizens of the better grade gathered at the hotel and Joseph asked them if he appeared to be the "desperate character" he was pictured by his foes. They replied that outwardly he appeared all right, but they could not judge what lay in his heart. To this he gave assent. "You can not see what is in my heart," he replied, "but I can see in yours, and will tell you what I see. I can see that you thirst for my blood and nothing but my blood will satisfy you. It is not for crime of any description that I and my brethren are thus continuously persecuted and harassed by our enemies, but there are other motives and some of them I have expressed, so far as relates to myself; and inasmuch as you and the people thirst for my blood, I prophesy in the name of the Lord that you shall witness scenes of blood and horror to your entire satisfaction. Your souls shall be perfectly satiated with blood, and many of you who are now present shall have an opportunity to face the cannon's mouth from sources you think not of, and these people who desire this great evil upon me and my brethren shall be filled with sorrow for the scenes of desolation that await them. They shall seek for peace and shall not be able to find it. Gentlemen, you will find what I have told you will come true."

This utterance was sixteen years in bearing fruit, but it came true, as the Prophet had said, and fell heavily upon Illinois and Missouri. R. F. Smith, a local justice, held the Mormons in seven thousand five hundred dollars bail for the next term of the Hancock County Court. This was for the "riot" at Nauvoo; it did not cover the treason charge. Joseph and Hyrum had not considered this and were amazed when the constable called to take them to jail, as Ford had promised protection should they appear at Carthage on the "riot" charge. The constable had a mittimus signed by the justice, averring that the Smiths had appeared on the treason charge and had been held. This was

not true, but the justice appealed to the governor to
let the mittimus stand, and was told he could call
on the militia to enforce his decree against the pro-
testing Saints. John Taylor, one of the Prophet's
followers, reminded the governor of his promised
protection, and said this was mob rule. Nothing
availed. Joseph, his brother Hyrum, John Taylor
and Willard Richards then went to the prison and
lay all that night on the floor. This was on the
twenty-fifth of June. They were taken from jail
the next day by Frank Worrell, Captain of the
Carthage Grays, for a further hearing before Justice R. F. Smith, who adjourned it until the twenty-
ninth. During the night a shot was fired near the
jail. All the following day, the twenty-seventh, the
mob, mainly militiamen out of ranks, filled the little
town. The Carthage Grays were encamped, as a
guard, near the prison, with only blank cartridges
in their guns, and no honest purpose in their hearts.
About five o'clock the mob rallied and charged the
jail. The guard fired a few shots, naturally without
effect, was speedily "overpowered" and the cells
invaded. Smith had an Allen revolver on his person
and used it bravely in defense, wounding four
assailants, but not until Hyrum had fallen with a
bullet through his brain. Taylor stood by him and
beat down bayonets with a stout walking stick;
then, in a shower of bullets, tried to escape through
a window. He was wounded and fell back within;
Joseph followed, to be riddled as he balanced himself on the sill. He fell outward but had strength

enough to raise himself against the curb of a near-by well. Another spray of bullets ended his life. Richards escaped injury and Taylor was at once cared for. The death of the brothers had slaked the anger of the mob.

It is given to a divine few to be both mystic and practical. Joseph, according to Monsieur Violet, was "a noble-looking fellow, a Mahomet every inch of him," and like Mahomet, he could combine mysticism with the workable in daily affairs. From the day in 1827, when the vision or impulse, whatever it may have been, mastered him, he became a force in America, the impetus of which shows no sign of being spent. Colloquially his people are Mormons. To themselves they are the Church of Jesus Christ of Latter-day Saints.

Their missionaries go forth without reward; their converts leave poverty behind them to become self-helping and helpful to others. In one state they are masters politically; in four others they hold the balance of power. The chairmanship of the most powerful committee in the United States Senate has been held by one of their kind and religion. Unlike the Jews, they have succeeded in keeping themselves apart and acquiring a heritage. Zion with them is an accomplished fact. The tall Yankee from Vermont holds unshaken his place in history!

CHAPTER II

WHEN the rifles of the Carthage mob had stilled the voice and ended the energies of Joseph Smith, Mormonism was deemed to be doomed. The fate of the "false prophet" caused much rejoicing in orthodox circles, religious and political. He had defied the rules and paid the price. Divine power had asserted itself. Great causes seldom die with their leaders, but Mormonism seemed little better than a whimsy, fathered by an adventurer. He had passed on, and his dupes were destined to be dispersed. Nothing of the sort followed. The bodies of the victims were borne to Nauvoo and buried in state. For the moment, Gentile commotion died down under a sense of shame. It broke out among the Saints. The thought of dispersing never seemed to have arisen among them, but the question of leadership became acute. Sidney Rigdon, Smith's associate in the formation period, had been sojourning in Pittsburgh and came forthwith to Nauvoo. On arrival he asserted it to be his province, under a "revelation" received in the Smoky City, to become guardian of the church. He had fallen out with Smith and several years

before lost his status. The church, subject to
the revelations of the Prophet, was under the ex-
ecutive rule of twelve apostles, whose ranks often
suffered from apostasy. In 1844 these were Brigham Young, chief; Heber C. Kimball, Parley P.
Pratt, Orson Hyde, Willard Richards, John Taylor, Wilford Woodruff, George A. Smith, Lyman
Wight, Orson Pratt, Amasa M. Lyman and Ezra
T. Benson. When the crisis came but few of these
were in Nauvoo, being scattered in missions to the
East. Rigdon called upon Elder William Marks
to summon the Saints on Tuesday, August 6, 1844,
for the purpose of selecting a successor to Smith,
slated to be Rigdon. He issued the call for the
eighth instead. By this date a sufficient number
of the twelve had arrived in town to complete a
quorum. The effort of Rigdon to seize the
sovereignty fell to the ground and there arose in
Mormondom one of the strongest figures in history. Again the strange psychology of perverted
Puritanism came into play. As in the case of
Smith, Vermont supplied the material.

Rigdon had made an impassioned appeal to a
large assemblage the previous Sunday, but his
words were without avail against a "vision" conveniently beheld by Brigham Young, who rose
"transfigured" before the meeting. George Q.
Cannon, who lived to become a Saint of large
power and who was present, saw Smith as another
Elisha with Elijah translated in his presence. "The
spirit of Joseph rests on Brigham," said the people,

and Rigdon beat an ignominious retreat. Something more than Joseph's spirit rested on Brigham. He had a large supply of his own. As Louis XIV said "I am the State," so Young curtly informed the congregation: "I will tell you who your leaders or guardians will be. The twelve—I at their head." And so to quote the *Book of Mormon*: "It came to pass."

Brigham Young, who was to save the Saints, was born in Whitingham, Windham County, Vermont, June 1, 1801, the youngest of nine children. Like Joseph Smith, he was of pure colonial descent with Massachusetts forebears. John Young, his father, was a Revolutionary soldier, whose father in turn had served as a surgeon in the French and Indian War. When Brigham was three years old his parents joined the considerable migration of Vermonters to the virgin lands of Western New York, where he grew up in narrow surroundings, to become a painter and glazier. When thirty years old, in 1831, he was converted to Mormonism and in 1832, joined the flock at Kirtland and became from that time on, a figure to be reckoned with.

Young's services to the church had been important from the beginning. On August 3, 1839, he was sent on a mission to England in search of converts. At that time he lived at Montrose, opposite Nauvoo, on the Missouri side of the Mississippi, with his first wife, Mary Ann Angell, and a number of small children. He was ill and so weak he had to be carried to the ferry. Reaching Nauvoo he was too feeble to go on, but after a four-day stay started on the long journey to England. Heber C. Kimball kept him company and they set out, true to Scripture, without purse or scrip, in the trust that luck or the Lord would take care of their ague-smitten families. They sailed for Britain by different routes, but met there, and combined their efforts with amazing success, sending shiploads of new-made Saints to Nauvoo.

For two years Young labored abroad, to return in 1841, when he was made head of the twelve apostles and began his career of power. Yet with his coming to the front the evil days in Nauvoo were not done. When it was seen that Mormonism declined to die with its founder, new friction arose. The city, being a law unto itself, became a place of refuge. The ne'er-do-wells resorted to it and, claiming citizenship, were protected. Thus shady characters, cattle-stealers and their like, found shelter in its environs. The counterfeiting of wild-cat bank notes was a thriving industry and it was claimed, without proof, that Nauvoo was a center for the nefarious work. The city prospered beyond all its rivals, and the old competitive jealousies broke out again. Mobs began their dreadful work. Twenty-nine Mormon houses were burned in a little settlement called Morley, and the occupants shivered in a chilling rain until dawn. Finally, the citizens of Quincy, eighty miles away, took the matter in hand to peacefully urge the Mormons to depart in the interest of common safety. On September 24, 1845, the much harassed Saints agreed to leave, as fast as their property could be sold or exchanged. Where to—they did not know. By the sixth of October, preparations to start were under way. It had been planned to remove in the spring, but the mob became so threatening it was deemed wise to expedite the exodus. Accordingly, on February 11, 1846, the twelve, leading four hundred families, crossed the Mississippi on the ice to face the winter in the waste beyond. By April nearly all were in motion. Those who lingered through the summer to save their property had a sorry time, being harassed and threatened on every side. By September the town, including many new non-Mormon inhabitants, was in a state of siege. Five cannon were fashioned from a steamboat shaft and redoubts thrown up. On September tenth, it was plain that the mob would make a determined assault. Fighting followed for a few days, in which three of the townfolk were killed. Receiving no support from the state authorities, the defenders finally asked a truce and surrendered the city to "Colonel" Thomas S. Brockman, a Campbellite preacher, who led the assailants. This was on September thirteenth. About two thousand men entered the town. The Mormons, and some others, fled precipitately and crossed the river, leaving homes and food behind.

In the meantime, the main body, under Brigham Young, and the rest of the twelve, had gath-

ered at Council Bluffs, on the Missouri River. The
Mexican War was under way and President James
K. Polk called upon the Mormons for recruits to
send to Mexico. They were not needed, but it was
thought a shrewd way to decimate the host. The
astute Brigham responded with alacrity, and eight
hundred men soon formed the "Mormon Battalion" and were en route to Santa Fé—provisioned
and transported by a government that was anxious
to be rid of them. When they were a thousand miles
on the way toward their goal, Brigham instructed
each one to make for California when discharged
from the service. He had not yet decided where
the abiding-place was to be. Fate might send them
to Oregon, as Henry Clay had suggested, and California was the nearest point thereto. Like boys
stealing a ride, the battalion went cheerily on its
way, doing no fighting, but feeding prodigiously
at Uncle Sam's expense!

Yet who shall say that they were not guided
by a higher hand than that of the head of the
church? Some of their number reached the coast
and found work on the ranch of John Augustus
Sutter, located on the north fork of the American
River above Sacramento. On January 18, 1848,
their foreman, James Wilson Marshall, while
deepening a mill race, discovered gold. Within
Brigham Young's lifetime the placers of California had produced more than one billion dollars'
worth of the precious metal.

Meanwhile the concentration at Council Bluffs

continued. New converts swelled the mass. The prairie was plowed for crops of grain and potatoes. Families lived in shacks, tents and huts of sod. The men scattered far and wide to work for wages among the Iowa and Nebraska farmers, already numerous. A great hall was built covered with cottonwood branches like a bower, where music and dancing could be enjoyed. Cheerfulness was the order of the day. They were free from fear and persecution.

Meanwhile their doughty leader had been looking about. He wished to place himself remote enough to be free from the causes that had led to so much strife and bloodshed. With this idea in mind he did his own exploring. Setting out with one hundred and forty-three men, women and children, in the late spring of 1847, he crossed the plains with this caravan, unmolested by the Indians, and came at last to the Uintah Mountains and into the dark defile of Echo Canyon. Pausing here, Orson Hyde and a score of the strongest were told to push ahead. This they did and creeping through another cleft in the mountains—now Emigration Canyon—on July 21, 1847, they beheld the Promised Land.

Here, indeed, was Zion. The great lake glittered in the sun like a second sea, while all about the valley circled the snowy peaks of the Wasatchs. It was another Palestine. The lake, like the Dead Sea, was below the level of the great waters; its waves, also, were bitter salt, and into them flowed a river like unto the Jordan. Satisfactory as was its scriptural resemblance, it had another agreeable side: the plain was well watered, the narrow pass through the Wasatchs was easily defended, and it was a thousand miles from the border of the hostile republic which rejected Brigham and his followers. No wonder he cried out: "It is enough: This is the right place," while his followers shouted "Hosanna."

So he decreed that this was the place to make a stand. Rapidly the faithful rallied to his call. Soon the valley rang with the din of hammers and buzzed with the swish of saws. The coarse soil was turned over by the plow, and the seed harrowed in with the brush. Irrigating ditches were dug and from the river now named Jordan, flowed lifegiving streams. Soon all the valley was green. But just as it was ready to turn yellow for the harvest, great swarms of locusts from the hills settled on it and the Saints, remembering the plagues of Egypt, fought bravely, but in vain, until clouds of seagulls from the lake swooped down upon the invaders and swept them away. Truly, thought the settlers, we are the chosen children of God and He has not forsaken us. Not all men were of this faith. James Bridger, the veteran hunter and scout, who knew the valley, offered to give one thousand dollars for the first ear of corn produced there. In the sterility lay its security.

Their city they laid out in great squares, built a tabernacle and soon a theater. Brigham was no austere prophet. He believed in music, the dance and the play. All went well and the colony thrived, so that when the great procession of gold-seekers began to pass, the farmers were enriched by selling them supplies. Again the hand of Providence had pointed things their way. So much had the unconsidered soldier Marshall done for his people!

On the fourth of March, 1849, a convention met at Salt Lake City and organized a territorial government for the State of Deseret, literally meaning: the "Land of the Honey Bee," in the jargon of the *Book of Mormon*. Salt Lake City became the capital, and at a general election, Brigham Young was chosen governor. Courts were established and the Nauvoo Legion revived with plenty of generals. Congress was next asked to take them into the Union, but the petition was rejected.

By the compromise legislation of September 7, 1850, California was admitted as a state, without the curse of slavery, and Deseret, somewhat shorn of its dimensions, became the territory of Utah. President Millard Fillmore appointed Young territorial governor and United States agent for the Indians. Mormons were selected as district attorney and United States marshal. The rest of the patronage went to Gentiles from the East. These were political tramps, so to speak, who cared more for their salaries than their duties. This bred scandal and dissatisfaction which, coupled with

Gentile exasperation at Mormon prosperity and polygamy, led in time to the Mormon War. The desert not filling as fast as it might, Brigham, bearing in mind the biblical injunction that man should increase and multiply, resurrected Joseph Smith's revelation of 1843, providing for the plurality of wives and "sealing" a select number for Heaven. By this time, thanks to the California rush, Gentiles were plentiful in the valley, but they were far from being Saints. Soon there was friction. Brigham's band of Danites, or Destroying Angels, headed by O. Porter Rockwell, were busy "regulating" newcomers. There was more than one murder, while a massacre of emigrants at Mountain Meadows was shocking in its savagery. This horror refused to down and twenty years after, John D. Lee, who led the Mormon raiders, was legally shot in the little valley where he and his followers had so cruelly obeyed whatever mandate sent them on their evil errand.

But Salt Lake grew, and Brigham remained supreme until James Buchanan came to the presidency. Buchanan could not deal firmly with the Confederacy, but he was stiff enough with the Mormons. He removed Brigham Young as governor in 1857, and sent Alfred Cumming to rule in his stead. In reply to Mormon objections that seemed to threaten armed resistance, he detailed Albert Sidney Johnston, with much of our small army, to subjugate the obstreperous Saints and their autocratic ruler. It is needless to relate the story of this luckless expedition. It suffered many hardships through winter in the Rockies and bid fair to be badly dealt with in the canyons, but Brigham saw a light. One civil war was enough. That between the states was brewing; he would have none. So he welcomed the soldiers, not warmly but not with ordnance, and they built Camp Floyd on an eminence where its guns commanded Salt Lake City and sat themselves to watch and wait. The new territorial appointees, who came with carpet-bags and the intent to fill them, were a sorry lot. Upon the recall of the regulars, Colonel Patrick Edward Connor, with a California regiment, commanded the post. Though he frequently occupied a box at the Salt Lake Theater, where he could see Brigham seated in his rocking chair in the parquette, he never called upon him. Scandal and conflict with the Gentiles continued and polygamy flourished.

Plural wives became plentiful, Brigham accumulating the most imposing list. To Mary Ann Angell, his first love, he added in order Emeline Free, Emeline D. Partridge, Clara Decker, Lucy Bigelow, Eliza Burgess, Margaret Pierce, Zina D. Huntington, Harriet E. Cook, Harriet Barney, Mary Van Cott, Susannah Snively, Eliza R. Snow, Naomi K. J. C. Twiss, Miriam Works, Martha Booker, Augusta Adams, Margaret Alley, Clara Ross, Harriet Amelia Folsom and Eliza Ann Webb—a neat total of twenty-one!

The last two occupy the largest place in his

Brigham Young

history. Amelia Folsom was about half the Prophet's age and a native of Portsmouth, New Hampshire. She was the much hated "favorite wife"
of his declining years. Most of the ladies
survived to be remembered in his will and to join
in an unsanctified lawsuit over its bequests. Brigham was not a frequent widower; but three wives
preceding him to Paradise. One, Eliza Ann Webb,
who starred as No. 19, left him by the divorce
route and caused a deal of trouble. She was a
grass widow with two children, who had played
small parts in the Salt Lake Theater and was deserted by her husband, James Dee. She had been
intimate with some of Young's daughters and at
one time on the stage felt that Brigham "had his
eye on her." As his gaze led him no further, she
married Dee, and being in misfortune after his
desertion, was taken up by the Prophet in 1869
and added to his collection. She left him in 1871,
to lecture and expose Mormonism in a viciously
written book, between the lines of which the cause
of her disgruntlement appears. She had expected
to reign, but Amelia Folsom, the "favorite," kept
her out of the family barracks and in an ill-fur-
nished house where her distracted husband seldom
came to see her. She was kept on an allowance,
closely rationed, and dressed skimpily. As even
the nineteenth part of his affections, she thought
she should fare better than she did at the hands of
the richest man in the territory, and cut up accordingly. The noise Eliza Ann made led to Brigham's

prosecution for polygamy in 1871, but he was not convicted.

Of children, forty-eight are mentioned in Brigham's will. Five of the ladies, including Amelia and the recalcitrant Eliza Ann, were childless. Of this swarm of children, only one, John W. Young, achieved any eminence. He acquired standing as a business man and financier. One daughter, Emily, who married Hiram B. Clawson, had moderate repute as an actress on the local stage, but killed herself in some passion of disappointment. One grandson, Mahonri Young, has achieved deserved fame as a sculptor.

Where the Prophet Joseph was easy with the erring, saving his severities of speech for his enemies, Brigham showered invective upon his flock. He was orthodox to his finger tips, and his hell fire the hottest to be had. Perhaps as one so much married might be moved, he was especially violent in his views on feminine vanity. Where the ladies of Joseph's retinue flaunted satins and fine feathers, Brigham required modest make-ups. He even went so far as to design an appropriate costume for the dames. It included a long surcoat over pantalettes, while for headgear a pot-shaped felt hat completed the horrors of the garb. Several of his more devoted wives wore it, but the sisters generally, rejected the forbidding combination. When that crowning frivolity, the "Grecian bend," came into being Brigham was beside himself at this attempt to distort the female form from its

God-given shape. He preached a furious sermon in the Tabernacle, in which he cavorted about the platform aping the contortions, and consigning those guilty of them to perdition. Yet he dressed well himself, and favored flowered waistcoats of vivid patterns.

Dignified in speech and action when out of the pulpit, he pranced and roared in it. Here he was vulgar—sometimes shockingly so—in his reference to women.

Liberal in providing amusements for his people, Brigham himself, unlike the Prophet Joseph, was an austere character. He danced and attended the theater more to lead others to enjoyment than from any delight of his own. He even appears to have acquired most of his wives from a sense of duty rather than from affection. He possessed an almost uncanny sagacity and knowledge of human nature, together with the New England ability to make money.

Samuel Bowles, editor the *Springfield Republican,* who accompanied Speaker Schuyler Colfax to Utah in 1865, heard one of his sermons. It "lacked logic, lacked effort, lacked wholly magnetism or impressiveness. It was a curious medley of scriptural exposition and exhortation, bold and bare statement, coarse denunciation and vulgar illusion, cheap rant and poor cant."

Brigham was credited with never having read a book and to have had a poor opinion of "book learning." Here is a quotation in point, answering

Orson Hyde, who believed in education: "The professor has told you there are many books in the world and I tell you there are many people there. He says there is something in all these books; I say each of those persons has got a name. It would do you just as much good to learn those somebodies' names, as it would to read these books. Five minutes' revelation would teach me more truth than all this pack of nonsense that I should have packed away in my unlucky brains from these books."

Despite this belief, he did not stand in the way of schools, and they flourished in Utah. It was a small melting pot and needed them. Brigham once boasted that he had fifty-one races under his rule. The leaders were men like himself, the flock all sorts of low grades, due to lack of opportunity where they were born. People who knew both Joseph and Brigham, declared that Smith had ten times the intellect. This is plain from a comparison of their spoken and written words. Smith could enter the lists with Clay and Calhoun and come off more than even. Brigham won against the Gentiles in Utah more by strength of mind than by any acquired intelligence.

Mrs. T. B. H. Stenhouse, wife of an English journalist, who became a trumpeter for Brigham and postmaster at Salt Lake, in her book, *Tell It All,* describes the head of the church when a little past fifty as "of medium height, well-built, upright and . . . with the air of one accustomed to be obeyed. His hair was light—sandy I suppose I ought to call it—with eyes to match; and the expression of his countenance was pleasant and manly."

She thought his hard early life had made him grasping. He certainly took good care of his own, so much so that Joseph Smith once informed him he would be a better Saint if he displayed a little less love for filthy lucre.

Brigham quoted Scripture: "Thou shalt not muzzle the ox when he treadeth out the corn."

"True, Brother Brigham," replied Joseph, "but Moses did not say the ox was to eat up *all* the corn."

Much as polygamy was denounced and deplored by churches and women in the East, Brigham Young found use for plural wives as a political support, and so granted female suffrage in Utah. The completion of the Union Pacific Railroad in 1869 brought in a flood of Gentiles, and to offset this opposition, women were given the vote—to use in Mormon fashion, that is, cast solidly for whomever Brigham willed. Thus out of darkness came this much light, fifty years before it reached the United States as a nation.

According to Eliza Ann, Brigham lived very simply, rising early and breakfasting alone. At three o'clock he dined *en famille* at the Lion's House. "The appearance of Brigham's family at dinner," wrote the lady in her memoirs of her unhappy days as a nineteenth spouse, "is very similar to that at a country boarding-house, when the gentlemen are all away at business in town and the wives and children are left together. At a short table, running across the head of the dining-room, Brigham sits with his favorite wife by his side. . . . At a long table, running lengthwise of the room, all the other wives are seated, each with her children about her." After grace by the patriarch food is served. "The family table is plainly spread," she observes, "while the smaller one is laden with every delicacy the market affords." In the evening Brigham presided at "family prayers" and prayed "with great unction."

On one occasion a venturesome "wife" left the poor fare of the commons and helped herself from the savory dishes at the head table. She never did it again.

His lot as a husband and father could hardly have been a happy one. This crops out in his sermons, or rather harangues, at the tabernacle, where he often tells the women to learn contentment with their lot and to accept without "whining" the dominion of their lords. He is very emphatic in his objection to "whining" women. "My wives have got to do one of two things," he remarks. "Either round up their shoulders to endure the afflictions of this world and love their religion, or they may leave, for I will not have them about me. I will go to Heaven alone rather than to have fighting and scratching about me. I will set all at liberty."

From all over the world he gathered trees and plants and blooded stock that would flourish in

Zion. To his enterprise the West owes the introduction of alfalfa, a matchless forage trifoil that restores nitrogen to the soil. The best grades of peaches, apples, pears and plums grow in the orchards he caused to be developed. He made money, even acting as a mail contractor for the government on the overland route, kept a general store and established manufactures in which he held a commanding interest. Preacher, politician, financier and shepherd of his flock; he was all these.

Though the mountains were full of treasures he would not permit them to be tapped. He concentrated on the soil, always the soil. It must produce more and more, yield each year better returns. Indeed, I once asked Patrick Lannon, Gentile sheriff of Salt Lake, what he thought Brigham's underlying principle was. "I asked a Mormon bishop that question," he replied. "He said as near as he could get at it it was 'plow deep and plant alfalfa.'"

Whatever the founder of the faith may have been, visionary or charlatan, his successor was sanely practical. He was a builder and planter. The city he laid out has grown on noble lines; the settlements he established are comely and comfortable. He made the desert blossom like the rose. That he was deeply religious can not be questioned. In all his contentions, and these were nearly ceaseless, he bore himself like a Lion of Israel. The petty adventurers sent out to govern the territory were made smaller in his hands. He alternately befuddled and outwitted the various Administrations at Washington. During the Civil War Utah did its share for the North, though garrisoned as a hostile country.

He left the world and its burdens behind, August 29, 1877. His will showed a total property of $1,626,510.08. The numerous heirs, though well cared for, thought the accounting a million too low and sued the executors, but were content to take $75,000 in settlement of their claims.

The church operates with undiminished energies. Its missionaries are to be found in the tropic islands of the Pacific, in the chill plains of Canada, in the great cities of the East and of Europe. It is still determined to seek and save. Where shall we find a greater example of "the undiscouraged, resolute, struggling soul of man?"

CHAPTER III

MARTIN SCOTT—WHO MADE THE 'COON COME DOWN

CAPTAIN SCOTT'S 'coon is the most famous American animal. Mr. Artemus Ward's Kangaroo, though justly celebrated, was an exotic, while the Teddy Bear is a stuffed imitation of the real article, made mainly in Germany. But Captain Scott's 'coon is truly indigenous, as was the man who gave it its reputation for celerity.

During his journey through what was the United States in 1837-38, Captain Frederick Marryat, the noted novelist, made some studies of our idiomatic terms for the benefit of benighted Britain, and recorded them in his diary first published in 1839. Included in their number was this item:

" 'I'm a gone 'coon' implies 'I am distressed—or ruined—or lost.' I once asked the origin of this expression and was gravely told as follows: 'There is a Captain Martin Scott in the United States Army who is a remarkable shot with the rifle. He was raised, I believe, in Vermont. His fame was so considerable through the State, that even the animals were aware of it. He went out one morning with his rifle and spying a raccoon upon the upper branches of a high tree, brought his gun up

to his shoulder; when the raccoon, perceiving it,
raised his paw for a parley. 'I beg your pardon,
mister,' said the raccoon very politely, 'but may I
ask if your name is Scott?' 'Yes,' replied the Captain. 'Martin Scott?' continued the raccoon. 'Yes,'
replied the Captain. 'Captain Martin Scott?' still
continued the animal. 'Yes,' replied the Captain.
'Captain Martin Scott?—Oh! then,' says the animal, 'I may just as well come down, for I'm a gone
'coon!' "

The "gone 'coon" remains secure in his fame
through endless repetition of the fact, but Captain
Scott is obscure to modern Americans. Yet he did
much besides enrich the language with a telling
phrase, though he is often robbed of the credit for
this. Sundry editors still insist on promoting the
'coon to be "General" Scott's captive, thus assign-
ing the glory of the bloodless conquest to Major-
General Winfield Scott, "Old Fuss and Feathers," who deserves no such distinction, while others
assign the achievement to Colonel David Crockett.
It is therefore an agreeable as well as an incumbent
duty to reveal all that need be known concerning
Martin Scott.

Like the two extraordinary characters who
have previously passed in review, Martin Scott
opened his amazingly accurate eyes in the state of
Vermont, adding to the fame already enjoyed by
Bennington through John Stark's promise to
make his Molly a widow before night, if he did not
defeat the despised Hessians on August 16, 1777.

His father was a farmer who "made a living" and nothing else on the difficult soil, so Martin grew up to be a likely lad with no prospects. The ability to shoot straight with an unflinching aim, developed early and gave him a reputation when a boy of twelve. The country about Bennington, though long settled, bordered on the wild. Deer, turkeys, bears and panthers roamed in the woods and the howl of the wolf was not unknown. The bear, though an amiable animal, has a penchant for sheep and once having tasted mutton, loses its regard for berries and wood-maggots as articles of diet. A sheep-eating she-bear with two cubs descended upon the neighborhood and caused consternation among the farmers. Up to this time young Martin had never been allowed to "go gunning" alone. Indeed, it was all he could do to lift the heavy musket with which his father hunted. Occasionally he would be allowed to rest it on the lower rail of the fence and blaze away, a proceeding that filled him with bliss. When the three bears appeared the whole country rose in a round-up. "Some had rifles," said the captain in telling the story, "and others what weapons they could get; the blacksmith shouldered his sledge, the farm laborer his pitch fork; for all I know to the contrary, the barber carried his pole."

Two boys named Pratt joined the hunt and one of these, placed near the mill "more to keep him out of harm's way than anything else," was at that post when one of the cubs went by and blazing

away laid it low. The rejoicing hunters loaded the
bear on a litter, with Pratt on the carcass and carried both in triumph through the town. The sight
filled little Martin with jealousy. He could not
sleep that night from the passion that stirred his
soul. The next day the other Pratt boy killed the
second cub. This was Saturday. Sunday the
hunters paused, but Martin, keen not to be outwitted, called on a neighbor in the evening and
persuaded the friendly soul to lend him a capable
hunting dog. He took the cur to his room and
tried to sleep with the animal tied to his wrist.
Rising before daylight he found his father irate
because he had employed time on Sunday looking
for a dog and he received a severe licking. "On
this memorable occasion," narrates the captain, "he
held me by the wrist with one hand, while he chas-
tised me with the other. I found the best plan was
to run round him as fast as I could, which obliged
him to turn round after me with the stick and then
for a short time he left off; not because he thought
I had had enough, but because he became so giddy
he could not stand." On top of this refreshment
he was told he could not join the day's hunt for the
bear. Martin made a strong appeal, asking his
father how he would like to have been kept home
from the Battle of Bennington, at which he had
been present as a lad. This moved the parental
heart and the boy was allowed to go. The family
musket was a heavy burden, but a kindly neighbor
agreed to look out for the lad. So he went forth

with a high heart. In a hollow by the mill the borrowed dog began to bark and a rustle in the bushes announced the coming of the bear. The neighbor leveled his rifle, but in the excitement he forgot to raise the hammer. So Martin was able to fire first and he sent a ball into Bruin's shoulder. She slid into a quarry followed by the dog, which was soon fast in her embrace. Martin caught the dog by the tail—remembering that it was a borrowed dog— and roared out: "Save the dog! Save the dog—or I'll have to pay ten dollars!" He thrust his musket barrel down the bear's throat, so it was out of use, but another hunter came up and handed the young Nimrod his gun. With this he shot the beast through the head and then in wild excitement fell to beating it with a stone, though life had fled. His triumph over the Pratts was supreme. They had killed cubs; he, a grown specimen, and he was paraded through the village on his quarry's back. Father Scott, seeing him thus riding in state, called out:

"Come down, sir; what are you doing up there, sir?"

"Let the boy alone," said the escort. "He killed the bear."

This was the beginning of what was to be an ever-growing fame as hunter and marksman. It made him a public character, and to sharpshooting he added another accomplishment—riding race horses. The sport of kings was not regarded as moral by Martin's father. There being no county fair tracks or licensed courses, racing was surreptitious and conducted against the moral opinion of the country. The senior Scott sternly interdicted attendance by his son on such occasions. But his skill as a jockey was known to the sports. There was no "circuit" then, but owners of fast steeds went about from town to town laying wagers against local speeders, and usually departing with all the loose cash in the neighborhood. One such adventurer came to Bennington with a nag whose prowess was known to be considerable. None of the local talent owned a horse that could match him. There was a belief, however, that a speedy Morgan owned by a local Presbyterian deacon could turn the trick. Now the deacon abhorred horse racing, but the pride of the fraternity was aroused and it was determined to draft the steed. Martin Scott was selected as jockey and assigned to the task of abducting the animal. This he did, skilfully muffling the hoofs so they made no sound and in the dark, rode, as he thought, undetected to the track, which was a straight mile on the country road.

The race was so close that great excitement was aroused. At its last quarter the deacon's horse fell a neck or so to the rear and his lagging legs indicated defeat. At this tense moment the good man himself rose from behind a board fence and shouted: "Put the whip to him, Martin! Put the whip to him."

Astounded, but stimulated, Martin applied the

whip and won by half a length. Victor, he faced the deacon, who in the moment of triumph had further so forgotten himself as to throw his hat in the air and give a rousing hurrah! Then a sense of his iniquity overcame him and he dealt thus with the abashed boy: "Martin Scott, you young reprobate, you have stolen my horse, and, unless you instantly lead him back to the stable and give him a good rubbing down, I'll report you to your father, sir!"

Martin meekly obeyed, but to his reputation as a shot was now added that of a superior horseman. So he grew up an all-round country sport, evading the stern rule of his parent by "sparking" adventures after dark when he was supposed to be safely in bed and doing the wild things that enliven the austerities of rural life, until the year 1814. He was following a plow one late spring day when the village postmaster came to him much excited, bearing an envelope with the frank of the War Department on it. Opening the missive he found within a commission that made him an ensign— now second lieutenant—in the Regular Army of the United States, with instructions to report at Sackett's Harbor on Lake Ontario, where there was and still is a military post. Who caused the appointment he never knew, nor do the records of the adjutant general's office shed any light on the subject. Rejoicing at his luck, however it might have arrived, he packed up and duly reported for duty. The War of 1812 had faded out and the only service was on the frontier where a thin line of soldiers faced the raiding warriors and were kept busy avenging or preventing massacres of the steadily encroaching settlers. On these outposts Scott spent most of his life and in the opportunities for game shooting, perfected his aim with pistol and rifle. As an old regular colonel once remarked to a prospective West Point cadet: "Jim, there's a good deal of ennui in the army," and so the young officer discovered. He found relief by increasing his skill as a shot and as a horseman.

Unlike many of his fellow-officers, Scott never drank, smoked or gambled at cards. He spent little of his pay upon himself, but was generous with others. Taking care of his money and keeping strictly sober seems to have been taken as an affront by sundry of his associates who began systematically to annoy him. This hazing became so pronounced that the young officer consulted his friends as to his best course with the tormenters. He was told he could either throw up his commission or challenge the next man who insulted him. Word got around that it would hereafter be risky to ruffle the feelings of a dead shot and the gentlemen became polite. This, however, was only pretense, for under it they plotted against him and brought from another post an officer with a reputation as a marksman. The visitor wantonly provoked a quarrel at the mess table and was promptly called to account. The affair was soon arranged, not to Scott's taste, however. His decent ideas deplored dueling and he had determined to fire in the air, when word reached him that his antagonist had remarked in the hearing of others that he had the disagreeable job of shooting "a damned Yankee" on his hands. Vexed by this news Scott met his man, who was no novice, and received a slight flesh wound, but his antagonist fell with a bullet through his lungs. Here comes the queer part of the story. The shot should have proved fatal, but its victim was suffering from consumption and the ball performed a cure. He recovered and lived for many years as the result of this strange specific. At the next meeting of the mess the company was informed that no more insults would be in order without consequences, which were likely to be fatal. Scott's social position was soon assured.

Besides his skill with firearms Captain Scott possessed extraordinary courage and resolution. Stationed at Fort Snelling, near the present cities of St. Paul and Minneapolis, he was not on terms with the colonel in command. Orders came from Washington to put Captain Scott in charge of an escort, which was to attend an eminent scientific gentleman into the wilds. Pleading lack of force the colonel sent Scott to Prairie du Chien, three hundred miles away, to secure more men. He made the trip by row-boat in remarkable time, to find on his return to Fort Snelling that the expedition had been sent off without him. It was headed for Pembina and had a two weeks' start. Scott asserted his rights under War Department orders and with but four men and a winded horse, began the trying task of catching up. The horse broke down before night and was cut loose. The captain and his men shouldered its load and pushed on. Shoes wore out, clothes became ragged and provisions exhausted. The four men were so worn that Scott turned them back on the trail, and for two days, without food, pushed on alone, catching up with his command at the Red River and performing his allotted duties thereafter.

Not only was the captain imposed upon in this fashion, but when winter came his superior turned him into a lumberman and he spent the bitter cold period with a squad of men cutting logs on Red River to be floated down to the fort in the spring.

All this while he kept up his practise, becoming so skilful with a pistol that he could toss two potatoes in the air so spaced that one was rising while the other fell, and perforate both with a single shot. He also trained race horses and hunting dogs, being an excellent judge of the qualities of each. He made much of both occupations while stationed at Prairie du Chien. Here he owned a half-breed setter and pointer named Mark. General Randolph B. Marcy, father-in-law of General George B. McClellan, was with him at this post and vouches for this in his *Army Life on the Border:* "Mark," Captain Scott would say, "I want you to go over to the island and ascertain if there are any woodcocks there and come back and tell me."

Mark would swim to the island, scare up some birds and return with a wagging tail, running to his master and then to the gun rack as a sign that sport was possible.

"Get the canoe ready," would be the next command and the dog would pick up a paddle and take it to the boat. Mark was rather dissolute in his habits and was regularly castigated for undue absences. He would return from a night's debauch, walk straight to the cabin wall, stand up against it and look about with an "I am ready" air for the cowhide which was sure to be applied. Stern as the captain was with his dogs—he always kept a pack of hounds—he was deeply attached to them and when one died it was given a formal burial with a hunting horse draped in black leading the funeral procession to the grave.

As he grew older he became very formal and meticulous, creating a code of sporting terms and practises that bore heavily upon his less accomplished comrades, who were apt to be sharply reproved for infractions.

Probably one of the most interesting episodes in the captain's career was his return in state to Bennington, after a long absence on the frontier— indeed, he had been absent ever since the mysterious message from Washington sent him to Sackett's Harbor. He owned two magnificent horses and a colored boy whom he had bought in the South for five dollars a pound, but had made a free man-servant. One of the horses on the occasion of his return, drew a splendid gig in which the captain sat in all the glory of full uniform, while black Jack followed on the other, clad in livery and making an imposing outrider. He in turn was followed by a pack of twenty dogs, full-bloods of various breeds. Bennington had seen nothing to equal it since Braun and his Hessians had called sixty years before. The procession stopped at the tavern and the town turned out to view it with wondering eyes. No one knew the splendid stranger who took up his quarters in the best room and seated himself comfortably at a window commanding Main Street.

Soon he saw his brother ambling up the road, goading a fine pair of oxen. The captain went out and halted him. "Do they belong to you?" he asked. The reply was that they were another's; the driver was too poor to own them. The captain asked their value and pulling out his purse handed over the needed sum, but did not reveal his own identity. The astounded recipient, being a Vermonter, took the money, though dazed at the liberality of a man he did not know. Further inquiry revealed that the brother was a tenant farmer in mean circumstances. The price of the farm was ascertained—but by this time the captain had been found out. He bought it and, content with putting his brother on his feet, he left for the frontier.

Captain Marryat met Captain Scott at Fort Snelling in the late 'thirties, when his fame was wide-spread enough to have produced the 'coon yarn. In his diary, Scott records two hunting stories that are worth repeating in his own language:

"I was once buffalo hunting in Arkansas. I was on a strong well-trained horse, pursuing a bull, when we arrived at a rent or crack in the prairie, so wide, that it was necessary for the animals to leap it. The bull went over first, and I, on the horse, following it close, rose on my stirrups, craning a little, that I might perceive the width of the rent. At that moment the bull turned round to charge; the horse perceiving it, and knowing his work, immediately wheeled also. This sudden change of motion threw me off my saddle, and I remained hanging by the side of the horse, with my leg over his neck: there I was, hanging on only by my leg, with my head downwards below the horse's belly. The bull rushed on to the charge, ranging up to the flank of the horse on the side where I was dangling, and the horse was so encumbered by my weight in that awkward position, that each moment the bull gained upon him. At last my strength failed me; I felt that I could hold on but a few seconds longer; the head of the bull was close to me, and the steam from his nostrils blew into my face. I gave myself up for lost; all the prayer I could possibly call to mind at the time was the first two lines of a hymn I used to repeat as a child—'Lord, now I lay me down to sleep'; and that I repeated two or three times, when, fortunately, the horse wheeled short round, evaded the bull, and leaped the gap. The bull was at fault; the jolt of the leap, after nearly dropping me into the gap, threw me up so high that I gained the neck of the horse, and eventually my saddle. I then thought of my rifle, and found that I had held it grasped in my hand during the whole time. I wheeled my horse and resumed the chase, and in a minute the bull was dead at my horse's feet.

"I was riding out one day in Arkansas, and it so happened I had not my rifle with me, nor indeed a weapon of any description, not even my jack-knife. As I came upon the skirts of a prairie, near a small copse, a buck started out, and dashed away as if much alarmed. I thought it was my sudden appearance which had alarmed him; I stopped my horse to look after him, and, turning my eyes afterwards in the direction from whence it had started, I perceived, as I thought, on a small mound of earth raised by an animal called a gopher, just the head of a doe, her body concealed by the high grass. I had no arms, but it occurred to me, that if I could contrive to crawl up very softly, the high grass might conceal my approach, and I should be able to spring upon her and secure her by main strength. 'If I can manage this,' said I to myself, 'it will be something to talk about.' I tied my horse to a tree and commenced crawling very softly on my hands and knees towards the gopher hill; I arrived close to it, and the doe had not started; I rose gently with both hands ready for a grab, and prepared to spring, slowly raising my head that I might get a sight of the animal. It appeared that the animal was equally inquisitive, and wished to gain a sight of me, and it slowly raised its head from the grass as I did mine. Imagine what was my surprise and consternation, to find that, instead of a doe, I was face to face with a large male panther. It was this brute which had so scared the buck, and now equally scared me. There I was, at hardly one yard's distance from him, without arms of any description, and almost in the paws of the panther. I knew that my only chance was keeping my eyes fixed steadfastly on his, and not moving hand or foot; the least motion to retreat would have been his signal to spring; so there I was, as white as a sheet, with my eyes fixed on him. Luckily he did not know what was passing within me. For some seconds the animal met my gaze, and I began to give myself up for lost. 'Tis time for you to go, thought I, or I am gone: will you never go? At last, the animal blinked, and then his eyes opened like balls of fire; I remained fascinated as it were; he blinked again, turned his head a very little, then turned round and went away at a light canter. Imagine the relief. I hastened back to my horse, and away also went I at a light canter, and with a lighter heart, grateful to Heaven for having preserved me."

On September 8, 1847, the end came to Scott's saga. The American forces investing the City of Mexico were instructed to take its defenses by storm. To General William J. Worth, who now

sleeps at the junction of Broadway and Fifth
Avenue in New York, was given the job of re-
ducing Molino del Rey (The King's Mill). A
brigade composed of the Fifth, Sixth, Eighth and
Eleventh Infantry, with guns from the Second
and Third Artillery, all under Colonel J. S. Mc-
Intosh, was assigned to the task. Advancing on
the Casa Mata, McIntosh, at the head of the column, fell mortally wounded in what was destined
to be the bloodiest battle of the war. Command of
the brigade then shifted by seniority to Martin
Scott, Lieutenant Colonel of the Fifth Infantry.
He led the line up the slope to the very edge of the
parapet. There a musket ball found him and extinguished his stout spirit. This heroism is no
longer remembered, but the 'coon story survives
and refuses to be forgotten.

CHAPTER IV

A MAN who could send eight shiploads of bed-warming-pans to the West Indies and nearly double his money by the speculation, is bound to survive in the annals of New England and his story deserves a modern recital.

Born in Malden, a suburb of Boston in 1743, Timothy Dexter came of a Massachusetts family that had long cut a figure in the commonwealth and of which he was the most striking member. He grew up decorously enough and made money modestly in Boston as a dresser of leather, so that by the time the Revolution had come and gone he had what was for the day a substantial fortune—not large, like that of John Hancock, or Thomas Russell, both great merchants who rivaled each other in magnificence, but still much above his fellows. The currency with which the Continental Congress paid for supplies and rewarded its soldiers for Bunker Hill, Saratoga, Valley Forge and Yorktown, having lost most of its value, deflated the bonds Massachusetts issued for war purposes until they were worth about one shilling, sixpence to the pound. Hancock and Russell, like later patriots, "stabilized" the bonds at their petty figure as a patriotic duty and, money being scarce, were able to acquire huge holdings. Dexter, the leather dresser, seeing that the president of Congress and the rich Thomas Russell were stowing away such securities in the hope that the state would some day redeem them at par, bought to the limit of his spare cash and shared the good fortune of the others when the state made good. Riches transformed him from a modest morocco merchant into what has been truly termed the most eccentric man of his time, and as such he still stands supreme.

It would be easy to call him mad, but more difficult to prove it. Finding it impossible to obtain entrance to society in Boston on the ladder of his dollars, he turned to Salem for solace. Snubbed there, he bought a great estate at Newburyport and began the second stage of his career. The ships of the port had traded far and gained great wealth to their owners, which faded with the war. Newburyport was a "dead" town in 1783 and has never revived. Dexter at a small price bought two estates of ruined sea kings cheaply. One he sold at a profit—he always sold at a profit—the other he rehabilitated to suit his new state of mind. A wooden palace of late colonial design was turned into an ornate box. Minarets with gilded balls graced the roof of the mansion and bizarre painting gave the house the look of a pile of barbers' poles. Rows of columns were placed to line the walks and drives, each surmounted by a high wooden statue of some celebrity. Not content with so decorating the landscape, Dexter designed a costume for himself that was unlike anything ever worn before by mortal man and gave its wearer the deepest delight. An enormous cushion adorned with tassels rested on his head, while a coat with skirts dropping to the heels touched trousers tied with ribbons at the ankles. But this was not all; he yearned for a title. None was to be had in the newly liberated land, so he bought a country estate at Chester, New Hampshire, and called himself King of Chester, but Chester would not have it. Kings were not to be tolerated even if only fustian. He reverted to Newburyport and dubbed himself Lord. The neighbors took kindly to this and "Lord Timothy" he remained the remainder of his days.

For further effect he proclaimed himself a sage in these terms: "I am the first in the East, the first in the West and the greatest philosopher in the known world." This was a large claim, but he did the best he could to live up to it by uttering strange fancies and taking queer attitudes in public affairs.

Whether from shrewdness or good luck all his ventures turned out amazingly. For example, he was quite sympathetic, as became a lord, with the misfortunes of the French royal family during the Revolution and announced that he would provide a proper home for them should they reach America. To feed the royalities in case they arrived he bought a great supply of provisions. Their majesties went to the guillotine instead of Newburyport and Dexter sold out his store at a liberal advance. When Louis XVI lost his head Dexter happened to be in Boston and carried the news to Newburyport, where he bribed the Congregational sexton to toll the church bell. Thus the town first learned the dismal tidings. The selectmen silenced the bell, but Dexter took huge delight in the sensation he had caused.

Surely the sour officials might have let the bell ring on. Louis XVI had made it possible to have a free America, and Liberty rewarded him with Death! Pining, himself, for immortality, Dexter planned a mock funeral—a rehearsal of what he hoped his would be. All was arranged with great splendor. Hearse, coffin and tomb were prepared and invitations on mourning cards went to the elect of the town. As no parson would aid the mockery, a local wag uttered a satisfactory eulogy and after the coffin had been entombed the guests were richly entertained with food and wine. The feast was marred by the momentary absence of the host and disturbed by the sounds of lamentation below. In the basement Lord Timothy was found vigorously caning his wife for failing to weep with sufficient sincerity at the ceremony!

To crown his career Lord Timothy must needs write a book, which he called *A Pickle for the Knowing Ones*. It is written in uncouth jargon, the spelling so rudimentary as to be sub-phonetic and below the par of Chaucer. Jokes lurk between its lines, while the author seeks to prove that he is not a fool—as if it made any difference, but such, alas, is human vanity, with which his lordship was well laden. Either from lack of confidence in his grammar, or in contempt of punctuation, he left out all marks, printing a sufficient quantity of the vexatious little signs on the last page, so that the reader could "salt and pepper" as he pleased. Declaring his purpose in these terms, "I wans to make my Enemys grin in tune Lik A Cat over A hot pudding," he proceeds to recite the profits of his "crazy" ventures—seventy-nine per cent. on the warming-pans, seventy-five per cent. on a cargo of whalebone. The refitter of a vessel in which Dexter had an interest asked money to buy new stays —that was the word for corsets those days—and the request suggested to his mercurial mind a corner in the elastic material of which they were made.

He further profited by forty-seven thousand dollars on twenty-one thousand Bibles sent to the West Indies after the warming-pans, with a message to the Africans there dwelling that those who did not buy and read would go straight and speedily to hell!

The enigma of the warming-pans is easily solved. Cuffee found the long-handled articles served admirably to fry fish and yams over open fires and to skim the scum off boiling cane sirup. He sold forty-one thousand—as he says at a profit of seventy-nine per cent.

Dropping his early English, Dexter occasionally aired his views in the *Impartial Herald* of Newburyport at run-of-paper rates: "Seeing mankind is so bad by nature," he once proclaimed, "I think when the candle goes out, men and women is done; they will lay as dirt and rocks till the great gun fires, and when that goes off the gun will be so large here that the gun will contain nine hundred million tons of the best of good powder, then that will shake and bring all bones together, then the world will be to an end." Some explosion!

Spiritualism not having been invented, Lord Timothy took kindly to astrology and weird witch women, who flourished despite the hangings at near-by Salem a century before. Besides these he took under his patronage a character as rare, but not so successful as his own, who set up with the tools of a mystic and made a living with his fooleries, Dexter being his chief patron. To test his belief that the spirits of a departed good man could not injure a child, he shut a small boy up in the tomb of George Whitefield, the great preacher of Newburyport and left him alone for hours. Luckily the lad had a steady head or the spirit of the good man was merciful for the boy took it coolly and was quite unconcerned when rescued by command of his alarmed mother, to whom some one had related the nature of the experiment that was being tried.

The astrologer made one prediction that came strangely true. He declared that he would not die until the sun was blotted from the heavens, and as narrated by Samuel L. Knapp, Dexter's biographer, the seer was stretched upon his bed, June 16, 1806, the day of a total eclipse of the sun and died at the moment when the glowing disk became dark!

One of the witch women who beguiled Dexter was a certain Madam Hooper, a left-over from the Peace of 1763, who had come to America as the follower of a British officer and drifted to Newburyport where she gave up teaching for fortune-telling, at which she became an adept, having excellent facilities for knowing what was going on. She could use firearms accurately and wielded a broadsword with the skill of a man. She won Dexter's patronage by locating a thief who had stolen his melons and she long held him under her sway, to be succeeded at her death by Moll Pitcher, who had been a gunner in the Revolution and had become a mystic for money. Dexter collected a library of dream books and works on astrology, to aid him in peering into the beyond. Besides astrologers Lord Timothy took on a poet to sing his praises and dubbed him Laureate. Jonathan Plummer was his name, born at Gravel Hill in Newbury. He had a fine voice that intoned loudly the virtues of his patron, who not only paid him a salary, but devised a costume in keeping with his own—a long black frock starred with gold and fringed with silk. Buckled shoes, a cocked hat and a gold headed cane completed his splendor. That

he was a true Laureate and not without the gift of
rhyme can be seen by this sole surviving scrap—a
pæan poured out in his patron's praise:

Lord Dexter is a man of fame;
Most celebrated is his name;
More precious far than gold that's pure,
Lord Dexter shine forevermore.

His noble house, it shines more bright
Than Lebanon's most pleasant height;
Never was one who stepped therein
Who wanted to come out again.

His house is filled with sweet perfumes,
Rich furniture doth fill his rooms;
Inside and out it is adorn'd,
And on the top an eagle's form'd.

His house is white and trimm'd with green,
For many miles it may be seen;
It shines as bright as any star,
The fame of it has spread afar.

Lord Dexter, thou, whose name alone
Shines brighter than King George's throne;
Thy name shall stand in books of fame,
And princes shall his name proclaim.

Lord Dexter hath a coach beside,
In pomp and splendor he doth ride;
The horses champ the silver bitt,
And throw the foam around their feet.

The images around him stand,
For they were made by his command,
Looking to see Lord Dexter come,
With fixed eyes they see him home.

Four lions stand to guard the door,
With mouths wide open to devour
All enemies who dare oppose
Lord Dexter or his shady groves.

Lord Dexter, like King Solomon,
Hath gold and silver by the ton,
And bells to churches he hath given,
To worship the great King of Heaven.

His mighty deeds they are so great,
He's honor'd both in church and state,
And when he comes all must give way,
To let Lord Dexter bear the sway.

When Dexter dies all things shall droop,
Lord East, Lord West, Lord North shall stoop,
And then Lord South with pomp shall come,
And bear his body to the tomb.

His tomb most charming to behold,
A thousand sweets it doth unfold;
When Dexter dies shall willows weep,
And mourning friends shall fill the street.

May Washington forever stand;
May Jefferson, by God's command,
Support the rights of all mankind,
John Adams not a whit behind.

America, with all your host,
Lord Dexter in a bumper toast;
May he enjoy his life in peace,
And when he's dead his name not cease.

In Heaven may he always reign,
For there's no sorrow, sin, nor pain;
Unto the world I leave the rest,
For to pronounce Lord Dexter best.

Though not remembered in Dexter's will the bard saved enough to live comfortably for twenty years after his patron's death. Then his mind slipped and going on a hunger strike, he died of starvation—like many another poet.

Pleased with his Laureate, Dexter added a fool to his entourage, William Burley, a giant six feet seven inches high, ironically called "The Dwarf," who served to amuse and as a bodyguard, though the best protector the lord ever had was Lucy Lancaster, a colored nurse of Newburyport, who came of high African lineage and was a person of character. She never robbed her employer or permitted any one else to, as far as she could prevent.

Dexter drove about in a gorgeous coach drawn by a beautiful team of cream-colored horses. He lost his fancy for these after a time and commanding them to change color sold them for failing to obey. His house was extravagantly furnished. He sent an agent to Europe to buy paintings who returned with some fine canvases—others not so good.

These Dexter kept and is presumed to have made money on the sale of the others. He bought many books but gaged their merits by their bindings. A son and daughter made up the family. The son was half-witted and died a dissolute dolt. The daughter married a sensible man, but became addicted to drink herself and lived miserably, leaving behind a daughter who grew up creditably.

Like some other men less eccentric, Dexter had a fancy for clocks and collected odd varieties of faces and works. He treated them as living things, talked to them and roundly scolded those that got out of order. Time, he thought, was part of the atmosphere, a shadow that could not be caught with a net like a butterfly, or brought down with a gun. This theory out-Einsteins Einstein.

He once ordered his half-witted son, under threat of death, to shoot at a passing stranger who stared too long at the palace. The curious one was not hit but he lodged a complaint with the magistrate which earned Lord Timothy two months in jail at Ipswich, whither he went in great state with coach and four. At first he enjoyed the novelty, but soon becoming bored bought a remittance of the sentence and was set free. Yet with all these freaks he could not help making money. He speculated in the distant lands of Ohio, opened up as the Western Reserve of Connecticut, with great resulting profit.

His wealth was very large for the times; he once boasted of having nine tons of silver in store,

and a visiting savant, curious to know the extent
of his philosophy, declared he never saw so many
diamond rings as his lordship exhibited. His property was sensibly disposed of by will; indeed, in his
last days he became quite a reasonable person. He
died in his palace October 26, 1806, insisting that
his "tomb" should be carved on his last resting
place. "Otherwise," he observed, "how could it be
known that it was not a potato cellar?" The estate,
with all the trimmings, remained one of the sights
of Newburyport until what we may call modern
times.

CHAPTER V

FOR half a century before the outbreak of the War between the States, Americans took their religion like their whisky—straight. There were no fancy frills, no trifling with the temperature in hell. Satan was fought in the open. The fires of perdition were at white heat and Heaven was a paradise for those who accepted the faith. The pioneer preachers were robust in mind and body. Chief among them in militancy were the circuit riders of the Methodist church, who covered large districts on horseback and laid hard hands on the devil.

Most notable of these strong men of the Gospel was Peter Cartwright, born September 1, 1785, in Amherst County, Virginia. The family moved to Kentucky in 1791 and there began the development of his brawn and brain. It was a rough country, and men took care of themselves. Of religious life there was little or none. "Sunday," says Cartwright in his autobiography, "was a day set apart for hunting, fishing, horse racing, card playing, balls, dances and all kinds of jollity and mirth."

71

In these surroundings he grew up. There was no pious pressure at home and he lived like his fellows until at sixteen years of age a sense of wasted life came over him. He fell under the spell of John Page, a Methodist preacher, and left his idle ways, to become in a few years one of the foremost leaders of the church, a soldier of the Cross and a tireless pursuer of Satan.

At seventeen he was at school, seeking to remedy defects in his education. Scoffed at by a pair of fellow-pupils for his Methodism, he lost his temper and threw them both into a stream. Vexed at his own lack of control, he left the institution, but was at once licensed as an exhorter, set to work with a zeal that never left him, and soon organized the Livingston Circuit in the wild and sparsely settled Cumberland country. At eighteen he became junior pastor on the Red River Circuit and his fame grew in the land. "I literally gave up the world," he said, on accepting the charge. To perform his duties he had to find his way through dark forests by the barest trails, sleep beside his horse in the open, ford rivers and brave the scorn of the various ruffians whom he sought to convert.

He soon found a text upon which to make a moving appeal: "Behold the Lamb of God." On this he rang the changes for over half a century. As he heard the call when young, he married young, joining hand and soul with Frances Gaines, August 18, 1808. She bore him nine children and lived to close his eyes. No man could have given greater devotion to his cause. "If I had been seeking money," he records, "I would not have travelled, for I knew I could have made more splitting rails than I could travelling a circuit when I started. It was not honor, there was no honor about it. It was to fulfill my own convictions of duty." So he sang, exhorted, argued and fought for righteousness. His life was one long campaign and most of his victories were in the field. He spoke to his congregation in the open, prayed before fireplaces or under the trees, and fought unbelievers and mockers with his fists, as well as his tongue. In the first twenty years of his career he preached eight thousand sermons.

Physically, Cartwright was a man of might. "His mouth and eyes," writes one who saw him in the fullness of his energies, "as well as the radiant play of the upper part of his cheeks, tell of a kindly, sociable nature. His head is large, and firmly supported between ample and compact shoulders. His brow is broad and overhung with a mass of iron-gray hair. His eyes are intensely deep in color, and shine like dark fires beneath his shaggy eyebrows, while crow's-feet wrinkles mark their corners, and add to the peculiar expression of his countenance. His complexion, never fair, is deeply tanned by the sun." That he had to be robust goes without saying. He rode hundreds of miles on horseback, preached day in and day out, prayed morning, noon and night, and wrestled with sinners not only mentally but physically.

While the population was scattered he "rode the circuit" and later, as presiding elder, covered all Illinois from Springfield to Cairo—a tough country. The people were barbaric; rough and strong. He gloried in the "camp-meeting", an indigenous American institution, peculiar to the early West. Indiana, Ohio and Illinois affected this form of exciting spirituality. Whole families traveled, sometimes as much as a hundred miles, to these centers of uplift, thousands of men, women and "young folks" attending. White cities sprang up in great groves of the tall noble trees that then garbed the landscape. In later years, permanent camp sites came into being, with cottage accompaniments and capacious auditoriums. Other amusements were scarce, so this form of exhilaration was hugely popular. They were at their apex of glory in the late 'thirties when Cartwright was at his best. Captain Frederick Marryat, in his *Diary in America,* graphically describes one of these affairs:

"The camp was raised upon . . . a piece of table-land comprising many acres. About one acre and a half was surrounded on the four sides by cabins built up of rough boards; the whole area in the center was fitted up with planks, laid about a foot from the ground, as seats. At one end, but not close to the cabins, was a raised stand, which served as a pulpit for the preachers, one of them praying, while five or six others sat down behind him on benches. There was ingress to the area by the four corners; the whole of it was shaded by vast forest trees, which ran up to the height of fifty or sixty feet without throwing out a branch; and to the trunks of these trees were fixed lamps in every direction, for the continuance of service at night.

"Outside of the area, which may be designated as the church, were hundreds of tents pitched in every quarter, their snowy whiteness contrasting beautifully with the deep verdure and gloom of the forest. These were the temporary habitations of those who had come many miles to attend the meeting, and who remained there from the commencement until it concluded—usually a period of from ten to twelve days, but often much longer. The tents were furnished with every article necessary for cooking; mattresses to sleep upon; some of them even had bedsteads and chests of drawers, which had been brought in the wagons in which the people in this country usually travel. At a farther distance were all the wagons and other vehicles which had conveyed the people to the meeting, whilst hundreds of horses were tethered under the trees, and plentifully provided with forage. Such were the general outlines of a most interesting and beautiful scene.

"The major portion of those not in the area were cooking the dinners. Fires were burning in every direction; pots boiling; chickens roasting, hams seething; indeed, there appeared to be no want of creature comforts.

"But the trumpet sounded as in the days of

yore, as a signal that the service was about to re-
commence, and I went into the area and took my
seat. One of the preachers rose and gave out a
hymn, which was sung by the congregation, numbering seven or eight hundred. After the singing
of the hymn was concluded he commenced an ex-
tensive sermon; it was good, sound doctrine and
although Methodism, it was Methodism of the
mildest tone and divested of the bitterness of denunciation, as, indeed, is generally the case with
Methodism in America. . . . In front of the
pulpit was a space railed off, and strewn with
straw, which I was told was the anxious seat, and
on which sat those who were touched by their conscience or the discourse of the preacher. On . . .
one side . . . about twenty females, mostly
young, squatted down on the straw; on the other a
few men; in the center was a long form, against
which some men were kneeling, with their faces
covered with their hands as if occupied in prayer.
Gradually the number increased, girl after girl
dropped down upon the straw on one side, and
men on the other. At last an elderly man gave
out a hymn, which was sung with peculiar energy;
then another knelt down in the center and commenced a prayer, shutting his eyes and raising his
hands above his head; then another burst into
prayer and another followed him; then their voices
all became confused together; and then were
heard the more silvery tones of women's supplica-
tion. As the din increased so did their enthusiasm;

handkerchiefs were raised to bright eyes, and sobs were intermingled with prayers and ejaculations. It became a scene of Babel; more than twenty men and women were crying out at the highest pitch of their voices, and trying apparently to be heard above the others.

"Every minute the excitement increased; some wrung their hands and called for mercy; some tore their hair; boys lay down crying bitterly, with their heads buried in the straw; there was sobbing almost to suffocation, and hysterics and deep agony. One young man clung to the form, crying: 'Satan tears at me, but I will hold fast. Help! Help! Help! He drags me down.'

"It was a scene of horrible agony and despair; and, when it was at its height, one of the preachers came in and raising his voice high above the tumult entreated the Lord to receive into His fold those who now repented and would fain return. Another of the ministers knelt down by some young men, whose faces were covered up and who appeared to be almost in a state of frenzy, and putting his hands upon them, poured forth an energetic prayer, well calculated to work upon their over-excited feelings. Groans, ejaculations, broken sobs, frantic motions and convulsions succeeded; some fell on their backs with their eyes closed, waving their heads in a slow motion, and crying out—'Glory, glory, glory!'"

This dropping to the ground represented the highest state of religious ecstasy, or auto-intoxica-

tion. The preacher who could cause the greater
number of such prostrations was reckoned the most
efficient of his kind. Cartwright excelled at de-
veloping this curious form of emotion in his hearers. Recording one occasion, when at the call of
the trumpet, he responded to the text: "The gates
of Hell shall not prevail against it," he says in his
autobiography: "In about thirty minutes the power of God fell upon the congregation in such a
manner as is seldom seen. The people fell in every
direction, right and left, front and rear. It was
supposed that not less than three hundred fell like
dead men in a mighty battle; and there was no need
of calling mourners, for they were strewed all over
the camp ground. . . . Our meeting lasted all
night; and when we closed on Tuesday, there were
two hundred who had professed religion, and about
that number found the church." A splendid spoil,
as he reckoned it.

Conducting a camp-meeting on the edge of
Tennessee, he brought "tall sons and daughters
of Belial" down to "cry for mercy." For this
prowess some of their brothers, still loyal to their
parent, decided to mob the powerful preacher.
They rode their horses to the threshold of the anxious seat. Here Cartwright ordered them to halt.
The leader sought to ride him down, but was jerked
from his saddle by the stalwart saver of souls, while
his horse bolted and demoralized the ranks of the
squadron. The "captain" thus unhorsed, was held
captive and fined fifty dollars, which insured
"peace on all our borders" during the meeting.

Bluntness of speech was Cartwright's greatest asset. He indulged in no finesse with sinners. They were all clay in his eyes. Visiting Nashville during a Presbyterian conference he was invited to speak at a Monday night service. With the invitation came a caution to have decorous regard for Presbyterian sensibilities, for the church in which he was to talk was the most aristocratic in the town. The edifice was crowded and the pastor sat beside Cartwright in the pulpit. He had just read his text: "What shall it profit a man, if he gain the whole world and lose his own soul," when he saw General Andrew Jackson enter. There were no vacant seats and the tall general leaned against a pillar. The pastor tugged Peter's coat-tail and whispered: "General Jackson has come in." Peter did not seem to hear. Again the pastor whispered: "General Jackson has come in, sir." Instead of being impressed, "I felt," says Cartwright in his autobiography, "a flash of indignation run all over me like an electric shock, and purposely speaking out audibly, I said: 'Who is General Jackson? If he doesn't get his soul converted, God will damn his soul as quick as he will a guinea negro.' "

The pastor ducked behind the pulpit as a titter ran through the crowd and even the grim Jackson smiled. The incumbent was sure Jackson would flog Cartwright for his impudence, and made a formal apology to the great man. A day or so later Cartwright and Jackson met on the street:

"You are a man after my own heart," was his greeting. "A minister of Christ ought to love everybody and fear no mortal man."

To Jackson, Cartwright was more than a man. The preacher had been a chaplain in his army and was present at the famous Battle of New Orleans. Besides this he was a Jacksonian Democrat of the truest type.

More than one challenge to mortal combat resulted from this frankness of speech. A loudly dressed gallant, who persisted in standing up on a seat, and who failed to respond to a call to order, got this direct remark: "I mean that young man there, standing on the seats of the ladies, with a ruffled shirt on—I doubt not that ruffled shirt was borrowed."

The fellow threatened to whip the preacher, at which Cartwright boldly approached him and invited him out in the grounds to settle the affront. On the way a cramp seized Cartwright, which caused him to clap his hand to his side. The challenger thought he was reaching for a dirk and so accused him. "Yes," said Cartwright, "I will give you the benefit of all the dirks I have."

The bully fled. Asked what he would have done had the man stood his ground, he replied: "I should no doubt have importuned him to have prayer first and then followed the openings of Providence." He called the unruly son of a militia major to account for disturbing a meeting, and the father challenged him, according to the custom of the time. This gave Cartwright the choice of weapons. He proposed cornstalks, and the laugh so raised smoothed the ruffled feathers of his foe.

The young men were especially vicious and disorderly. It is difficult to understand how the drift from Kentucky, Virginia and Tennessee to Ohio, Indiana and Illinois produced such wild people, but it did, and to these Cartwright came to save them from their sins. Since Hercules cleaned the Augean stables there had been no greater task. Sometimes he was mobbed and once had to fight seven magistrates, who sided with the unrighteous. He led a party on behalf of law and order and made thirty prisoners. Some of the cases were too hard for conversion, but readily yielded to his spell.

The Calvinistic fundamentalists of the day were severe critics of Cartwright, who opposed their doctrine and accepted that of Arminius. As the result, a pamphlet was circulated against him purporting to describe a council in hell where Diabolus, Apollyon and Lucifer gave their reasons for supporting the milder belief. It was aimed at Cartwright, who responded with a series of reasons why the report could not have been written in the infernal regions, viz:

1. The devil, who was familiar with the old Romans, would certainly show a greater knowledge of Latin than is manifest in this letter.

2. The author is evidently unfamiliar with the constitution of the hierarchy of hell.

3.   There is more truth in the document than could easily be put to the credit of the devil.

In concluding his response Cartwright observed: "If any friends of his Satanic Majesty think that anything I have said is not correct, and if they feel any disposition to set me right, they are at perfect liberty to do so, provided they will sign their proper names." There is no evidence that any of the "friends" ever came forward.

In one of his controversies a young clergyman fresh from the theological seminary sought to confound the "unlettered backwoodsman," as he deemed Cartwright, by throwing at him a section of the New Testament in Greek. To this Cartwright promptly replied in German, a language unknown to either his auditors or his opponent, who, supposing it to be Hebrew, surrendered with the remark that this was the first learned Methodist he had ever met.

"I do not wish to underrate education," says Cartwright in reciting the experience, "but really I have seen so many of these educated preachers who forcibly remind me of lettuce growing under a shade of a peach tree, or a gosling that had got the straddles by wading in the dew, that I turn away sick and faint."

He throve on controversy with his fellow-orthodox. The Baptists, being next in strength, were his most frequent antagonists. It was a contest, so to speak, between the Army and the Navy of the Lord. He once narrowly escaped a Baptist

trap when induced, with twenty-three of his own
converts, to take part in a "union" meeting. At
the climax of fervor the Baptist preacher called on
all true believers to come forward for baptism. To
the astonishment of all, Cartwright followed the
command with his little band. In the presence of
the pool he balked. He would accept baptism by
sprinkling but not submit to immersion! The plot
failed and the Methodists were saved, as the Baptist revivalist would have no part in half-way
measures.

Severe as Cartwright was with Calvinists and
Baptists, he was kind as a cooing dove with Universalists and Unitarians. Though he used the
fires of hell as a persuader he did not wish to con-
demn any one to everlasting punishment and always gave the most hardened sinner a chance.

Having settled in Sangamon County, Illinois,
the Democrats capitalized Cartwright's popularity
and nominated him for the Legislature. He succeeded in winning the election after a hot campaign, in which he was charged with trying to
"swear off" a note of indebtedness. He faced the
man who started the story as he was telling it on
the hustings in Springfield.

"I want to know something about this lying
report you have been circulating about me," was
his introduction to the speaker.

"Who are you?"

"Did you ever see me before?"

"No, sir, not that I know of."

"My name is Peter Cartwright, and if you do not here acknowledge yourself a liar I will sweep the streets with you to your heart's content."

The defamer ate his words with a relish, rather than be used as a street cleaner.

Crossing a ferry on the Sangamon a group of men were aspersing him profanely, and one declared he would thrash "the Methodist horse thief" the first time he met him.

Cartwright stepped up to him. "Come," he said. "I am the man you propose to thrash. Either whip me as you threaten, or quit cursing me, else I will put you in the river and baptize you in the name of the devil."

The awful alternative cowed the profane passenger. Indeed, he became converted and voted for the valorous parson. Two terms in the Legislature were so well spent that his constituency decided to promote him to Congress in 1846. His Whig opponent was a tall lawyer twenty-four years his junior, known as a wit, who was becoming popular on the circuit. He told funny stories to illustrate his points and had organized the "rough young fellows," into a considerable following. His name was Abraham Lincoln.

At the beginning of the campaign all the advantages appeared to lie with Cartwright. Abolitionism was splitting the Whigs. Many objected to the annexation of Texas, with its promise of increase in slave territory and would not follow their party. Lincoln was well known, but not a drawing card on the hustings, compared with his competitor. Cartwright threw the fervor of a revival into the campaign and coupled politics with his religion. He used the pulpit liberally, and a "revival" held in Springfield under his auspices was really part of his well-conceived canvass. Lincoln attended one evening. The preacher made his customary passionate appeal for sinners to come forward to the mourners' bench. Catching sight of his opponent he turned the fire in his direction, ending with this perorative query: "If you are not going to repent and go to Heaven, Mr. Lincoln, where are you going?"

The tall personage so summoned to the bar arose tranquilly and responded:

"I am going to Congress, Brother Cartwright."

This was correct. He went, defeating the popular pulpiter by 1,511 votes. This had not been thought possible, but the district did not want a preacher in Congress who had been pretty hard on its sins, and the anti-slavery feeling underneath was great. Yet Cartwright was not a believer in slavery, but his party fell, unfortunately, into its alignment. He had been one of those to take the stand for freedom in the general convention of his church held at Cincinnati in 1844, a convention that split the Methodist church into North and South, to be followed in this respect by Baptists, Presbyterians and Episcopalians.

An elder in the Sangamon district had a termagant wife. She ran counter to her husband's piety, refused to let him hold family prayer and lashed him unmercifully with a profane and bitter tongue. Cartwright, calling one evening, had to run a gauntlet of abuse and determined to take her in hand. Believing she was possessed of the devil he proceeded to exorcise the evil one in this fashion:

"I caught her by the arm and swinging her round in a circle, brought her right up to the door and shoved her out. She jumped up, tore her hair, foamed; and such swearing as she uttered was seldom equalled and never surpassed. The door was very strongly made to keep out Indians. I shut it tight, barred it and went to prayer, and I prayed as best I could, but I have no language at my command to describe my feelings; to conquer or die in the attempt. While she was raging and foaming in the yard and around the cabin, I started a spiritual song and sung loud, to drown her voice as much as possible. . . . I sang on and she roared and thundered outside till she became perfectly exhausted and panted for breath. At length when she had spent her force, she became calm and still, and then knocked at the door, saying: 'Mr. Cartwright, please let me in.' 'Will you behave yourself if I let you in?' said I. 'O, yes,' said she, 'I will.' She had roared and foamed until she was in a high perspiration and looked pale as death. After she took her seat 'O!' she said, 'what a fool I am.' "

Satan was vanquished. She sat meek and quiet and within six months, as Cartwright triumphantly records, "was soundly converted and became an exemplary wife and mother, and an earnest worker for Christ."

Living as he did a life of extreme emotion he wore well. He throve on the extraordinary and was unyielding in his assaults on evil. He was Union to the core in the wartime. Southern Illinois, though the home of Lincoln, was filled with southern sympathizers. Called to christen a child at Springfield the parents gave "Jefferson Davis" as the desired appellation. He handed the infant back to its mother, dismissed the congregation and went home to pray over the problem. The next day the parents selected "George Washington" as more likely to pass muster and Cartwright accepted it with joy. "I thanked God," he said afterward, "and dedicated the child to Him with that revered name."

So he fought, exhorted and labored through all his life, dealing with rough people and standing by the right as he saw it with his clear shining eyes. These closed for the last time on September 25, 1872, at Pleasant Plains, Illinois, where he had made his home for more than fifty years.

CHAPTER VI

CONTEMPORARY with Cartwright, though beginning his active career at a later date, was Charles Grandison Finney, a remarkable revivalist. Unlike Cartwright he worked in towns and cities. His creed was that of Calvin and he was merciless toward all foes of that austere doctrine. His wrath fell heaviest upon the Universalists, who were very active from 1830 to 1860, spreading the doctrine of the Fatherhood of God and the Brotherhood of Man, with faith in the final salvation of all mankind. Just what objection there should be to this amiable belief is difficult to understand at this day, but at the time when the controversy raged hottest, Universalists, and their even more liberal, if ultra-aristocratic fellows, the Unitarians, were anathema to the orthodox. Finney was born in the Congregationalist garden, Litchfield County, Connecticut, August 29, 1792, in the town of Warren. Litchfield, the county-seat, is where the amazing brood of Beechers first saw the light, their father, the great Lyman Beecher being the pastor in that lovely village. Though Connecticut born, Finney was New York State bred. When he was two years old his parents removed to Oneida County, New York, along with many other natives of New England. Like Cartwright he had no special impetus toward religion in his surroundings. His father and mother were not strongly inclined to the church. There were no stated services in their neighborhood, though a district school was maintained, which the boy attended until fifteen years old. An occasional itinerant made himself heard, but Finney was usually shocked by the ignorance of the stray exhorter, who was more apt to excite laughter than repentance among his hearers.

The neighborhood finally built a church edifice, but the restless elder Finney moved away to carve out another farm in the wilderness of Ontario County, near Sackett's Harbor. There were no religious advantages in the vicinity. Here the lad lived until twenty years of age, when he set out on his worldly pilgrimage, first to Connecticut, then to New Jersey, where he began his struggle with life as a school-teacher, so earning money enough to enjoy a term in a Connecticut high school. Here he sought to fit himself for Yale, but was dissuaded by his instructor, who told him he would waste his time, though himself a Yale graduate. Four years of teaching and attending school brought him to the conclusion that he would take up the law as an occupation. Accordingly he entered a country office at Adams, Jefferson County, New York. "When I went to Adams to study law," Finney says in his autobiography, "I was almost as ignorant of religion as a heathen. I had been brought up mostly in the woods. I had very little regard for the Sabbath and had no definite knowledge of religious truth."

The local Presbyterian preacher, a Princeton product, Reverend George W. Gale, taught "hyper-Calvinism," and the young man was "rather perplexed than edified by his preaching."

The old books he read in the squire's office cited Scripture as authority for many of the main principles of common law. His curiosity stirred by this the student bought a Bible and checking up on Coke and Blackstone, developed his interest in the logic of the book which he studied assiduously, taking issue in consequence with Pastor Gale on much that he preached. These disputes leading nowhere, after several years "my mind, as I have since known, was so much impressed by the Holy Spirit, that I could not long leave this question unsettled," and he accepted the faith of Christ in orthodox fulness.

This did not come about without a considerable mental struggle, accompanied with hysteria and much exhausting prayer, but in the end: "My sense of guilt was gone; my sins were gone—and I do not think I felt any more sense of guilt than if I had never sinned." This result was reached in 1821, when he had certainly reached years of reasonable discretion. He at once abandoned the law in a determination to preach the gospel. Like Don Quixote he went out prepared to meet all comers in his new delight and by chance his first encounter was with a defender of Universalism. "In a moment," says Finney, "I was enabled to blow his argument to the wind." The vanquished believer in universal salvation climbed over a fence and disappeared in the woods, returning at night "a bright convert," who during his stay in the timber belt "gave his heart to God."

"My conversion," he records, "had created a good deal of astonishment in the village," especially as he accosted every person he met and insisted on taking account of the state of each one's soul. One old lawyer thought the youth was perpetrating a hoax—simply trying to see what he could "make Christian people believe."

Soon he had the chance to make a public test of his powers. He attended the next prayer-meeting night, finding the house packed. The spirit moving no one he arose and recited his experiences. "What the Lord enabled me to say," he wrote, "seemed to take a wonderful hold upon the people." The skeptical old lawyer was present. "He is earnest," was his comment. "There is no mistake, but he is deranged, that is clear."

Pastor Gale then made a public apology for himself, having doubted the conversion and called upon Finney to lead in prayer. He had never uttered an invocation in his life, but rose to the occasion. "We had a wonderful meeting," he records, "and, from that day we had a meeting every evening for a long time. The work spread on

every side." The young people of his class rallied
and followed him into the fold. His heart was so
full that "for more than a week" he did not feel
the need "of food or of sleep," and went on thus
for many days until his strong mind reacted under
the strain, convinced that unless he became nearer
normal he would go insane. His next step was to
visit his father and mother and in a short time
thereafter "they were both hopefully converted."
That he had subconsciously learned to play upon
the psychic chord that controls human emotion is
very clear. He began spending an early morning
hour in the meeting-house in solitary prayer.
Others joined him momentarily, and broke away,
to his great distress, but he was consoled one day at
dawn when as he entered the edifice "a light perfectly ineffable shone in my soul . . . like . . .
that light that prostrated Saul on his way to
Damascus." He came to fast at stated intervals
and his fantasies were naturally heightened by hunger.

All did not go well, however. A young woman
over whom he had cast a spell became a Universalist. The discovery of which "so astounded me that
I could not break through with my faith, and get
hold of God in reference to her case." She remained in her sins several months in consequence.
There was even a worse case, a magistrate who had
been elected to the Legislature, who declined to
become converted until he had served his term, or
as he said in his case-hardened way: "I stand com-

mitted to my political friends to carry out certain measures in the Legislature that are incompatible with my first becoming a Christian; and I have promised that I will not attend to the subject until after I have returned from Albany."

Alas, when he "returned from Albany" he had become almost an insane Universalist. No argument could move this statesman who "remained in his sins, finally fell into decay, and died at last, I have been told, a dilapidated man, and in the full faith of his Universalism."

In the spring of 1822 Finney became a candidate for the ministry, but declined the suggestion that he should take a theological course at Princeton, as he would not put himself "under such an influence." He thought the preachers who came from the University had not been properly educated and so preferred to continue his studies under Mr. Gale, with whom he differed widely and argued interminably. He was finally ordained in the face of much opposition in the hope that the Lord would give him "deliverance." Mr. Gale was not sound on the subject of eternal punishment, holding that the atonement was made for all men. This view was seized by a Universalist proselyte to prove that universal salvation was the inevitable result, as God could not justly punish those whose debt was paid. Seeing that Mr. Gale was in "a tight place" Finney came to the rescue. He silenced the Universalist with the assertion that the "atonement did not consist in the literal payment of the debt of sinners—it simply rendered the salvation of all men possible. Christ had not cancelled sin in the sense of literally paying the indebtedness of sinners."

Finney received full license to preach in March, 1824, having conquered all doubts as to his sincerity or ability. He began his great career humbly enough at Evan's Mills, in the Jefferson County town of Le Roy. There was no church edifice but the Baptists and Congregationalists took alternate Sundays in the schoolhouse. This gave Finney two Sundays a month to spare and he added Antwerp, eighteen miles away, to his task. Here there was a Presbyterian church, the key of which was in the possession of the village innkeeper. There had been no settled pastor, but a deacon who lived five miles up the road had read service until the pranks played by some belligerent Universalists who took the wheels off his buggy caused him to give up the effort. Finney found haven in a friendly parlor, began to preach and as attendance grew, shifted to the schoolhouse, where the little meetings expanded into the zealot's first revival and gave impetus to what was to become the main work of his life. The obdurate landlord who held the church key was moved to relax and opened the building, which was soon overfilled. The fire spread. Called to a near-by school district, "an awful solemnity" settled upon the congregation "which began to fall from their seats in every direction and cried for mercy." Indeed, he says, "if I had had a sword in each hand, I would not have cut them off their seats as fast as they fell." Nearly all were prostrate within two minutes after they first felt the psychic shock, each praying for himself or herself. The preacher was compelled to stop to await the fading out of the ecstasy. Finney's heart so overflowed with joy at the scene that it was with much difficulty he refrained from shouting and giving glory to God. The revival penetrated to every part of the town and some of the neighboring ones "shared the blessing."

As to his method, he borrowed his illustrations from the occupations of his hearers, used language they would understand, that of the common people. Indeed, his singling out sinners was painfully plain. "Hell" was as definite a place in his adjurations as the railroad depot at Watertown. Naturally the decorous dominies of the day viewed him askance, but he had bound on his buckler and was soon on his way to larger triumphs.

Governeur, in the adjacent county of St. Lawrence, next called on the revivalist to save its sinners. It was a sizable place as communities average in the North Country, settled mainly from New England, by way of Vermont. It was a Universalist stronghold and he at once challenged their leader to debate. The liberal's valor faded after a few encounters: "His agony became intense, and as soon as the way was opened for him to speak out, he surrendered up his convictions and soon after expressed hope of Christ. In a few days his companions were brought in, one after the other, till I believe the revival made a clean sweep of them." If the Universalists were easy the Baptists were not. They "used very objectionable means" to stop the progress of the revival, rallying a corps of young men actively to oppose Finney's efforts. He took to prayer and prayed for the softening of their obdurate spirits with such effect that before the end of a week, nearly, if not all of them "were hoping for Christ." Parenthetically, it may be observed that Finney's colleague, Brother Nash, had given the young men a week to be converted or go to hell. Finney singled out individual "sinners" and argued with them at homes and places of business. This was his special method with free thinkers or "infidels" as he prefers to call them. One of these in Governeur confessed that he "deserved endless damnation" for "the way he had treated God."

The dreariest place in the known world is Dekalb, a railway junction between Governeur and Canton. This was Finney's next stopping-place. There was a schism in the town between the Methodists and Presbyterians who had fought a revival incited by the Wesleyans several years before, as the Calvinists resented having their fellows proselyted during the excitement. Finney decided they were wrong and preached with his customary power. A man "fell" as several had fallen for the Methodist exhorter. The hard-headed Presbyterians laid this to hysteria. Finney was satisfied that "it was a case of falling under the power of

God." He kept on and a number of Presbyterians "fell" but no Methodists! Many heard the call.

Finney's fame had now spread over northern New York and after a brief exhibition of his powers at Western, he moved upon Rome, through an "exchange" with the Reverend Moses Gillett, pastor of the Congregationalist church. His hearers were magnetized as usual, to the alarm of Brother Gillett, though "they did not shriek but went out sobbing and sighing, and their sobs and sighs could be heard till they got out into the street."

From Rome to Utica is a short step. Here the revivalist repeated his triumph, converting full five hundred souls; he was credited with salvaging three thousand during this, his first real campaign. The knowledge of his efforts troubled the more conservative divines who began to inveigh against him, even the great Lyman Beecher taking a hand in the deprecations.

Auburn was the next point of attack, and after some success in this cultured community, he assailed the wicked city of Troy, where he spent the fall and early winter of 1826. He met with a good deal of opposition from church people, influenced by Doctor Beecher's disapproval, with the result that the Presbytery appointed a committee to investigate, which was to report to a convention at New Lebanon. Here he faced Doctor Beecher, who resented Finney's attitude and that of his defenders. When asked for the authority upon which he had asserted the claims made for the revivalist were "unintelligent" Beecher replied: "We have not come here to be catechised; and our spiritual dignity forbids us to answer such questions." While the conference was willing to accept the accounts as truthful—all except Beecher and one other—it passed a resolve condemning the methods of the revivalist and Beecher said to him: "Finney, I know your plan and you know I do; you mean to come to Connecticut and carry a streak of fire to Boston. But, if you attempt it, as the Lord liveth, I'll meet you at the state line, and call out all the artillerymen, and fight every inch of the way to Boston, and then I'll fight you there."

This proved to be a vain fulmination. Finney met the situation with dignity, declined to enter upon any personal controversy and went on with his work. Stephentown, adjacent to New Lebanon, was in "a state of impenitence," and he responded to a call for its redemption. While so employed in the rescue of souls made dormant by the neglect of an endowed Presbyterian parson, he had for an auditor, Honorable Z. R. Shipherd, a Washington County lawyer, who was attending court in Albany. He was "converted" before he left the house. It is worthy of recording that his son, Reverend J. J. Shipherd, was to found Oberlin College, the scene of Finney's greatest work, and his grandson, Jacob R. Shipherd, was to get Secretary of State James G. Blaine into a dispute over some Peruvian guano concessions and so aided in spoiling his chance to become president of the United States. The revival was a success, "the converts turned out to be saved," and the church renewed its vigor.

The next "call" came from Wilmington, Delaware, where it appears there was stagnation due to a belief "that God would convert sinners in His own time," a view with which Finney had no sympathy. This corrected, he proceeded to attack Philadelphia, at the church of Reverend James Patterson, a Princetonian, but who had no objections to emotional salvation. He made the rounds of the various Presbyterian churches, laboring for a year and a half in revival effort, to be accepted with the customary Philadelphia placidity. Reading furnished a further field, then Lancaster, where he found religion "in a low state." Conversions multiplied during his stay, but this was brief. After a short effort at Columbia, Anson G. Phelps invited him to a test of strength in New York, hiring a vacant church in Vandewater Street as an arena. He could lease this for but three months, and at the end of that time bought a disused Universalist edifice at Broadway and Prince Street, where the campaign against the city's supply of sinners was vigorously carried on. Mr. Phelps, it may be noted, was the founder of the Phelps-Dodge metal business, with its great and ramifying fortunes that continue until this day. For the period of his stay in Vandewater Street, the revivalist, with his wife and young daughter, were guests of the Phelps.

After successful assaults upon the sinners of Rochester, Auburn, Buffalo and Providence, Finney made the invasion of Boston, which Doctor Lyman Beecher had threatened to forfend. The Beechers were intrenched in the modern Athens. Lyman was pastor of Bowdoin Street church and his son Edward was filling the pulpit at Park Street, at the corner of Tremont, a church made celebrated in later years as "Brimstone Corner" by the Reverend Doctor J. L. Withrow. Instead of the threatened hostility, Finney was welcomed with the customary Boston courtesy— one of coolness prepared for developments. He preached around among the churches and held week evening services at Park Street, delivering what he called "sermons to Christians." These assailed the perfections of Boston orthodoxy and gave great cheer to the local Unitarians who were a power and eager for controversy. He heard again and again the query: "What will the Unitarians say; if such things are true of us who are orthodox?" Also this further thought: "If Mr. Finney preaches to us in this way, the Unitarians will triumph over us, and say that at least the orthodox are no better Christians than the Unitarians"—a frightful implication. Besides this he found in Boston "a method of dealing with inquiring sinners that was very trying to me." For example, after exhorting a group of these recalcitrants to give up all and follow Christ, he was disturbed by Lyman Beecher's saying in echo:

"You need not be afraid to give up all to Christ, your property and all, for He will give it right back to you." This was repentance with a string to it in Finney's opinion and he took strong, though diplomatic, exception to the view. He produced some good results, but slipped on more ice than he broke and was glad to return to New York where, having now a family of three children, he was happy to accept a call from the Second Free Church and settle down for a period. The anti-slavery movement was beginning to show strength. *The Evangelist* took strong grounds in its support and Leavitt, its editor, soon found himself in trouble with many of his readers. Finney, who was to become foremost in the cause, cautioned Leavitt to go slow lest he ruin the paper. As an antidote he began to write a series on revivals, that quite drowned the disaffection and brought a multitude of new subscribers—a splendid tribute to American hypocrisy.

Finney had in the meantime secured the support of Arthur Tappan, a rich and worthy merchant. Lane Theological Seminary at Cincinnati had been the scene of an uprising due to the suppression by the trustees of the student activity against slavery. Tappan proposed that Finney should go to Ohio and establish a class in theology that would continue the orderly production of evangels. The revivalist had started many students on their course and felt the need of doing something, but was at a loss how to proceed, when in January, 1835, the Reverend John J. Shipherd, son of Finney's New Lebanon convert, came to New York and offered him the post of Professor of Theology in his recently established college at Oberlin, Ohio. With him was the Reverend Asa Mahan, of Cincinnati, who had been the only trustee of Lane to object to the suppression of free speech. He joined in the request. The rebellious students from Lane had formed the nucleus of the new school. Both Arthur Tappan and his brother Lewis were strong supporters of anti-slavery and urged Finney to go. He finally assented on condition that the Oberlin trustees should not interfere with the conduct of the school, and that there should be no discrimination against students on account of color. "After a great struggle to overcome their own prejudices and those of the community" the terms were accepted. Finney's New York friends got together and endowed eight professorships. Whether he then realized it or not, Finney had forced one of the greatest forward movements in the history of the republic. To this Arthur Tappen guaranteed, from his own great income (for that time) of one hundred thousand dollars a year, to provide for the support of Finney and his family. With the added promise that he might serve his church part of each year he went to Oberlin at the beginning of summer in 1835.

The rebellious Lane students followed in force and were lodged in barracks built by the trustees.

There was no chapel. Finney's friends bought a great tent to use for the purpose. It served also for the revivals, from which he could not stay his hand. The college grew, new buildings were rushed and students came in swarms. In the midst of the undertaking the panic of 1837 ruined Tappan, and the college went on the rocks. The crash, coming at the time when large obligations had been incurred, left Finney and his associates in a painful position. Besides, as he wrote, "The great run of people of Ohio were utterly opposed to our enterprise because of its abolition character. The towns around were hostile to our movement, and in some places threats were made to come and tear down our buildings. A Democratic legislature was, in the meantime, endeavoring to get some hold of us, which would enable them to abrogate our charter."

His revival lectures had been published in book form and enjoyed a great sale, especially in England, to which country Oberlin now sent an embassy to ask for help. John Keep and William Dawes, who bore the appeal, came back with six thousand pounds, given by supporters of anti-slavery. This helped, as did other contributions from the slender following in the western states. Finney became impoverished. Thanksgiving Day found him with an empty purse. Despite this he preached and "greatly enjoyed" his own effort. Going home to a lean dinner his wife met him with a letter from Josiah Chapin, of Providence. It contained a check for two hundred dollars, with a hint that there was more where that came from. There was. He supported the Finneys with an allowance of six hundred dollars a year for several years, when loss of income compelled him to discontinue the benefaction. It was carried on, however, by Willard Sears, of Boston. So the struggle went valiantly on until "by the grace of God we outrode the gale." By 1842 Oberlin was a substantial and much hated institution.

Boston was violently pro-slavery and Mr. Sears' sympathy with the cause made him many enemies. He bought the Marlborough Hotel in Washington Street and turned it into a chapel where free speech might be heard. To this Finney now came and in it reached the apex of his career as a saver of souls in the fall of 1843; or, as he put it: "The Lord gave my own soul a very thorough overhauling, and a fresh baptism of His spirit." Altogether he favored Boston with five visitations and seems to have converted all who came his way except the clergy, whose fear of the aristocratic Unitarians and the numerous Universalists "kept them back from preaching and holding forth the danger of the impenitent," as set forth by Jonathan Edwards, to wit: "The doctrine of endless punishment, and the necessity of entire sanctification."

During one of the great Boston revivals the Finney family became saturated in the prevailing atmosphere of high-power piety. One day a gentleman called on business. The small daughter of the house responded to the bell.

"Is your father in?" inquired the visitor.

"No," was the startling response, "but come in, poor dying sinner, mother will pray for you."

In 1849 the revivalist went to England. His wife had died and he had taken to himself a second, Mrs. Elizabeth Atkinson, a widow of Rochester, who joined him in his revivalistic efforts. The stay was successful, terminating in 1851 when Finney returned, a year later to become president of Oberlin, which position he retained until 1866. Two of his daughters had grown up and were married to Oberlin professors, James Monroe and Henry E. Peck. Both were great workers in the cause of anti-slavery and were frequently under arrest and occasionally in jail. Finney was also pastor of the church, to which all students were compelled to go. Indeed, their evangelization was his chief aim. He left instruction to others.

The severity of Finney's attitude toward what he considered sin is well illustrated by the following anecdote:

In his congregation was the worthy wife of a well-to-do farmer who brought her children to church and preserved exemplary piety. Not so the husband. Though a man of means he did not accept the faith, indeed, was suspected to be little better than an infidel, while he consorted with the wicked who played cards and drank corn whisky. In the course of events, he died—one of the best things he ever did. The family, with some trepidation, invited Finney to preach the funeral sermon.

This he agreed to do. Now at Oberlin, whatever the occasion, when the church doors opened, the student body had to attend. This included funerals. So all were there when the farmer came to that finality. Finney preached a terrible sermon, picturing the evil life of the deceased and painting a powerful picture of the status of his soul. Needless to say it was in the hottest part of hell.

While the family knew the worldly facts were correctly stated, they could not rest under the conviction that the husband and father was perpetually damned, and besought Finney to review the case and see if he could not locate some hope for the redemption of the lost. He was agreeable, promised to pray over the matter and announce the results from the pulpit the next Sunday. This he did, detailing the request of the relatives and his pleas to Heaven. Then he recited his previous indictment and left the old man where he had put him—with a doubly locked door!

Oberlin, as the best organized center of Abolitionism in the North, was under constant fire and suspicion, and once came near being the scene of a great tragedy. One morning while my father and his chum were in the chapel with a thousand others, the janitor, chancing to visit the cellar, saw a spark fizzing in the earthern floor. Being a man of swift mind he stepped on the flame. Digging revealed two kegs of powder, to which was attached the fuse that the quick-witted man had extinguished. Two "students" hailing from Tennessee disappeared at the same time and were never heard from again.

It was regarded as a pro-slavery plot and naturally created intense excitement. The student body certainly had a narrow escape.

One of the iron rules of Oberlin was that all students should cultivate a grave outward aspect. Such frivolity as smiles and laughter in public was strictly barred. To tame the innocent impulse of nature would seem an impossible task, yet it was done save in one notable case. There came to the college a charming girl whose eyes flashed merriment, and whose dimples gave her a perpetual smile. She bubbled with a humor, that, backed by beauty, made her irresistible, to the great discomfiture of her sober sisters, who, at last moved by the girl's popularity, complained to the president.

"Leave her to me. I'll settle her case."

It was not long before the opportunity came to crush the butterfly. Meeting her on the street, Finney was greeted with an engaging smile, which he returned with a look of marble coldness:

"Good morning, daughter of the devil."

"Good morning, father," was the ready response. This ended the efforts of the reformer, and the charmer kept on charming.

Leaving the presidency of the college in 1866, Finney continued as pastor and lecturer on theology. He visited England anew and kept high his revival spirit. For all his activities, he remained strong, dying August 16, 1875, after but three hours' illness, from an acute heart attack. He was an unfaltering soldier of the Cross, a friend of freedom and a great soul.

CHAPTER VII

ROBUST New England of colonial days had its exemplification in Israel Putnam, the Pomfret, Connecticut, farmer, who perhaps, next to Washington, enjoys the greatest fame as an American soldier. He was not Connecticut born, but saw the light in Danvers, a Massachusetts town near Salem, January 7, 1718, the twelfth child of Puritan parents. Putnams are still plentiful in Danvers, all from this tribal strain. History says the English name was Puttenham, that of a Buckinghamshire family which bred besides the soldier, a poet of some small fame, who did not shorten the nomenclature of his kin. On his mother's side were Hawthornes, from whom came Nathaniel Hawthorne of Salem and the world of letters.

With eleven children ahead of him Israel proved the most vigorous of the lot, muscular and venturesome. As a boy of eighteen he ran the farm, his father having died when he was but five, and there showed his prowess. He tamed a vicious bull by donning spurs and riding the beast around a field until the animal bellowed "enough." Called to aid in whipping a refractory negro (this was in

108

the days of colonial slaveholding) he lassoed master and man together, swung them to a beam in the barn and left them there until the owner's wrath was transferred from the slave to the joker.

His bold temperament led him to marry Hannah Pope when twenty-one. The old farm had no room for his growing family and so he followed the tide that had turned to the new lands in Connecticut, moving thither with his wife and first born in 1740. Henceforth his name is identified with that sturdy state as the most famous of its citizens.

A she-wolf was responsible for the beginning of his repute, though he deserved honorable mention as the planter of the first orchard of Roxbury Russets, on his Pomfret farm. The she-wolf harried the flocks and did great damage among the sheep. Her cubs were caught and killed, but the cunning animal long outwitted the hunters. Traps were set in vain, though once she left the claws of one paw behind. She was not content with killing sheep for food, but murdered them for amusement, as do wanton dogs that have tasted blood. Putnam lost seventy in a single night and this massacre sealed the doom of the prowler.

With five of his neighbors he set out to hunt her down and followed a long trail in a light snow that ended in a den amid some rocks, only three miles from Putnam's house. She was at home but could not be dislodged. The countryside was aroused and the den surrounded by excited farmers. Dogs were sent in only to come out lacerated and whimpering. Straw and sulphur were burned without result. The siege lasted all day and until late in the night, when fires and torches lit up the strange scene. At that hour Putnam determined to enter the den himself and end the affair.

Fastening a rope to his legs so he could be pulled out on signal, he lit a torch of birch bark and crept into the hole between the ledges. He had to crawl something like forty feet before he saw the red eyes glowing. He had a prearranged signal—tugging at the rope—that should let the crowd know he had found the enemy. In their excitement they misread the signal and pulled him out, skinning him on the rough rock and stripping his shirt over his head. He had gone in uncoated. Returning with a musket loaded with buckshot he crawled in again and ended the incident. Taking the dead wolf by the ears he signaled a recall and was dragged out with the varmint in his stout hands. The countryside rang with the exploit and for several days the wolf was exhibited to curious crowds. Putnam became the recognized leader of the neighborhood. This spirit of rough daring never left him. Coincidentally, the Puttenham family crest carried a wolf's head on the escutcheon. It became apropos now for its American branch.

By firing on a scouting party of French at Will's Creek, in Pennsylvania, not far from Pittsburgh, then Fort Duquesne, George Washington, a young major of Virginia, began the Seven Years' War—known on this side of the water as the French and Indian conflict— that was to settle forever the destiny of the continent. Putnam, in the meantime, had become prosperous; he was thirty-seven and already enjoyed a competence due to his industry. Connecticut called for volunteers and he was one of the first to respond. His wife and young sons assumed the burden of the farm, while Putnam marched to Albany with the Connecticut forces. Albany had been selected as a rendezvous for descent upon the French strongholds of Ticonderoga and Crown Point on Lake Champlain. The control of this sheet of water gave the French a great military advantage, while the two fortifications had been designed by the best engineers of France.

The movement got under way in July, 1755, some three thousand Colonials being in line together with a band of Mohawks under a celebrated chief called Hendrick, while all were subject to the general command of Sir William Johnson, who set them in motion on August twenty-sixth, cutting their way through the forests to Lake George. They came into contact with the French on September seventh, when Baron Dieskau reached the ground with a force about equal to their own. On the eighth, Dieskau checked the Colonial advance and drove it back with great loss. His were seasoned soldiers; Johnson's, the greenest of the green. Hendrick was killed as was Colonel

Ephraim Williams, who led the line, and under whom Putnam served. His place was taken by Colonel Nathan Whiting and after an all-day conflict Dieskau gave way. Putnam, a second lieutenant in the third company of the Sixth Connecticut Regiment, greatly distinguished himself in the battle. The victory was not followed up. Johnson intrenched himself and Dieskau retired to Ticonderoga.

Desultory fighting followed; Putnam, joining the company of rangers led by Major Robert Rogers and promoted to a captaincy, was kept busy with arduous and dangerous employment. Winter soon befell and there was little activity. In May he was relieved and went home, where the Legislature awarded him fifty Spanish milled dollars for "extraordinary services and good conduct in ranging and scouting the winter past for the annoyance of the enemy near Crown Point and discovery of their motions."

Montcalm, a great general, had succeeded Dieskau in the operations around Lake Champlain and the colonies had again to bestir themselves. Putnam rejoined and again devoted himself to scouting, in company with the resourceful Rogers. There were constant skirmishes and hair-breadth escapes. For two years this went on without either side gaining visible advantage. In July, 1758, General Abercrombie made his disastrous attack on Ticonderoga and was signally defeated. The great brunt of loss fell upon the regulars. Aber-

crombie retreated with his shattered forces and
Putnam resumed ranging. He was now a major
and Robert Rogers had become a colonel. Heading a scouting party on August eighth, the column
was here ambushed by Indians and Putnam taken
prisoner. He was tied to a tree during a lively skir-
mish, while musket balls flew dangerously near him.
When the fight was over he was released, loaded
with baggage and carried with the Indians on a
forced march. He was badly treated and sustained
a gash from a tomahawk, that ever after marked
his features. The Indian who had made him prisoner was absent during these indignities and, returning, forced better treatment. This did not last
long. The Conawaughas had suffered severely in
the fight and decided to burn Putnam at the stake.
He was bound, faggots piled about him and set on
fire. The flames had begun to scorch when a
French officer came up, kicked the brands aside,
cut the thongs and saved the prisoner. He, however, remained a captive with the Indians, but was
not badly treated beyond being bound and closely
watched. Reaching Ticonderoga, he was freed
from the Indian thrall by Montcalm himself and
sent a prisoner of war to Montreal, and from there
to Quebec. An exchange soon followed and in
November he was on his way home.

Jeffrey Amherst now became commander of
the forces facing Ticonderoga which Putnam rejoined as lieutenant-colonel of the Fourth Connecticut Regiment. Amherst prepared to attack

the place on July twenty-seventh, when word came
that the French were in retreat. A week later
Crown Point was abandoned and French resistance was centered at Montreal and Quebec. Putnam was relieved and went home. By spring
Quebec had fallen, Wolf and Montcalm were dead,
and to Amherst remained the task of taking Montreal. Once more Putnam journeyed to the
Canadian frontier, this time proceeding to Oswego,
whence Amherst proposed to approach his prey.
By September sixth, Montreal was invaded. On
the eighth, the city surrendered and France was
no longer a power in the Western World.

The Seven Years' War was over, but England
took on a clash with Spain and called her faithful
Colonials to assist in taking the Island of Cuba.
Putnam, now forty-four, became lieutenant-colonel
of the First Connecticut Regiment and put to sea
for Havana. Lord Albemarle commanded the
expedition. He took all the forts but the Cabanas.
Then the Spaniards surrendered. England gave
Cuba back to Spain in season, to become a problem
for the United States a century and a quarter
later. By autumn Putnam was back in Pomfret,
not a whit worse for his campaign in the tropics.

The conspiracy of Pontiac, by which the tribes
between the Ohio and the Mississippi rose in a last
effort to resist the white invasion, brought on a
brief Indian war in 1764. Detroit was beleaguered
and Colonel John Bradstreet raised an army for
its relief. Putnam promptly joined. The expedi-

tion set out from a point near Buffalo and moved along the lake shore, expecting to punish the Wyandots, Miamis and Ottawas on the way to Detroit. These tribes preferred peace to fighting and volunteered to accompany the expedition. Detroit was relieved, but desultory warfare followed for a time. Putnam was placed in command at Sandusky to watch the Wyandots and a settlement of so-called Senecas, really refugees from many tribes. Bradstreet managed things badly, but Putnam averted trouble in his territory. The country was at peace and the "army" was allowed to get home the best way it could, which it did after much hardship. By November, Putnam was again at Pomfret, after nine years of severe campaigning in arctic and tropic lands.

He had now reached the eminence, the years and the prosperity that entitled him to ease. Family bereavements, ending with the death of his wife, left him with seven children, three sons and four daughters, the youngest but three months old. For several years he devoted himself to peaceful pursuits. Then the smoldering that was to end in the flame of revolution began. The Sons of Liberty came into being with Putnam as an active organizer. Resistance to the Stamp Act was the order of the day and Putnam's Sons of Liberty included enough members of the militia to permit his pledging that body to the cause. The ferment began a decade before the actual outbreak, and all this time Putnam was in evidence, a factor in what was to end in final separation from the Crown. He married again June 3, 1767, Deborah Gardiner, widow of John Gardiner, of Gardiner's Island, a domain in Peconic Bay, and set up a public house in Brooklyn. Old soldiers who did not pay were the best customers. He sang in the church choir in a deep and lusty basso and rang the bell o' Sundays.

General Phineas Lyman, his old commander, had secured from the Crown the fee to lands in West Florida with which to reward the colonial soldiers for their services, and an organization of military adventurers was formed to explore and exploit it. Putnam became an active member and left for the new land on the sloop *Mississippi,* January 10, 1773, headed for Pensacola. There they found old comrades of the French War, General Frederick Haldimand and Major John Small, but no word from the king that would permit them to proceed with their enterprise.

Not wishing to be idle, the adventurers decided to work their sloop up the Mississippi and spy out the land. They went into the Choctaw country, but were warned off by the chiefs. It took a month to get back to Pensacola, where the hoped-for authorization had not yet come from His Majesty. There was nothing left to do but go home.

The repeal of the Stamp Act had not removed the friction between the colonies and the king. When Putnam returned from his adventure the excitement over the tax on tea arose, terminating

in the overt act of the celebrated Boston "party,"
the members of which, disguised as Indians, threw
a cargo into the sea. There followed the enact-
ment of the Boston Port Bill, which stopped trade,
while a Regulating Act took away the liberties of
Massachusetts. Connecticut rallied to the relief of
her neighbors and Putnam was most active in the
cause. He drove a flock of sheep a hundred miles
to Boston, as a gift to the foodless and was received with the distinction he deserved, by no less
personage than Joseph Warren, whom he was to
meet again, and for the last time, on Bunker Hill.

Events now shaped themselves rapidly. Towns
began withdrawing their powder stored in Boston
and keeping it instead, nearer home. A supply
belonging to the province was removed by General
Gage, the British commandant, and placed in
Castle William. Word came to Connecticut that
this act had led to bloodshed. This was incorrect,
but it made a mighty stir. Putnam caused a call
to be issued mustering the militia. They began to
rally, when the rumor of bloodshed was proved
false, and the soldiery disbanded. Meanwhile the
colonists were actively arming and accumulating
military supplies. On April 19, 1775, Gage made
the fatal raid on Concord and Lexington.

Word of the battle reached Putnam while he
was plowing in his fields in Brooklyn. Leaving
the plow in its furrow he mounted a horse, dressed
as he was, and rode to Lebanon for orders from
Governor Jonathan Trumbull—"Brother Jona-

than"—raising the country as he went. He was told to proceed to Boston. Returning to Brooklyn, he found the village green covered with eager volunteers. Leaving these to await a mustering officer he proceeded to Concord, which the patriots held after the British retreat. He was there on the twenty-first, having galloped a hundred miles in eighteen hours. Troops accumulated rapidly at Cambridge and Roxbury. While the situation was shaping Putnam was called to Hartford, where the Legislature, gathered in special session, made him a brigadier general.

Gage was reluctant to force the issue and tried to reach old comrades of the French War, including Putnam, but without avail. The colonists occupied Bunker and Breed's Hills, throwing up rude entrenchments. There were occasional clashes with the regulars and the harbor men o' war now and then tested the range with their cannon. Each side was waiting on the other. One fight, in which Putnam took part, came off on May twenty-seventh. Some of his men were wounded. It was thought the British lost a number in killed. The clash came through "cutting out" a schooner from which some needed cannon were secured. These bold enterprises were much in his line. Each day saw some such exploit. When Gage at last moved on Bunker Hill, June seventeenth, provoked thereto by active work in the entrenchments, Putnam became the center of the fighting. The militia fought like heroes under his lead until their powder gave out. Then they fought with clubbed muskets. Putnam himself served a cannon. When it was over the regulars held the field, but the prestige was with the Colonials. The British lost heavily. Putnam's command to hold fire until the whites in the eyes of the enemy were visible had been obeyed with terrific effect.

Washington now became commander-in-chief and invested Boston with great military skill. There was no work in this for Putnam. The British held out until March 17, 1776, and then ingloriously evacuated the city forever, thus transferring the seat of war to New York, to which point the retiring forces proceeded, occupying Staten Island, much augmented by reinforcements from abroad. The city was in the hands of the Colonials, but it was in an undefended state. Putnam was sent to secure its defenses against the coming of the invaders. He busied himself enormously, but ineffectively, the defeat at the Battle of Long Island making all fortresses useless. On August 22, 1776, fifteen thousand choice British troops were moved across the narrows to Long Island and, reenforced by five thousand Hessians on August twenty-seventh, pushed Washington before them across the East River and beyond the Harlem, although he had nineteen thousand men at his disposal. They were, however, scattered at defensive points and could not concentrate effectively, while Washington's main body was outflanked. He made a masterly retreat and saved his army, but lost New York, which remained in enemy hands until the end of the war.

Putnam was actively engaged on Brooklyn Heights, again commanding his men to hold their fire for the whites of British eyes, but he, too, had to join in the retreat that followed a further action on August twenty-fourth. Much in evidence during the mixed campaign that followed, Putnam was given command of Philadelphia December ninth. He was there to receive the Hessians taken prisoners by Washington when he crossed the Delaware on the ice and surprised Trenton.

Promoted to major-general, Putnam was now sent by Washington to command the Hudson Highlands and prevent any movement from New York by the river to join Burgoyne on his march from Canada. The river was barred at West Point by a gigantic chain forged by Lord Stirling at his Morristown furnace, and the heights were well fortified. The British never essayed an assault, though keeping a formidable fleet at hand and holding Stony Point, near Haverstraw, which was taken from them in a gallant assault led by Anthony Wayne. They made a poor showing with all their power. While in command here, Putnam caught one Edmund Palmer, an English agent, within his lines. He was held as a spy. Sir Henry Clinton sent Captain Montague in the *Mercury* to claim Palmer as a lieutenant in His Majesty's service. Putnam's reply to the bearer of the flag of truce, is his best literary effort:

Headquarters, 7 August, 1777.

Edmund Palmer, an officer in the enemy's service, was taken as a spy lurking within our lines; he has been tried as a spy, condemned as a spy and shall be executed as a spy, and the flag is ordered to depart immediately.

Israel Putnam.

P. S. He has been accordingly executed.

Burgoyne beaten, and the peril past, Putnam was assigned to recruiting service, after a clash with Washington's brilliant young aid, Alexander Hamilton, which ended in disobedience of orders. Putnam was old, hot-tempered and in no state of mind to obey a youngster, forgetting the great commander behind him. He asked to be relieved, the death of his second wife leaving affairs confused at home, and was assigned to recruiting service in Connecticut. He began his efforts in April, 1778, and did well, forming a training camp in Redding—now a state park bearing his name.

Camp life at Redding was not comfortable and the men were poorly provided with food and clothing. This bred a mutiny and a determination to march on Hartford and force the Assembly to redress the grievances. Putnam speedily brought the men to their senses by a combination of firmness and good humor that won Washington's warm commendation.

Putnam's command extended over Connecticut and the British lines were on the border of the state near Greenwich. Visiting his outposts here,

Putnam enjoyed what was his most famous adventure. He had been attending a dance at Pecksland, a back district of the town, and brought the Widow Bush home on the pillion of his saddle at an early hour, February 26, 1779. The lady lived in Cos Cob, another hamlet in the township, in a house still standing. Putnam's quarters were in a stone cottage, now preserved as a museum in Greenwich, on an avenue named in his honor. He reached home and was about to shave himself when he caught a glimpse of a red coat in the mirror, and leaping through the window, mounted the first horse that came handy and rode for Stamford, coatless and unarmed. Tory cavalry chased him to the brow of Horseneck Height, now "Put's Hill," from which then led a long flight of stone steps. Down these he sent his horse leaping, while the troopers paused at the top and then took the spiral roadway that wound its way to the valley below. In this way he evaded the shower of bullets that came after him and reached Stamford in safety. The Tories, under Tryon, were baffled and their raid failed of its purpose. The incident still rings in history. For the rest of the wartime he was not active, though present at Tappan when André's plot ended on the gallows. Unlike the luckless Palmer, who is forgotten, André's memorial graces Westminster Abbey.

The Putnam legends are many. Challenged to a duel by a British officer who was a prisoner on parole, Putnam, as chooser of weapons, selected an open keg of powder and set a lighted candle in the explosive. The challenger did not await the result. An American who challenged him was met, not with sword and pistols, as he expected, but found Putnam blazing away with a musket and announcing his firm purpose to kill him. He fled from the violent presence of the old fighter.

It has been stated that Washington had a better opinion of "Old Put" as a man than as a soldier. This is readily understood. Putnam was a much better fighter than strategist. Washington, with limited means, could take few risks and his Fabian tactics earned much complaint from the combative. He was wise in his prudence and so saved the day and the cause of liberty.

Putnam is well summed up in these lines left by Margaret Moncrieffe, daughter of an old English companion in arms, whose life was spoiled by Aaron Burr, but who as a girl in New York during the American occupation was befriended by Putnam: "General Putnam was certainly one of the best characters in the world; his heart being composed of those noble materials which equally command respect and admiration."

The general's life of storm ended May 29, 1790, in his seventy-third year. He is buried in Brooklyn under a modest monument, for which Timothy Dwight wrote the inscription. It contains one immortal line:

"Who dared to lead where any dared to follow."

CHAPTER VIII

To BECOME a soldier after forty years of civil life and earn lasting renown by exploits of the highest enterprise, which left him the ranking cavalry leader in the War between the States, was the remarkable fortune of Nathan Bedford Forrest.

He was not a member of the southern chivalry, but was born a twin and a "poor white" at Chapel Hill, near Duck River, Tennessee, July 13, 1821. He had a mixture of English, Scotch and Irish in his blood, like most of the dwellers in that region, few of whom ever reached distinction or escaped from the ignorance and poverty of their environment.

William Forrest, his father, stirred by the opening of the Chickasaw lands in northern Mississippi, migrated thither in 1834, taking up a leasehold in the wild country. Here he died three years later, leaving to Nathan, then a lad of sixteen, the care of the mother, who had been Miriam Beck, and a family, seven brothers and three sisters—one an infant who arrived four months after the father's death.

The boy met the responsibility bravely. Sacrificing education to necessity he toiled early and late until, by 1840, he had the plantation tamed and productive enough to pay its rental and support the household. In that year an epidemic of typhoid swept the newly settled land, always to be one of fever and affliction. The three sisters died and two of the brothers, one his twin, while he himself fell prey to a wasting malady that sapped his energies and well-nigh ended his life. After a long ordeal his strength returned and found him a man. He then began to make his mark in conflict with others. A wandering steer had been making free in his fields. Its owner, frequently warned to stop the marauding, paid no heed. Forrest then gave notice that he would shoot the beast at the next trespass, and did so. The owner came full armed, seeking vengeance. A bullet too close for comfort gave hint that two could play the game. He took to his heels and the corn-fields were thereafter safe from beast and man.

The times were restive. Texas, in constant friction with Mexico, from which she had parted by force, invited volunteers. One Wallace Wilson formed a company which Forrest joined. The company fell apart at New Orleans, but Forrest, then close to age, kept on with a few comrades and reached Houston to find that the promised fighting had faded out. Forrest split rails on a plantation for four months and so earned money enough to get back home.

Here he did not return to the farm, but engaged with an uncle in the uncertain business of trading horses. A quarrel between this uncle and one William Matlock placed the future general under fire for the first time. With three others, Matlock waylaid Forrest in the little square of Hernando, Mississippi, and opened fire. Forrest was armed and unflinchingly replied. Revolvers emptied, the bowie knife came into play. Forrest beat off his assailants and suffered little damage, but the uncle who had come out to see what it was all about received a mortal wound.

The social custom of the day was to regard such affairs leniently, but community sympathy for Forrest was strong enough to force an appeal to the law. The assailants were arrested, prosecuted and fined, but escaped the gallows. Forrest was held to have acted properly in self-defense.

This was beginning young. Yet a few months later when riding to Holly Springs in company with a local lawyer, James K. Morse, James Dyson, a planter with a grudge against Morse, shot him out of his saddle. He fell dead in the road, but Forrest, covering the assassin with his revolver, forced his surrender to the law. Dyson was convicted of murder, though not executed.

By this time "Bedford," as he was known, had reached twenty-five and married Mary Ann Montgomery, a kinswoman of the Richard Montgomery who fell at Quebec in the Revolution, and who is buried in St. Paul's Chapel, New York. He continued active in horse trading and opened a brickyard. The breach of trust of an agent emptied his pockets, but he began over again and soon filled them. He had an instinct for success, coupled with tireless industry.

The financial crisis brought him to Memphis where he began dealing in slaves and real estate. This traffic in human property was often used against him as he rose in repute during the war. Even in the South it was considered discreditable to deal in black flesh, though not to buy it. There is testimony that he was a humane trader who would not separate families, and indeed, often united them in his deals. He continued to prosper and in a dozen years was a rich man possessing two plantations on which a thousand bales of cotton grew, besides investments of value in various enterprises. His strength of character was always exerted on the side of law. In a city where the percentage of murders seems still to be the highest in America he tried to keep legal forces in motion. Once a Memphis mob took a prisoner from jail for the purpose of lynching him. The noose was in place and the rope over a limb. Forrest faced the furious crowd alone and cut the cord. He then restored the prisoner to his cell and the law for once took its course. This feat gave him fame and he was elected alderman, an office not much respected as a rule. He tried to stop pillage, but did not always succeed. The city's stock in the Memphis and Charleston railroad was sold by a vote of the board over his strong protest. He said the price was too low and proved it by buying some at the accepted figure and making twenty thousand dollars on its resale.

By 1860, Forrest was a rich and respected citizen. Then the Civil War broke. He enlisted at once as a private in the Tennessee Mounted Rifles, organized at Memphis by Doctor Josiah S. White. This was in June, 1861.

His services as private were brief. Governor Isham G. Harris sent for him early in July and gave him a colonel's commission, under which he was authorized to raise a regiment of cavalry. Tennessee had not gone out of the Union officially, but Harris had. The state never did. Harris traveled with the Confederate army as a governor without a state, throughout the war, and when the Union forces took and kept Nashville, Andrew Johnson ruled in his stead.

Beyond giving authority to raise the regiment Harris did nothing. As governor his power had oozed with his secession. Neither did Memphis indulge in any exhibition of zeal in enrolling troopers. Forrest therefore turned to the rural regions of Kentucky, taking in Paris, Mount Sterling, Lexington and other blue-grass towns. He had expected a warm welcome but did not receive it. Determined in his purpose he went on to Louisville and, although it was in Union hands, bought at his personal expense, five hundred revolvers and equipment for one hundred horses. His call had now been heard and Frank Overton, of Bradenburg, Meade County, on the river below Louisville, sent word that he had recruited ninety men. Forrest went thither and mustered in the troop as "The Boone Rangers" and these became the nucleus of his celebrated command.

He had much difficulty in getting his revolvers and equipment out of Louisville, but with the aid of Colonel Richard C. Wintersweet and M. Harrison, the thing was done. Overton's men reached an agreed rendezvous and safely carted off the supplies. Joined by Forrest they rode away through Bowling Green to Clarksville, Tennessee, being well received along the way. Following this route the troop reached Memphis August first, and there found that Charles May had recruited a fine company and named it "Forrest Rangers." It took two months more to raise the command to eight companies. In mid-October the regiment was ordered to Fort Donelson to receive its first lesson in war.

The inglorious end of the defense brought no shame to Forrest. Defending intrenchments is not the forte of horsemen. Suffice it to say he was among those with sufficient foresight to get away, riding safely with his men through a gap in the Federal lines and rounding up at Corinth, where the command became part of Albert Sidney Johnston's army that was to come so near to victory over Grant at Shiloh and Pittsburg Landing. Here once more he had small chance to show his mettle, but brought his forces safely away.

Indeed, Forrest knew the value of saving man-power. Most of the generals on both sides were wastrels. Not he. In after-days, when operating successfully as an independent raider, he ventured no hazards. When the odds were visibly too great, the men were told to scatter, and a brigade would vanish for the moment, each man looking to himself, only to reassemble when the peril was past and resume operations with full saddles and plenty of vigor.

The fighting and falling back tactics of Braxton Bragg, to whose forces Forrest next belonged, based upon the insistent effort of President Jefferson Davis to hold territory instead of destroying the enemy, put the palsy of failure upon every move. It was only when free of the road that Forrest showed his true metal, taking Murfreesboro from a brigade of sleepy Federals, riding across Kentucky to return laden with arms, powder, percussion caps and more food than could be conveniently carried, and capturing Colonel Robert G. Ingersoll and his Fifth Illinois Cavalry. All these were exploits successfully performed while the army of Bragg was supine or in retreat.

When the gigantic conflict at Chickamauga was over, with Union defeat as the result and its cause a-tremble, swift use of Forrest would have done much to have completed the near-triumph. He was not used. Instead, although now a brigadier, Bragg demoted him to a subordinate place under Wheeler, as a result of which Forrest resigned. Meeting Jefferson Davis at Montgomery, he received assurances such as led him to recall this step, and to accept a transfer to northern Mississippi in what was practically an independent command. He had to patch up a new force, feeble at first, to march in mid-November, 1863, to Okolona, where it may be said his career truly began. Thus it befell that it was not until the last days, when the sun was setting on the South, that the intrepid leader did his most dashing work.

Cutting loose from "headquarters" and military formalities he was ever in the field, discomfiting his opponents with lightning strokes that added to his glory, but could not help a cause already lost. General Sherman has well described the sort of men who rallied to his banner: "—Young bloods of the South, sons of planters, lawyers about towns; good billiard players and sportsmen—men who never did work and never will; . . . fine riders, bold to rashness and dangerous subjects in every sense. . . . As long as they have good horses, plenty of forage and an open country they are happy—the most dangerous set of men which this war has turned loose upon the world. They are splendid shots and utterly reckless."

The change put Forrest under General Joseph E. Johnston, who gave him permission to do practically as he pleased. The command at first numbered only about five hundred men, and operations were hampered by a wet spell that rivaled the one that embarrassed Noah, lasting forty days, during which the whole country was a mass of mire. Before Christmas, despite the continuing rain, about seventeen hundred horsemen had been rallied.

The Federals knew what was going on; they did their best to prevent the anticipated irruption and active skirmishing was soon in order, while with the coming of 1864, Forrest was made a major-general and Lieutenant-General Leonidas Polk became his inconsiderate superior. Fighting grew heavier and in a four-to-one conflict at Okolona, Forrest's youngest brother, Jeffrey, who had attained the rank of colonel, was slain. He was the son born after the father's death and had been the pride of the elder who had given him the education he himself had been denied.

Forrest held the field. The Federals lost six hundred killed and wounded and had three hundred taken prisoners—almost as many as were arrayed against them at the onset.

In the spring the cavalry were ceaselessly active. It would be too long a tale to recite the numberless clashes and daring raids. Like Marion in the Revolution, Forrest seemed everywhere and at all times, so active were his movements and so cunning his plans. His force grew to a division and its sections ranged at will. The fall of Fort Pillow was the next considerable achievement. This victory was darkened by the slaughter of the colored garrison by troops under command of Brigadier-General J. R. Chalmers, who suffered obloquy all his life, though elected to Congress and

turning Republican in his later years. Only fourteen Confederates were killed and eighty-six
wounded.

While fortune favored Forrest he was alone in
his luck. The Confederate commanders failed one
by one. Johnston had succeeded Bragg and
Hood followed Johnston, each with equal ill-
fortune, Hood crushing himself against the redoubts at Franklin and receiving his *coup de grace*
soon after from George H. Thomas at Nashville.
The great Army of the Tennessee was gone.

From this debacle Forrest escaped to dodge a
few weeks longer the circling cavalry of his foes,
under James H. Wilson, and in this last campaign
showed the utmost courage and skill. He served
as a rear-guard for the remnants of Hood's army
as it moved brokenly toward the Southwest, ever
in peril. The fragments turned toward Selma,
held by Zachary Taylor's son Richard, better
known as "Dick" Taylor, all the while closely pursued. Forrest, riding alone, was assailed by four
troopers. He engaged them with sword and pistol,
beating them off, as well as three others who came
to their support.

The road lay through a thicket. When he
turned to flee the way was blocked by a wagon
which cut off escape. His horse had been badly
wounded, but never lacking in courage, Forrest
plied his spurs and the noble animal leaped over
the obstruction just as the trap seemed about to
close. Safely beyond the barrier Forrest halted

for a moment when one Taylor, a Federal captain, rode him down and a hand-to-hand encounter followed. Forrest killed his adversary with a pistol shot, but in a moment had other foes to face. Two members of his staff came to the rescue. The little band killed something like thirty men in this short fierce encounter, being armed with revolvers, while the Union cavalry had nothing but sabers as weapons. So Forrest went free. The last important stand was at Selma. It was then the second of April and the life of the Confederacy was near its end. Dick Taylor, in command of the regular forces, had made a retreat that was in its nature a rout leaving Forrest to hold the town. They got away safely, but the enemy was too powerful to be withstood. By night the city fell.

Within a week Lee had surrendered; Davis was in flight and the war over. Yet during the month or so of his wanderings Davis clung to the belief that the cause was not lost, and that the war could be resumed in the Southwest, where he proposed to go, with Forrest as the leader. When the faithful few who stood by Davis shook their heads at this proposal he bowed to the inevitable and said, "All is indeed lost"—and it was.

Forrest, himself, had no such thought. He had fought bravely and well. He could be equally brave in defeat. "I have never," he wrote in his formal farewell to his command, "on the field of battle, sent you where I was unwilling to go myself; nor would I now advise you to a course which

I felt myself unwilling to pursue. You have been good soldiers; you can be good citizens. Obey the laws, preserve your honor, and the government to which you have surrendered can afford to be and will be magnanimous."

This farewell word was not written until the ninth of May, 1865. Davis had been captured near Washington, Georgia, on the tenth.

Forrest's rule or strategy—though he often succeeded without it—was to "get there first with the most men." He did not indulge in formal military commands. "Get over there and get to fighting," was the usual dictum. The wild young men believed him invincible and followed accordingly. A constructive commander, capable of accumulating and directing large forces, he was not and could not be. Romance, however, must continue to cling about his name. The long night rides, the swift attack, pillage and away, have in them a thrill denied the serried ranks and the solemnity of fighting in columns paraded to die.

Returning to face the ruin wrought by the war, Forrest bestirred himself with his customary energy. It was not long before he was called again to public duty, this time at the behest of the organization that lives weirdly in history as the Ku Klux Klan, in its original form and purpose. Briefly it came into being on December 24, 1865, at Pulaski, Tennessee, where six ex-soldiers met in the law office of Thomas M. Jones and sought some relief from the ennui that followed peace.

John C. Lester, who had been a Confederate captain, proposed that they form a club to break the monotony of their lives. A committee was appointed to formulate a plan and at the next meeting reported. The club lacked a name. Captain John B. Kennedy suggested "Kukloi" from the Greek "Kuklos," meaning circle. This James R. Crowe amended to "Ku Klux" and Captain Lester added "Klan" as they were all Scotch-Irish. The fantastic uniform was next devised. There seems to have been no purpose but that of idle amusement behind the prank. A parade in sheet and mask sent a chill through the colored population that caused it suddenly to take an interest in industry. Like wildfire the idea spread from town to town as a device whereby the disfranchised and outvoted whites could assert their power over the former slaves and their "carpetbag" leaders from the North. The rest is a long story of outrage and rough justice too intermingled to disentangle. By 1870 the Klan had become all-powerful throughout the late Confederacy. Forrest all this while had been toiling to rehabilitate his fortunes. Feeling that the uncontrolled "Invisible Empire" was working more harm than good he called a meeting of the best-known leaders, at Florence, to put a curb on its undertakings and make the Klan either a decent force or abolish it. The gathering was held at the home of General George S. Houston. General John B. Gordon, of Georgia, was one of the conferees. The meeting resulted in Forrest's acquiring complete control of the organization, or as much of it as could be managed. In the rôle of Grand Wizard he deployed its forces politically throughout the South, just as he had sent his horsemen on errands during the conflict, and bent the bayonets that surrounded the ballot boxes.

When the troops were withdrawn from the South by President Rutherford B. Hayes, the excuse for the Klan's existence passed away.

After twelve long years the conquered country was free to operate on its own lines and at its own will. Forrest called a meeting of all the Grand Dragons, or sub-rulers of the Klan, at Elkmont Springs. There was a full attendance. This was late in August. The general was in failing health and knew his end was near. To dissolve the Klan became the last and crowning action of his life. In a general order issued early in September he closed its work with these words: "There never was a time before or since its organization when such an organization as the Ku Klux Klan could have lived. May there never be again."

Though yet young in years the general's life ended with the passing of the Klan. He died at Memphis, October 29, 1877, having passed but a little way into his fifty-seventh year.

CHAPTER IX

WARFARE, when carried on by partisans, speedily takes on a severity and cruelty that rarely develop between organized forces. The most bitter chapter in the War between the States was that written by Mosby's irregulars, usually designated as "guerrillas," and so dealt with by the Federal military authorities, although their commander bore a regular commission from the Confederate States. The men had no headquarters save in the saddle, coming and going from their homes or hiding-places as required by the raiding or scouting operations in which they were engaged. They were young, some mere boys. Notable among these juniors was the late Joseph Bryan, of Richmond, Virginia, who became an eminent lawyer, capitalist and philanthropist, whose name lives in high honor.

John Singleton Mosby, who gave his name to the rangers and led them through all their dangerous adventures, was born in Powhatan County, Virginia, December 6, 1833, and graduated from the University of Virginia just before the outbreak of civil strife. He had settled down to the prac-

138

tise of law in Bristol, Virginia. The call to arms led him to join the cavalry forces under General J. E. B. Stuart, which he soon left to organize his "guerrillas." This force never exceeded five hundred men, but it made more disturbance than as many thousands usually do. Their quality was superb for the service in which they were employed. They knew every road and mountain path in Northern Virginia, were fearless riders of horses trained to speeding and to jump obstacles, such as fences or hedges, and that often saved their riders when closely pursued. As one of their number, John W. Munson, has written:

"His men had no camps nor fixed quarters, and never slept in tents. They did not even know anything about pitching a tent. The idea of making coffee, frying bacon or soaking hard-tack was never entertained. When we wanted to eat we stopped at a friendly farmhouse or went into some little town and bought what we wanted. Every man in the command had some special farm he could call his home. . . . As a command we had no knowledge of the first principles of cavalry drill, and could not have formed in a straight line had there been any need for our doing so. We did not know the bugle calls and very rarely had a roll call. . . . Two things were impressed upon us well, however—to obey orders and to fight."

Furthermore:

"Whenever we made a successful raid, we made it a point to repay the farmers and country people

whose bounty we enjoyed in live stock and supplies. The return from a sutler's raid was a holi-
day occasion, for everybody got something. On
one occasion we captured about two hundred and
fifty fat cattle from General Sheridan's supply
train, and we gave our friends half of them, divid-
ing them among all the people living within
range."

Not all of the "guerrillas" were Virginians.
One captain was a British veteran of the Crimea;
another, Robert Von Massow, was a German
baron.

They were exasperatingly active, cutting off
supply trains, raiding outposts and vexing their
opponents almost beyond endurance. They were
declared outlaws and a war of extermination was
decreed. Brigadier-General George A. Custer,
who was to die with all his men in an Indian massacre, captured six of Mosby's command and ordered them hanged at once. The sentence was immediately carried out, though the mother of one, a
lad of seventeen, begged for his life on her knees in
the street at Front Royal. He died before her eyes.
A seventh man was taken by Colonel Powell, in a
raid on the Rappahannock and hanged, with a label
affixed to his coat saying this would be the fate
of Mosby and his men, should they be taken. Mosby had recently gathered in seven hundred Union
prisoners. By order of General Robert E. Lee,
he selected seven of these by lot and they were
hanged in retaliation. This policy, he announced,

would be continued, though prisoners in general would be well treated. There were no more executions on the Federal side, though neither gave much quarter in combat.

The "guerrillas" brought great suffering on the regions in which they were active, for the Federals regarded the farm-houses as hiding-places and burned them pitilessly upon suspicion or even less.

One of Mosby's greatest exploits was a raid with twenty-nine men on the Federal headquarters at Fairfax Court House, where Brigadier-General E. H. Stoughton was taken and borne away captive. Stoughton was in bed and asleep when Mosby entered his room and unceremoniously woke him up by spanking him on his bare skin.

The general was properly horrified at such a liberty, and, when asked if he had ever heard of Mosby, quickly answered:

" 'Yes. Have you got him?'

"Mosby replied:

" 'No, but he has got you!' "

Besides Stoughton he carried away two captains, thirty-five privates and fifty-eight horses. President Lincoln took a grimly humorous view of the incident, remarking that he could easily make brigadiers, but horses were a real loss and difficult to replace. The crestfallen Stoughton asked that he be turned over to General Fitzhugh Lee, who had been his classmate at West Point. This was done. Lee gave him a warm welcome, with dinner and wine, but left Mosby and his men out in a chilly rain without food or further attention. Later the exploit raised Mosby in rank from captain to major.

In an audacious moment, scouting near Washington, he sent a lock of his hair by a farmer's wife to Abraham Lincoln, with the remark that he soon expected to snip one from the president's cranium in exchange. The lock and message were delivered. Lincoln laughed.

Mosby caught two *New York Herald* correspondents, Hårt and Hendricks. They had fine appetites, so he sent them to Richmond and kept their excellent horses for board. The pair was exchanged, no worse for the experience.

In all his operations the command took more than six thousand Federal prisoners; destroyed or captured millions in supplies. He once nabbed two of Sheridan's paymasters with one hundred sixty-eight thousand dollars in greenbacks, that were put to good use by the Confederacy. Burning railway equipment was another specialty that annoyed the cavalry branch of the Army of the Potomac.

Mosby surrendered at Lynchburg, after the fall of Lee, believing he was "about the last man to give in" as he expressed it in later years. His force had been disbanded, but his delay led to threats from General W. S. Hancock of further military proceedings, while Secretary Stanton specifically excluded him from parole.

Horace Greeley, in the *New York Tribune,*

JOHN S. MOSBY

was insistent that he be hanged. The passion for hanging was discouraged by General Grant, and no one died at the rope's end except Wirz, commander of the prison camp at Andersonville. Mosby was closely watched and often arrested by provost marshals acting in the old war area. He finally appealed to General Grant, who gave him a letter that stopped the uncomfortable practise. When Grant ran for president, Mosby became a Republican, earning much odium thereby. He continued in that faith and in 1876, when announcing his purpose to support Rutherford B. Hayes for the presidency, said: "Suppose Hayes is elected, what will become of our people with the *solid South* against him?" Thus he made a phrase that is still a fact and still in use. His idea was that a breaking of political forces would be to the advantage of all below Mason and Dixon's line. As a matter of history, Hayes broke the tyranny that followed the war, took the garrisons from the towns, and soldiers away from the ballot boxes, giving the South a chance to work out its own salvation.

Hayes rewarded Mosby by appointment as United States Consul at Hong Kong, a well-paid post, which he filled acceptably for six and one-half years. On his return he settled in San Francisco, opening a law office and receiving a retainer from the Southern Pacific railroad. Here he passed a number of pleasant and tranquil years.

In 1898, he tried to volunteer for the War with

Spain, but could not get by the bureaucrats in the War Department at Washington, though they accepted Fitzhugh Lee and Joseph Wheeler, Confederates, but West Pointers. Mosby said that he could take twenty-five thousand men and sweep Cuba from end to end. There was no doubt about that!

Six years later, at the instance of President Roosevelt, who wrote Mosby that he was himself "half Southern," he became an assistant in the Department of Justice, a post that he held until turned out by the Taft Administration in 1910. He rendered some important service in uncovering Indian and land frauds in the West.

Following his retirement, Colonel Mosby lived quietly in Washington, writing his memoirs and attending occasional Confederate reunions. It might be observed that he was not widely popular, "hero" that he was. Becoming a Republican after much aspersion as a soldier did not make him welcome. It was not known for a long time that Mosby reported solely to General Robert E. Lee, that model soldier, and that all he did was in obedience to Lee's orders. This Mosby would not reveal, nor did it become really public until the official records were published nearly half a century after the conflict.

In 1915, the University of Virginia forgave him for his political apostasy and presented him with a medal of honor, "The gift of the Alma Mater to her Son."

He took a vivid interest in the World War, and the possibilities fired his blood, though past eighty when it broke out. Incidentally, in discussing cavalry work at the moment he declared the saber to be an obsolete and useless weapon. The six shooter was the thing. He knew of few fatalities from a saber stroke. He was, he observed, the first cavalry commander to discard the blade and substitute the revolver.

His uniform hangs in the Military Museum at Washington, in company with a hat lost in what was his narrowest escape, when Company I of the Thirteenth New York Cavalry surprised him and Thomas Love, a trooper, at a Fauquier farmhouse. A bullet landed in his abdomen and as his identity was unknown he was left for dead as the party rode on. He had torn off his insignia and the farmer said he was "Lieutenant Johnson" in whom the Federals took no interest. Oddly enough, their captain, Selden L. Jones, met Mosby long afterward in San Francisco and was glad he had not identified him. In all Mosby was six times wounded and carried one bullet to his grave.

In stature he was rather short and quite spare. He weighed one hundred twenty-two pounds when he entered the war, and no more at the end. Rough riding and irregular meals were not fattening. I recall him in his last years, when the sight of one of his steel blue eyes had been destroyed by accident. His face was one of the coldest and calmest I ever saw.

He died in Washington, March 20, 1916, having entered into his eighty-fourth year, and lies buried at Warrenton, Virginia, in his native soil.

"Personally, I knew him well," wrote George Cary Eggleston, as the worn old leader lay dying. "His was a gallant soul. He never failed in a duty; never flinched from a danger. He had in him all that is admirable in the chevalier. In stature he was of medium height and weight. On foot he was in no way conspicuous, but on his horse he was every inch a cavalier. Sun-burned, weather-beaten and swarthy, he had a singularly winning countenance. It had gentleness as well as determination in it, delicacy as well as daring. He never posed, but was always a modest man, intensely in earnest. He had none of Stuart's dandyism, none of that great leader's love of personal display. He lacked the boyish vanity that has distinguished most of the world's great cavalry leaders. He did nothing for effect, but everything for the accomplishment of results. No man was ever gentler or more considerate of others; no man was ever readier to meet a challenge of any kind with fight. No man was readier to forgive a fault confessed— no man more merciless toward wrong-doing unrepented."

CHAPTER X

TALL, firm-featured, with the angularity usually employed to depict the typical school-teacher, Susan Brownell Anthony of Rochester, New York, has become an historical figure as the chief crusader for what was long called "Women's Rights." The word "suffragette" was not invented until Mrs. Elizabeth Pankhurst and her combative associates began their effective campaign in England. Miss Anthony affected a severe plainness in dress that accorded well with her figure and purpose. Silk of the best, without frills or ornament, was her usual garb, while her hair, parted in the center of her lofty head, was folded over the ears and tied in a plain knot behind. She never varied her dress or appearance. A woman of invincible courage, she faced not only the derision of mankind, but the scorn of genteel ladies who had been accustomed to faint if some one said "pants" in their presence.

Born in South Adams, a Massachusetts village amid the Berkshires, February 15, 1820, of a Quaker father and Baptist mother, Miss Anthony enjoyed an excellent education, in which three sis-

147

ters and two brothers shared. Her father, Daniel
Anthony, believed in the equality of sexes and saw
that his daughters had all the advantages given
sons. He was a manufacturer of cotton goods and
well-to-do. True to his Quaker cult, he would not
pay taxes to a government that made war and was
prosecuted accordingly, becoming the first martyr
in his family. His business went down with a crash
in the panic of 1837, and after a time he migrated
to Rochester, with ten dollars in his pocket, to begin over again. Susan was already self-sustaining,
teaching school at one dollar a week and boarding
'round. In 1846, she accepted a place in the Cana-
joharie Academy, and ceased to be a Quaker.
Here she delivered her first speech, at a temperance gathering, and made the acquaintance of Lucretia and Abigail Mott. She also fell in at this
time with her lifelong co-worker, Elizabeth Cady
Stanton, who with Lucretia Mott, called the first
"Women's Rights" convention to meet at Seneca
Falls, in 1848. It extended its session to Rochester,
where the Anthony family fell in line with its purpose, father, mother and daughters joining in a
petition to establish sex equality.

Miss Anthony did not, however, enter actively
in the cause until 1852, when, attending a convention of the Sons of Temperance, to which the
Daughters of Temperance, of which she was an
active member, were invited, she was snubbed by
the male chairman when she sought to make a motion. "Women," this tactful gentleman observed,

in refusing to recognize her, "are here to listen and learn."

This rebuke turned her to her lifelong labor, supplemented by a similar reminder from the presiding officer of a teachers' conclave, where she had the supreme audacity to rise and evince an intent to discuss a question before the assemblage. She really began her career as a crusader at Mayville, Chautauqua County, New York, the day after Christmas, 1854, and thenceforward never ceased her endeavors, so long as her physical energies permitted.

Miss Anthony had the serenity and dignity of a great lady, and never descended to the eccentric, as did other followers of the faith. She faltered only once. Amelia Jenks Bloomer, an Illinois pioneer in the "Women's Rights" cause, had invented a costume, the chief feature of which was a voluminous pair of trousers built after the Turkish pattern, which replaced the conventional skirt. This made a great stir. She was mobbed and mocked at until her fame spread over the land. Miss Anthony's coadjutor, Mrs. Stanton, thought they ought not to let Mrs. Bloomer suffer martyrdom alone. Each, therefore, made a pair, with the intent of trying them on before the other by way of prudent rehearsal. Mrs. Stanton carried her suit in a parcel to the Anthony residence, and was startled to be met at the door by Susan in full array. The effect was so startling that the merry visitor nearly had hysterics. On recovering from

her "fit," Mrs. Stanton was reproved by her stern-
er sister, and for a short time the two wore the
"advanced" garments. Popular prejudice proved
too great to be endured and both returned to the
conventional, Miss Anthony changing to her ele-
gant severity and the lovely Mrs. Stanton wearing
whatever was most becoming. Miss Anthony always objected to over, or under, dressing and succeeded once in defeating the accomplished and
beautiful Elizabeth Oakes Smith for a chairmanship, because of low neck and filmy flowing fab-
rics. Fifty years after, the bicycle made
"bloomers" an article of popular woman's wear
and preserved the name of their inventor for an
ungrateful country.

Besides taking up women's rights, Miss Anthony became an ardent advocate of the abolition of
slavery, and in the opening days of the Civil War
was mobbed in Buffalo for speaking her mind, and
finally was allowed to lift up her voice for freedom
only in an obscure negro church. The war once
on, as a member of the Loyal League, she agitated
for emancipation until Lincoln's proclamation
ended the need. Then she began the long campaign to eliminate "male" from the Federal Constitution and was a strong worker for the Fourteenth Amendment, which gave citizenship to the
black. It was ratified July 28, 1868, so that the
most ignorant ex-slave became the political superior of the most intelligent wife and mother!

In 1868, the National Democratic Party held

its convention in New York City, and Miss Anthony occupied a seat on the platform. When resolutions were called for she handed Horatio Seymour, who was destined to be nominated and defeated, a resolution endorsing female suffrage. The chronicles of the day recite that it was received with uproarious laughter. At the next New York City gathering of the Democracy, in 1924, fifty-six years after, many of the delegates were women; some spoke effectively and all were treated with marked respect. So the slow world moves!

The organization of the National Women's Suffrage Association followed, with Miss Anthony as its head, a place she was to hold with distinguished honor for half a century. It was formally set a-going May 15, 1869, to push a sixteenth amendment, the fifteenth having been added to perfect the fourteenth. She lectured over the country, going as far as California, but made no special stir until November 1, 1872, just before the Grant-Greeley election, when an appeal to voters to register, made by the *Rochester Democrat and Chronicle,* caught her eye and she determined to find out how much "equality" the new amendment provided. She rallied fourteen other women, including her sisters, and all registered, after refreshing themselves with a perusal of the amendments. The Democratic *Union and Advertiser* denounced the act and demanded that the election inspectors refuse to receive the "female" ballots on pain of prosecution. Such clamor was raised, that in all wards save the eighth, the officials refused to receive the ballots. Here the inspectors took the offered slips.

Miss Anthony voted early—at seven o'clock. Two weeks later, after a great furore, she was arrested by Deputy United States Marshal E. J. Keeney, and in due season the other fourteen were rounded up. They were not put in durance, but were held for examination by United States Commissioner Storrs. They had thoughtfully voted the Republican ticket, which tempered the severity of the proceedings. All gave bonds save Miss Anthony. She applied for a writ of habeas corpus, which was denied, and her bail raised to one thousand dollars. She preferred prison to yielding, but Judge Henry R. Selden, her attorney, gave the needed bond, as "he could not see a lady he respected put in jail." She was indignant, but the bond stood and saved her from a cell. There followed an indictment for illegal voting, under which she was tried in the United States Circuit Court at Canandaigua, June 17, 1873, before Justice Ward Hunt, who at the conclusion of the testimony, which admitted the act of voting, ordered the jury to bring in a verdict of guilty. Like that which refused to obey an order to convict William Penn, two hundred years before, the jury refused and was discharged without being formally asked for its verdict, which would have been "not guilty." Judge Hunt directed the clerk to enter a verdict of guilty, denied a motion for a new trial, and fined the defendant one hundred dollars.

SUSAN B. ANTHONY

"May it please your Honor," she said in protest, "I will never pay a dollar of your unjust penalty. All the stock in trade I possess is a debt of ten thousand dollars, incurred by publishing my paper—*The Revolution*—the sole object of which was to educate all women to do precisely as I have done, rebel against your man-made, unjust, unconstitutional forms of law, which tax, fine, imprison and hang women, while denying them the right of representation in the government; and I will work on with might and main to pay every dollar of that honest debt, but not a penny shall go to this unjust claim. And I shall earnestly and persistently continue to urge all women to the practical recognition of the old Revolutionary maxim, 'Resistance to tyranny is obedience to God.' "

Thus ended the famous, or infamous, trial and the last attempt to vote until the Constitution's nineteenth amendment gave the right.

My own memory of Miss Anthony is very vivid. I was an Albany correspondent for the *Brooklyn Daily Eagle* in 1887, 1888 and 1889. In company with her lifelong comrade, Elizabeth Cady Stanton, and Mrs. Mary Seymour Howell, wife of the assistant state librarian, she often sat in the outer row of seats in the Assembly Chamber, where each year the bill providing for female suffrage would be presented amid mockery and dismissed with contempt. The Assembly contained such men as Ernest Howard Crosby, a great humanitarian; Hamilton Fish, the second, whose grandfather was George Washington's chief aid, and Robert Ray Hamilton, great grandson of Alexander. None of these three, nor any Republican member, would father the bill. The only man to treat it with respect was Timothy D. Sullivan, a young Tammany representative from the Bowery district. He introduced it repeatedly, amid laughter and derision. The "gentlemen," including those named, were all alike in their scorn. Sullivan would blush red under the jeers, but never failed to stand behind the measure—and almost alone. When I asked him why he did it, he replied simply: "I respected those ladies."

Miss Anthony, with all her public activity, was a perfect housekeeper. Order reigned, and neatness was the law in her home. It was beautifully furnished with choice mahogany, and the delicate china and slender silver were inheritances from her grandmother. Linen of the choicest was another heirloom. Above all, she could cook and had a recipe for gingerbread that made the neighbors sniff with delight on baking days. She had no patience with idleness or neglect. To a woman who said she was praying for her, she answered smartly: "Well, pray with your hands and feet. I like prayers that take the form of work." Intensely practical, she lost all, or nearly all of her sense of humor. Decision and duty ruled her.

She died where she had so long lived in her house at Rochester, a little after midnight, at the beginning of March 13, 1906. A short time before she had attended the National Suffrage Convention in Baltimore and was there taken ill and hurried home, being unable to attend a banquet in her honor held in New York on February twentieth, the anniversary of her eighty-sixth birthday. Pneumonia was the primary cause, added to the weight of years. "Her name once a jest, now honored," was the *New York World's* head-line over its obituary notice. In Rochester, where she had endured arrest and contumely, the flags were lowered at half mast, shops were closed and all the city mourned. She left her modest fortune of ten thousand dollars to the cause for which she had long labored. Her grave in Mount Hope Cemetery has become a place of pilgrimage.

"Did you not get discouraged?" she was once asked, later in life, when discussing the old cruel days.

"Never," she answered. "I knew that my cause was just and I was always in good company."

She was, indeed!

Miss Anthony, Elizabeth Cady Stanton and Lucretia Mott are sculptured together in a memorial given to the United States for installation in the Capitol at Washington, by the suffragettes of America. It did not receive a warm welcome, and there was some difficulty in placing it decently.

CHAPTER XI

STUDENTS of nomenclature can find in the American Indian's method of naming children, a specificness that has long been lost among civilized peoples. Peculiarly apt were the selections of the Iroquois, who made the noble state of New York their home, and dominated the country from the Alleghenies to the sea, north to the St. Lawrence, and south to the Carolinas. Moreover they had a convenient custom of altering names to suit new developments of character or characteristics. So an Indian lad, of quick wit, born at Old Castle, near what is now Geneva, New York, about the year 1750, was first called O-te-ti-ani, or "Always Ready." When he grew up he became a matchless orator and was rechristened Sa-go-ye-wat-ha, meaning, "He keeps them awake"—a feat not always accomplished by spouters. In the annals of American history, where he plays a great part, he lives as Red Jacket. This designation he acquired during the Revolution, while a runner in the service of the Crown. Being remarkably fleet of foot, he won favor with the officers whose messages he carried, one of whom rewarded him with a scarlet

156

coat. It made him conspicuous among his people and "Red Jacket" was the lasting result.

For almost two centuries the Iroquois held their lines against the European invaders, fighting France in Canada, and astutely using the English to guard their interests. They faded against the pressure of the new republic, but without loss of dignity or prestige. They were simply surrounded and to this day some six thousand, about half their aboriginal total, remain on their own lands in New York. The names of their sachems survive in sonorous majesty, from Decanisora to Thayendanegea (Joseph Brant), as do the names given localities—Ticonderoga, Onondaga, Canandaigua —and the like, against puny Warsaws, Batavias and such. That so many live is a fine token of the survival of the fittest.

Red Jacket's repute, which was responsible for his later election as a chief of the Senecas, rests upon his ability as an orator, for like Cicero and Demosthenes, as one biographer has observed, his force lay in arousing, not leading his people. His birth was humble and he made his way on his merits. Joseph Brant was the great war chief of the Iroquois during the Revolution. He was a Mohawk, a section of the Six Nations that had become small through their fierce and warlike traits. Red Jacket was a Seneca, the largest branch then and now, of the Confederacy. Brant considered him cowardly and time-serving, as blunt soldiers are apt to regard orators and lawyers, and from

Brant's standpoint, this could be proved true. But as a patriot who tried to serve and save his people, Red Jacket measures up to a high standard.

When the wrath of the Americans fell, rather undeservedly, upon the Senecas, through Sullivan's expedition to Western New York in 1779, Red Jacket was but twenty-nine, and not a chief. His influence had, however, become marked, and Brant regarded him with an evil eye, especially as he caught him in negotiations with Sullivan for a truce that would have gone hard with his own fortunes. Brant caused the messengers to be waylaid and killed. Following the Revolution, Brant and his Mohawks, with sundry Oneidas and Cayugas, took up their residence in Canada, at Brantford, where their descendants live to-day. The Senecas, save for a few who ventured to the Indian territory, remain, and number well over three thousand souls. The statecraft of Red Jacket was more purposeful and successful than the armed forces of Thayendanegea. His people remain serene on their own land, ruled by their own chiefs, and protected in their rights, while the Mohawks are little more than a name.

In making their treaty with John Jay, in 1783, the chagrined British forgot all about their red allies and left them to shift for themselves. Of the Six Nations, two, the Oneidas and the Tuscaroras, had kept out of the conflict. The Senecas had suffered most, their farms and orchards being destroyed, as the Germans devastated Belgium in the

World War, and the Onondagas, Cayugas and Mohawks were left weak and without property or influence. The impulse of New York State was to exile them all to the distant wilderness of the West, but the great and good George Washington intervened and saved the tribes. There followed a conclave at Fort Stanwix in 1784, where terms of peace were agreed upon and there the voice of Red Jacket lifted him into a place that he never lost. He met men of ability such as Oliver Wolcott, Richard Butler and Arthur Lee, and won their high respect. That he practised mystic arts to secure his selection as one of the council may be true, as alleged by the historian, William L. Stone. But Stone was a partizan of Brant and does small justice to Red Jacket. By whatever means he arrived the results were highly to his credit as a statesman and speaker.

Speculators in Indian lands made most of the trouble that followed the Treaty, supplemented as a matter of course by clashes between low whites and drunken Indians, whom the former debauched. Out of these things came frequent councils to secure redress on one side or the other, at which Red Jacket always shone.

Here is an appeal from the orator for justice in a notorious land case, by which his people were cruelly robbed:

"Now, brothers, the Thirteen States, you must open your ears. You know what has happened respecting our lands. You told us, from this time the chain of friendship should be brightened. Now, brothers, we have begun to brighten the chain, and we will follow the footsteps of our forefathers. We will take those steps, that we may sit easy and choose where and how large our seats should be. The reason we send this message is, that the president, who is over all the Thirteen States, may make our seats easy. We do it that the chain of friendship may be brightened with the Thirteen States, as well as with the British; that we may pass from one to the other unmolested. We wish to be under the protection of the Thirteen States as well as of the British."

As satisfaction was not forthcoming, another council was held in Philadelphia, by choice of the Iroquois, who wished Quakers to be present, as they were honest and had never wronged them. Here again was Red Jacket supremely eloquent, saying:

"Brother:—You now represent the president of the United States, and when you spoke to us, we considered it as the voice of the fifteen fires. You desired that we would take the matter under our deliberate consideration, and consult each other well, that when the chain was rusty it might be brightened. We took General Washington by the hand, and desired this council-fire, that all the lines of dispute might be settled.

"Brother:—We told you before of the two rusty places on the chain, which were also pointed out by the sachems. Instead of complying with our request respecting the places where we told you the chain was rusty, you offered to relinquish the land on Lake Erie, eastward of the triangular piece sold by Congress to Pennsylvania, and to retain the four-mile path between Cayuga and Buffalo Creek, by which you expect to brighten the chain.

"Brother:—We thought you had a sharp file to take off the rust, but we believe it must have been dull, or else you let it slip out of your hands. With respect to the four-mile path, we are in want of it on account of the fisheries. Although we are but children, we are sharp-sighted and we see that you want that strip of land for a road, that when you have vessels on the lakes you may have harbors. But we wish that in respect to that land, the treaty of Fort Stanwix may not be broken. You white people have increased very fast on this island, which was given to us Indians by the Great Spirit. We are now become a small people. You are cutting off our lands piece after piece. You are a kind-hearted people,—seeking your own advantages.

"Brother:—We are tender-hearted and desirous of peace. You told us what you would give for our land, to brighten your end of the chain. If you will relinquish the piece of land we have mentioned, our friendship will be strong. You say you are not proud. Neither are we. Congress expects we are now settling the business with regularity. We wish that both parties may have something to

say in settling peace. At the time we requested a
conference, we also requested that our friends, the
Quakers, should come forward, as they are pro-
moters of peace, and we wanted them to be witnesses of what took place. We wish to do nothing
private. We have told you of the rusty part, which
the file passed over without brightening and we
wish you to take up the file again, and rub it very
hard. You told us that if it would not do without,
you would apply oil.

"Brother:—We, the sachems, warriors and
others, all depend upon you. Whatever is done
we regard as final and permanent. We wish you
to take it into consideration, and give us an answer."

Of the Senecas themselves, and of Red Jacket's
home life, William Savary, one of the unofficial
Quaker observers who attended a council near
Buffalo, has left this record in his journal:

"Fifth Day, Oct. 30. After dinner, John Par-
ish and myself rode to view the Farmer's Brother's
encampment, which contained about five hundred
Indians. They are located by the side of a brook,
in the woods; having built about seventy or eighty
huts, by far the most commodious and ingeniously
made of any that I have seen. The principal materials are bark, and boughs of trees, so nicely put
together as to keep the family dry and warm. The
women as well as the men appeared to be mostly
employed. In this camp there are a large number
of pretty children, who, in all the activity and

RED JACKET

buoyancy of health, were diverting themselves according to their fancy. The vast number of deer they have killed, since coming here, which they cut up, and hang round their huts inside and out, to dry, together with the rations of the beef which they draw daily, give the appearance of plenty to supply the few wants to which they are subjected. The ease and cheerfulness of every countenance, and the delightfulness of the afternoon, which these inhabitants of the woods seemed to enjoy with a relish far superior to those who are pent up in crowded and populous cities, all combined to make this the most pleasant visit I have yet made to the Indians; and induced me to believe that before they became acquainted with white people, and were infected with their vices, they must have been as happy a people as any in the world. In returning to our quarters we passed by the Indian council, where Red Jacket was displaying his oratory to his brother chiefs, on the subject of Colonel Pickering's proposals. . . . Red Jacket visited us with his wife and five children, whom he had brought to see us. They were exceedingly well clad, in their manner, and the best behaved and prettiest Indian children I have ever met with."

During the War of 1812, Red Jacket performed the important service of keeping the New York Indians in line, while Brant's exiles were with the British. Their services were not great and General Peter B. Porter has left an accusation of cowardice against Red Jacket. It would appear more likely to have been well-calculated prudence. Certainly he saved much anxiety by keeping the tribes loyal, and as the war faded out, the American record being as inglorious on land as it was glorious on the water, through his influence the warriors on both sides quietly laid down their hatchets.

For all this Red Jacket gained nothing for himself, or for his people, and became soured toward the whites. Where before he had been progressive and favored civilization, he now sought to preserve the ancient ways of the tribes and the rites of paganism. Many Indian girls married white men, and so spread much excellent red blood among the settlers, whose descendants now claim it proudly. He frowned on these alliances, became morose and bitter. His influence was steadily and strongly exerted to hold his people together and prevent their absorption by the dominant race. In this he succeeded. There are many pagans among them to-day and they do not advance, though individual cases are notable, such as that of Brigadier-General Ely Parker, who was General Grant's military secretary; and his nephew, A. C. Parker, who became state antiquarian of New York. They gain but little in numbers, and live poorly on ill-cultivated lands, yet they have undoubted latent talent. The Indian in them remains supreme.

As affairs settled down, and the red race accepted its limitations, Red Jacket slipped from view. In taking the pagan part he lost his leadership and the title of chief. It came back to him just before his death, when he was reinstated, more as a last tribute than for any other reason. The fire in his soul had burned out. Yet, as he said in his last recorded speech: "Many years have I guided the nation."

The great men at the national capital, from Washington to Andrew Jackson, thought well of him and treated him as an equal, which in many ways he was. The end was pitiful. With a failing mind, he was put on show in Boston and Albany by some sharp speculators in human curiosity, and then taken home to die.

He was buried in Buffalo, where for nine years his grave bore no mark. Then Henry Placide, the English actor, erected a stone on which was graven:

Sa-go-ye-wat-ha,

(He-keeps-them-awake)

RED-JACKET

Chief of the

Wolf Tribe of the Senecas,

The Friend and Protector of His People,

Died Jan'y 20, 1830,

Aged 78 years.

This remained until the orator was reburied under a splendid monument at the entrance to the beautiful Delaware Cemetery, where around him sleep numbers of his tribesfolk, including Deerfoot, the runner. Moved by its dedication, October 9, 1884, Walt Whitman wrote:

Upon this scene, this show,
Yielded to-day by fashion, learning, wealth;
(Nor in caprice alone—some grains of deepest
      meaning,)
Haply aloft, (who knows?) from distant sky-
      clouds blended shapes
As some old tree, or rock or cliff, thrilled with its
      soul
Product of Nature's sun, stars, earth direct—
      a towering human form,
In hunting-shirt of film, armed with the rifle, a
      half ironical smile curving its phantom lips,
Like one of Ossian's ghosts looks down.

CHAPTER XII

BOSTON, the brainery of America, produced George Francis Train, one of the most amazing of all Americans. He was born March 24, 1829, and early in life leaped into a large place in affairs. Soon after his birth his father ventured to New Orleans and set up in business. In 1833 an epidemic of yellow fever devastated the city, and the Train family was sorely smitten. His mother and three sisters died, and his grandmother, in Waltham, Massachusetts, wrote begging that some one of them come to her before all were dead. "Send George," she concluded. So four-year-old George was tagged and forwarded alone. The tag read: "This is my little son George Francis Train, four years old, consigned on board the ship *Henry* to John Clark, Jr., Dock Square, Boston; to be sent to his grandmother Pickering, in Waltham, ten miles from Boston. Take good care of the little fellow as he is the only one left of eleven of us in the house, including the servants. I will come as soon as I can arrange my business."

The "little fellow" was the only passenger on the ship and made the voyage safely though with

167

some moral impairment. The seamen taught him to swear. From the time of his setting sail he developed an extraordinary capacity for taking care of himself that continued all of his life. He lived on the Waltham farm until fifteen, going to the town school. Then he was placed in his Uncle Enoch Train's shipping office in Boston, and began an astonishing career of business success. He had an uncanny prescience that placed him far ahead of men of his time. So intense were his purposes, and so superior his abilities, that when he was twenty he had forced an interest in his uncle's house worth ten thousand dollars a year. The California boom following the discovery of gold set a great company of Argonauts flowing to the Pacific. Train was responsible for creating a fleet of forty sailing ships, for the trade, built mainly by Donald McKay at East Boston, the queen of which was the *Flying Cloud,* a matchless vessel for speed, outfooting the best of the famous Baltimore clippers.

The discovery of gold in Australia, following that in California, started a stream of adventurers to the Antipodes. On this Train rode, establishing a shipping and commission house in Melbourne, that earned for a time ninety-five thousand dollars a year. He literally turned everything he touched into gold.

The discontented Australian miners organized a sort of revolution and attempted to establish a Five Star Republic, offering the adventurous

American its presidency. He declined, and the movement came to nothing, but in the end won the colonies their present freedom. After this Train relaxed a bit by journeying to India and writing an interesting book on his experiences there and in Australia. Reaching Europe he visited Paris in the heyday of the second Empire, to become intimate with Louis Napoleon and the Empress Eugenie. He was dashing in manner and handsome of face, possessed of a magnetic, compelling temperament that carried him wherever it willed that he should go.

Street railways had come into vogue in the United States. Train introduced them to Europe, constructing the first line between Liverpool and Birkenhead. He followed this venture with three more in London.

Visiting Madrid, he acquired the regard of the Spanish Queen, Maria Christina, and proved an expensive acquaintance for the lady, for in projecting the Atlantic and Great Western Railroad, now a part of the Erie, he persuaded her to invest large sums, which never came back, the road becoming one of the choicest wrecks in American railway history.

During the Civil War he took to the platform in England, espousing the Union cause, and did much to keep that country from recognizing the Confederacy. The war over, he projected the Union Pacific Railway, organized the famous Credit Mobilier to finance it and founded Omaha,

where he owned five thousand lots, reckoned forty
years later to be worth thirty million dollars,
though he had lost title to them through litigation
that finally declared him insane.   The Credit
Mobilier scandals were not of his making.
Heavier financiers had taken the reins from his
hands and he had gone abroad to organize the
Commune in Marseilles, where he became first aid
to Cluseret, the ex-Union brigadier who had so
large a share in the uprising that almost ruined
France.   This followed a trip around the world in
eighty days, thereby anticipating, if not provoking,
Jules Verne's famous tale.

Some of his stunts were remarkable.   Not
liking a hotel in Omaha he complained to the proprietor, who told him to go and build one to suit
himself.   He did this in sixty days and mocking-
ly named it "Cozzens," after the boniface who had
scorned him.

During the Commune period he stood off a
file of soldiers sent to corral Cluseret.   This is
his own account of the incident:

"I saw from my window an army marching
down the street, and went out on the balcony shouting *Vive la République! Vive la Commune!*
echoing the cries of the people in the street.   There
was an ominous silence.   Then I saw the new
Prefect, M. Gent, Gambetta's man, riding in a
carriage with the troops.   Suddenly I heard a shot
and M. Gent dropped to the bottom of the vehicle.
Some one had tried to kill him, but missed, and the

Prefect did not want to be conspicuous again. The troops came to a halt directly in front of our hotel, and I saw that the officers were regarding with anger the flag of the Commune which floated from the balcony. Orders were given and a firing squad stepped from the ranks. I knew it was their purpose to shoot me. I felt that if I had to die I should die in the most dramatic manner possible. There were two other flags on the balcony—the colors of France and the United States. I seized both of these, wrapped them quickly around my body. Then I stepped forward and knelt in front of the balcony, facing the squad. Then I shouted to the officers in French:

" 'Fire, fire, you miserable cowards. Fire upon the flags of France and America wrapped around the body of an American citizen, if you have the courage.' "

The squad lowered its rifles and retired to the ranks. Train came home in time to announce himself as a candidate for president in the campaign of 1872. Victoria Woodhull and Tennessee Claflin, her sister, were then the sensation of New York with their free-love theories. Train came to Mrs. Woodhull's defense and was jailed for printing some salacious selections from the Bible to prove her innocence of moral turpitude. They put him in "Murderer's Row" in the Tombs, where Richard Croker, and John J. Scannell were held on a homicide charge. Another neighbor was Thomas J. Sharkey, who escaped and was

never found.   The two others were acquitted, to
become powerful politicians.   Train was also
freed.   He was wont to boast that he had been
fifteen times imprisoned without ever having committed a crime.   In all there were twenty-two
"murderers" in the "row."   They formed a club
and elected Train president.   The nature of his
actions was such that his sanity was made a matter
of court inquiry before Judge Noah Davis, who
directed the jury to declare him a lunatic and the
verdict went on record.   Train appealed and on
May 27, 1873, the verdict was set aside.   He had,
however, in the meantime suffered severe property
losses.   He had been a man of large means, owned
a villa at Newport, and spent two thousand dollars
a week—a great sum for the period.   The effect
of the litigation was to restrain him from throwing
away his funds, but when relieved of the ban he
lost all interest in money, and took delight in becoming, as he called himself, "the Great American
Crank."   This led him into some spectacular
whimsies.   For years he lived in an attic room
under the mansard roof of the Hotel Continental,
at Broadway and Nineteenth Street.   When
Darius Ogden Mills opened his "Mills Hotel No.
1," in Bleecker Street, Mr. Train moved thereto
and claimed to be able to subsist on three dollars
a week.   For thirty years he ate no meat, living
chiefly on cereals and fresh fruits, though profess-
ing to find much nutriment in the humble peanut.
These he shared with the squirrels that frequented

Madison Square, where on one of the benches he made his headquarters during the last decade or more of his life, cultivating friendly relations with the children of the neighborhood. The youngsters flocked about him, and hundreds of the boys and girls of the 'nineties became his friends.   For adults he had small use, though acquaintances of his greater days by no means forgot him.   E. P. Mitchell and Amos J. Cummings of the *New York Sun*, were steadfast in their regard for the brilliant self-constituted "crank."   Charles A. Dana was always tolerant of him, and the newspapers generally kept him in mind.   He would write weird post-card notes on current topics, using a double-ended red and blue pencil with striking effect.   I reproduce a sample from my collection, received while city editor of the *Brooklyn Daily Eagle*.

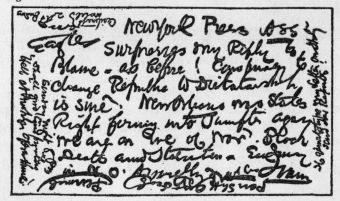

An incident, quite characteristic of his stay in Madison Square, is taken from the *New York World* of August 8, 1892:

"A tall, lank man walked across Madison Square Park yesterday morning and accosted nearly everybody he met with the query: 'Want to buy a mocking bird?'   He carried a flat pasteboard box about eight inches square in his hand. Inside fluttered a bird, which apparently did not relish its confinement at all.   Small holes punctured in the sides of this improvised cage gave the songster a chance to breathe.

"George Francis Train was occupying his usual bench.   As the vender approached he asked him to let him view the mocking bird.

" 'How much do you want for him?' inquired the philosopher.

" 'It's worth $1,' said the man, to whom it would appear such a sum was something as large as the side of a house.

" 'Can he fly?' queried the philosopher.

"The man nodded his head.   'My little boy ketched him in a trap,' he said.

" 'Will your little boy get the dollar?' went on Mr. Train.

" 'His mother will,' answered the man.

" 'Well,' returned George Francis, 'if this bird has been in seventy-five jails the way I have, he will appreciate getting out,' and fishing one dollar out of his white coat pocket, the sage handed it to the man.   Then untying the string he lifted the cover off the box.   There was a whirr as the bird flew out like a shot.

"The vender, who didn't appear to be a particularly industrious soul, looked at Train with an expression of disgust.   'You're a chump,' he said.

" 'You're another,' returned the Citizen.   'Why don't you go to work instead of peddling your little boy's pets?'

"The man muttered something and slunk off, as the bird, evidently weary with his cramped wings, sat on a neighboring branch and began to make his toilet, meanwhile thanking his liberator in a chirp or two.

" 'That gives me more real pleasure than a pint of peanuts,' said Mr. Train, and the mocking bird doubtless thought the same."

He could tell a lot of truth in his simulation of irresponsibility. Here is a sample from one of his speeches, made at the New York Grand Opera House:

"The newspapers took $7,000,000 of the steal of Tweed and then they poisoned the old cuss in Ludlow Street Jail, and my old friend Dana never said a word about the fund that he collected there. He built a monument for him. The *News* is down here on my list for $300,000; the *Times*, $34,000—for what? For five-column message of Oakley Hall's in agate at two cents a line, and because Tweed wouldn't pay it they opened fire on Tammany two years after. The *Herald* got $100,000 for young Jim to start the *Telegram*. The *Herald* has been the tool of Jay Gould for six years. The *Sun*—I don't want to say anything against my friend Dana, but the *Sun* is down for $64,000."

Arrested while on a visit to Boston in the 'eighties, for a debt that really was another's he was put into the new Charles Street jail where he made much out of the episode, amusing himself for one thing by filling out the required register blank as follows:

Registered No. Cell 10. Mittimus No. 2,000.

Name.

Geo. Francis Train, more commonly known as "Champion Crank."

Birthplace.

21 High street, Boston.

Residence.

Continental Hotel, New York City, now, but generally in some jail!

Color.	Age.	Sex.	Height.
Octoroon!	Sixty!	Male.	5 feet 11

Birthplace of Father.

Boston.   He founded Boston Port Society and Father Taylor's Seamen's Bethel!

Birthplace of Mother.

Waltham, Mass.   (My room, bed, desk, in homestead 200 years old, still shown strangers!)

Married.

Yes!   1851!   Wife died 1879!

Education.

Three months.   Winter school.

Temperate.

Yes.   (Never tasted liquor!)

Property

Own half Omaha when I choose to become sane!

Ever in Reform School?   Where?

Yes!   Three times 'round world, twenty-seven times across Atlantic!

No. of Children under 15.

None!   (Three living grown up!)

Occupation

Aristocratic Loafer!

When Committed.

Sept. 24, 1889!   (Tremont House, Boston.)

Offense Charged.

Helping poor printer buy printing press sixteen years ago.

No. of Times Committed.

Twice for this one offense!   In fourteen jails for telling truth!

Sentence or Otherwise.

So long as blackmailer pays my board.

Non-Payment of Fine and Costs.

Have not paid cent for anything, and don't intend to!

Witness.

Geo. Francis Train, who has Boston?   Bay State?   Republic?   American justice's generating power in steel trap!

Geo. Francis Train.

(Fifteenth Jail.)

The creditor was a man from Toledo, who soon tired of paying the prisoner's board. Train was quite comfortable and announced his purpose to spend his life there—at the claimant's expense. He was soon released, quartered himself at the Tremont House and easily made himself a center of attention.   A fire broke out in Houghton & Dutton's department store and one of the firemen was overcome by smoke.   Train broke into the hotel bar, closed for the night, and commandeering a bottle of whisky, revived the man with its contents.   Then he made a speech on whisky, of which he said he was a judge, although he did not drink it.   He had once laid fifteen Englishmen drunk with whisky under his table and uttered the dictum that Britishers could swallow more whisky than any people on earth—when it was free!

His Boston visit was topped off with a Christmas tree which he gave to the children in his old home at Waltham. He played Santa Claus himself, with signal success. He also lectured to a great audience in the Boston Music Hall, in which he gracefully called the city a "backwoods town" where a man could be imprisoned on a bogus affidavit; Harvard College was only a school for football players, and poor ones at that, while Massachusetts had produced no great men since Choate and Webster.

In 1890 he made another leap around the world. Interviewed in London on his way home, he gave this vivid summary of the then remarkable journey:

"Fifty-two days on the way and will finish my journey around the world in ten days more. Remember the fuss some people made when a young woman went around the world in seventy-two days and some hours? It's enough to make one sick. Nothing. Anybody could do it. Remember Jules Verne's *Around the World in Eighty Days?* He stole my thunder. I'm Phileas Fogg. But I have beaten Phileas Fogg out of sight. What put the notion into my head? Well, I'm possessed of great psychic force. I'm a pioneer of Tacoma. You know where it is, in Washington State, on Puget Sound. I went there. They asked me to go around the world. I said I would. I gave a lecture, and for it they paid me eight hun-

GEORGE FRANCIS TRAIN

dred pounds in these [these meant fifty pound bills, a number of which Mr. Train showed]. I told them I'd go around the world and make Tacoma famous.

"I left Tacoma on March eighteenth, chartered steamer *Olympia* for two hundred pounds to catch Vancouver boat; caught it. There were five hundred people to see me off. Made trip to Yokohama in sixteen days. There found that North German Lloyd steamer had been gone two days. She was at Kobe. I asked them to hold her by wire. They laughed at me. I held her by wire and engaged special train. I traveled three hundred and sixty miles through the interior of Japan; at Nagasaki the Consul told me that no foreigner could get a passport in less than three days. I said I'd get one in less than three seconds or see the Mikado or burst the empire. I went to Tokio and got my passport in thirty minutes.

"I took special train for Kobe. There I hired a steam launch to catch the steamship *General Werder*. I caught her, and went to Hong Kong, was delayed outside the harbor for two days by a fog, left Hong Kong on April thirteenth and reached Singapore, a distance of 1,428 miles, in three and a half days. Was detained thirty hours on way by rain and a cyclone.

"Jumped to Colombo, distance of 15,170 metres, in four days, and made another jump of 2,093 miles to Aden in six and one-half days, beating fast P. and O. sixteen-knot boat by eighteen

hours.   Went up Red Sea to Suez, distance of
1,308 miles, in three and one-half days and got
into the Canal before P. and O. boat.

"I had sent word on to charter a steam launch
in case of need, but didn't want it.   The steamship
Preussen couldn't catch the British mail, so I went
aboard the P. and O. steamer *Arcadia*, went
through the Suez Canal in sixteen hours, was at
Brindisi two and a half days later, and left Brindisi
at two P. M., on Thursday, May eighth.

"Upon arriving at Calais I found there was no
boat which I could catch.   I telegraphed to Dover
for a special boat and was told I could have one
for forty pounds.   All right.   The boat came, but
there were many people who desired to come, so
they charged the others 17s. 6d. a head and charged
me nothing; forty pounds saved.   I reached Calais
at nine o'clock this morning, telegraphed for special train from Dover to London, left Dover at
noon, arrived in London at five P. M., and will
leave at twenty minutes past eight."

The Columbian Exposition at Chicago in 1893,
did not start off very well.   Train, leaving his
park bench, announced his purpose to "save" the
show.   He went to Chicago, organized a grand
march to the grounds, leading it with a belle from
Dahomey on his arm, and with the help of Mayor
George P. Bemis of Omaha, his nephew, roused
the West to interest in the enterprise.   The man
had some right to believe himself a magnet.

When seventy-four, he dictated in thirty-five

hours, a hundred thousand word biography, *My Life in Many States and in Foreign Lands,* that told his story with vivid freshness. These samples of his practical quickness of thought are from it:

"Once in London I was astonished to see a man, after writing something with a lead pencil, search through his pockets for a piece of India rubber with which to erase an error. He had lost it, and could only smudge the paper by marking out what he had written. I said to him: 'Why don't you attach the rubber to the pencil? Then you couldn't lose it.' He jumped at my suggestion, took out a patent for the rubber attachment to pencils and made money.

"When Rowland Hill, the great English postal reformer, introduced penny postage into England he found it necessary to employ many girls to clip off the stamps from great sheets. I took a sheet of paper to him and showed him how easy it would be by perforation to tear off the stamps as needed. He adopted my idea; and now a single machine does the whole work.

"I noticed one day in England a lot of 'flunkeys' rushing up to the carriages of titled ladies and busying themselves adjusting steps, which were separate from the carriage and had been taken along with great inconvenience. I said to myself, why not have the steps attached? and I spoke about the idea to others. It was taken up and carried out. Now every carriage has steps attached as part of the structure.

"In '50 I was with James McHenry in Liverpool, and in trying to pour some ink from a bottle into the ink well the bottle was upset and the ink spilled all over the desk.   This was because too much ink came from the mouth.   'Give the bottle a nose like a milk pitcher,' I said, 'then you can pour the ink into the well easily.'   Holden, of Liverpool, took up the idea and patented it and made a fortune out of it."

In 1903, Mr. Train was stricken with smallpox while visiting his daughter at Stamford, Connecticut, and forthwith conveyed to the local, but little used, pest house.   He was not very ill, but contrived to make it interesting for the town.   He inveighed against the authorities for burning his garments and a mass of manuscripts, and threatened them with a fifty thousand dollar damage suit.   This was never filed but the eccentric's stay in the lazaret cost the community two thousand dollars.

Though once legally called insane, there was much doubt as to the accuracy of the diagnosis. Eccentric, he was indeed, but much of it was planned, not spontaneous.   He had heaps of fun with himself and the world at large.

Train died at Mills Hotel No. 1, New York, January 19, 1904, in his seventy-sixth year.   Doctor Edward C. Spitzka, the alienist, weighed his brain.   It ranked No. 27 among the heaviest known, 1525 grains, or 53.8 ounces.   He was buried in Greenwood Cemetery, Brooklyn.

CHAPTER XIII

TECUMSEH—PATRIOT AND WARRIOR

OF THE many natives of Ohio who have earned niches in the hall of fame, none more fully fills his place than Tecumseh, Chief of the Shawnee nation. He was a warrior and statesman of the first rank, and he was noble in character, lofty in his ideals and eminent in attainments. He deserves well of history as a great and unusual American. Son of Puckeshinwau, a noted chieftain, he was born on the Mad River, in what is now Clark County, in 1768. His people were of Iroquoian stock, who had wandered from Pennsylvania to the South and back again to receive territory from the Wyandots, and became members of the Northwestern Federation, an alliance next in power and intelligence to the Six Nations.

Elkswatawa, a younger brother, famous as "The Prophet," was largely responsible for the part played in pioneer history by Tecumseh. In 1805 he proclaimed himself a religious leader and began to arouse the Ohio, Indiana and Illinois tribes, to the great disturbance of the white settlers. His doctrines were not primarily revolutionary. Temperance and total abstinence were tenets, to-

gether with reverence for old age and sympathy
for the infirm.   He also urged his people to resist
intermarriage and to preserve their own customs
and costumes.   This was in the line of Indian
comity.   His preaching caused much excitement
among the Indians and fear among the whites.

Soon his exordiums were heard far and wide
by the red men, who were stirred to unite in the
common welfare, which was quite naturally viewed
with alarm.   The Spanish in Florida lent friendly
ears to representations that the tribes might be
made allies in resisting the American advance.
Tecumseh himself went on a mission to the Cherokees and the other more civilized tribes of the
South.   By 1810 the Delawares, Pottawattomies,
Chippewas and Ottawas had joined the Shawnees
and followed the Prophet.   The Wyandots and
Miamis kept out of it as tribes.

William Henry Harrison was governor of the
Northwest Territory and took active cognizance of
the movement, doing his best to arrest its growth
and allay hostile feeling.   To his efforts Tecumseh responded in kind, coming to Vincennes on
the twenty-seventh of July, 1811, with a following
of some three hundred warriors and women, and
expressing a longing for "peace and happiness."
His arrival caused great uneasiness and the militia
was called out, to the number of seven hundred and
fifty men.   The chief frankly explained that he
was endeavoring to form a confederation that
would protect the rights of his race, with no hostile

design against the then seventeen states of the
Union.   He also explained his purpose to unite
with the Cherokees, Creeks, Choctaws, Chicka-
saws and Seminoles and pledged himself to peace.
He then left on a mission to the South.   The settlers were greatly stirred, but Harrison was filled
with admiration for the chief, which wells up in a
report made to Washington:

"If it were not for the vicinity of the United
States, he would perhaps be the founder of an empire that would rival in glory Mexico or Peru.   No
difficulties deter him. For four years he has been in
constant motion.   You see him to-day on the
Wabash, and in a short time hear of him on the
shores of Lake Erie or Michigan, or on the banks
of the Mississippi, and wherever he goes he makes
an impression favorable to his purpose.   He is
now upon his last round to put a finishing stroke
upon his work."   To this he added: "I hope,
however, before his return that that part of his
work which he considered complete will be demolished and even its foundation rooted up."

In response to an invitation for further conference, Tecumseh came again to Vincennes with
his retinue.   The Indians were less friendly than
before and their leader held himself haughtily at
the council.   No chair had been provided for him.
The interpreter, noting that he seemed exhausted
after speaking long and with much vehemence,
handed one forward with the remark: "Your
father (Harrison) requests you to take a chair."

"My father!" retorted Tecumseh scornfully. "My father!   The sun is my father, the earth my mother; upon her bosom I will repose."

With that he sat himself upon the ground. Talking to Harrison about President Madison, as the responsible party in their discussion, he observed sententiously: "He is so far off that war will not injure him; he may sit still in his town and drink his wine, while you and I will have to fight it out."

The great earthquake at New Madrid had taken place, forming the Reelfoot lake and doing vast damage.   Tecumseh seized it as a retributive act from on high: "The Great Spirit is angry with our enemies; he speaks in thunder, and the earth swallows up villages and drinks of the Mississippi; the wide waters will cover their lowlands and the Great Spirit will sweep from the earth with his terrible breath, those who escape to the hills."

Harrison began a reply with a recital of the purpose of the Seventeen Fires, as the states were called by the Indians, to do strict justice.   Tecumseh commented in Shawnee that this was not true, and his warriors fumbled their weapons.   Harrison, being told the cause of the commotion (he did not understand the Shawnee tongue), dismissed the council.

Parleyings, however, were continued.   On August tenth, Tecumseh came again to Vincennes, accompanied as before.   He remained a fortnight, during which there were many conferences, at the

final one of which he made his purpose plain.   It
was that recent land sales made by petty chiefs be
abrogated and the deeds destroyed.   In pressing
his petition he said to Harrison:

"Brother, I wish you would take pity on the red
people and do what I have requested.   If you will
not give up the land, and do cross the boundary of
your present settlement, it will be very hard and
cause great trouble among us.   How can you
have confidence in the white people?   When
Jesus Christ came on earth, you killed Him and
nailed Him on a cross.   You thought He was
dead, but you were mistaken.   You have Shakers
among you, and you laugh and make light of their
worship.   Everything I have said to you is the
truth.   The Great Spirit has inspired me, and I
speak nothing but the truth to you. . . . Brother,
I hope you will confess that you ought not to have
listened to those bad birds who bring you bad
news.   I have declared myself freely to you, and
if any explanations should be required from our
town, send a man who can speak to us.   If you
think proper to give us any presents, and we can be
convinced that they are given through friendship,
we will accept them.   As we intend to hold our
council at the Huron village, which is near the
British, we may probably make them a visit.
Should they offer us any presents of goods we will
not take them.   Should they offer us powder and
the tomahawk we will take the powder and refuse
the tomahawk.   I wish you, brother, to consider

everything I have said as true, and that it is the sentiment of all the red people that listen to me."

Following this Tecumseh actively renewed his efforts to form a red federation. He traveled a thousand miles among the tribes of the South and was everywhere received with attention and respect. The five civilized tribes were ready to join but the Spanish promises came to nothing. Harrison improved on the leader's absence to take precautions against his return. The settlers were infuriated by sundry outrages, though there is no evidence that either Tecumseh or his brother could in any just way be held responsible. The Prophet had built up a considerable village at Tippecanoe, to which point some stolen horses were traced. They were promptly given up when demanded. Harrison now called for the surrender of several alleged murderers, who, naturally, could not be produced. In response to the clamor President Madison ordered the Fourth Dragoon Regiment to report to Harrison. With this force at hand the settlers demanded a move against Tippecanoe. The alarmed Indians sent a delegation to Harrison at Vincennes, deprecating the obvious hostility of their white neighbors and making every profession of good will. Despite this, Harrison, yielding to the clamor and fearful of Tecumseh, decided to move against the Prophet before he could return. Accordingly, on the sixteenth of September, 1811, he issued orders that set the force in motion. In all it numbered nine hundred and ten men. Remembering the fate of St. Clair, Harrison moved slowly. He did not reach the vicinity of Tippecanoe until the fifth of November. The Prophet sent a deputation to Harrison and proffered a peace, which it was agreed should be concluded on the following day. The Indians located a good camp-site for the army and this was utilized.

According to Harrison the Indians began an attack at about four o'clock in the morning, which drove back the pickets and routed the guards, penetrating even to the tents. The aroused regulars soon had the lines in hand, but the militia were in confusion. By the time matters were in shape some losses had been incurred, and when the warriors were at last beaten the toll of American dead was thirty-seven. Some one hundred and fifty-one had been wounded. The Indians' loss was credited with being about the same. How strong the red legions were is not known. They were estimated at all the way from three hundred and fifty to one thousand. The first figure is more likely the correct one.

The Prophet took refuge with the Wyandots and his following rejoined their tribes. Tecumseh returned, to find his work "demolished and its foundations rooted up" as Harrison had desired.

Resolutely he endeavored to repair the situation. Previous to his departure for the South he had been invited by President Madison to visit him in Washington. With the object of gaining time

Tecumseh sent word to General Harrison that he would go; but only as a chief.   To this Harrison replied that he might proceed as a member of a deputation, but not with the desired title.   Deeply hurt, the warrior declined to go.   Instead, he visited the Northwestern tribes in an effort to reunite them.   He collected a roving band of followers and menaced the much troubled frontier.   Harrison sought further council, and one was held in May, 1812, at Mississihniway, on the Wabash, attended by representatives of twelve tribes.   All were for peace save Tecumseh, who said he did not care for peace without justice, though he had no mind for war.   "If the whites come again and make an unprovoked attack on our village," he said, "we will die like men, but we will never strike the first blow."

He continued to urge that the Ohio River become the white man's boundary and that the purchase of tribal lands, without the consent of all members, should cease.   The War of 1812 loomed fast into view.   Wishing to take sides with neither he felt impelled by the interests of the cause to deal with the one that promised most.   This became the British.   Matthew Elliott, a renegade, uncle of Commodore Jesse D. Elliott, who was to serve with Oliver Hazard Perry at the Battle of Lake Erie and become a naval storm-breeder for many years, held out inducements that were accepted.   This occurred at a council held at Malden.

Tecumseh at once began active recruiting and

assembled some three thousand warriors. He was absent on this service in the Wabash country when the massacre of the River Raisin occurred—a lasting blot on the honor of English arms. Prisoners taken at Fort Meigs were being butchered by Indians when Tecumseh ran to their rescue and stopped the slaughter. He was in numerous skirmishes and attacks under the British General Proctor, a foolhardy and incapable officer, whom the chief warned in vain. Following Perry's victory, Proctor prepared to evacuate Malden. Tecumseh knew this was an error that spelled the ruin of his own hopes and remonstrated in these terms:

"Father—Listen to your children! You have them all now before you.

"The war before this, our British father gave the hatchet to his red children, when our old chiefs were alive. They are now dead! In the war, our father was thrown on his back, by the Americans, and our father took them by the hand without our knowledge. We are afraid our father will do so again at this time.

"Summer before last, when I came forward with my red brethren, and was ready to take up the hatchet in favor of our British father, we were told not to be in a hurry, that he had not yet determined to fight the Americans.

"Listen! When war was declared, our father stood up and gave us the tomahawk, and told us that he was then ready to strike the Americans;

that he wanted our assistance; and that he would certainly get us our lands back, which the Americans had taken from us.

"Listen!—You told us at that time to bring our families to this place, and we did so; and you promised to take care of them; that they should want for nothing, while the men would go and fight the enemy; that we need not trouble ourselves about the enemy's garrisons; that we knew nothing about them, and that our father would attend to that part of the business. You also told your red children that you would take good care of your garrison here, which made our hearts glad.

"Listen!—When we were last at the Rapids, it is true, we gave you little assistance. It is hard to fight people who live like ground-hogs.

"Father, listen!—Our fleet has gone out; we know they have fought; we have heard the great guns; but we know nothing of what has happened to our father with one arm. Our ships have gone one way, and we are much astonished to see our father tying up every thing and preparing to run away the other, without letting his red children know what his intentions are. You always told us to remain here and take care of our lands; it made our hearts glad to hear that was your wish. Our great father, the king, is the head, and you represent him. You always told us you would never draw your foot off British ground; but now, father, we see you are drawing back, and we are sorry to see our father doing so, without seeing the enemy. We must compare our father's conduct to a fat dog, that carries its tail upon its back, but when affrighted, it drops it between its legs, and runs off.

"Father, listen!—The Americans have not yet defeated us by land; neither are we sure that they have done so by water; we therefore wish to remain here, and fight our enemy, should they make their appearance. If they defeat us, we will then retreat with our father. At the battle of the Rapids, last war, the Americans certainly defeated us; and when we returned to our father's fort at that place, the gates were shut against us. We were afraid that it would now be the case; but instead of that, we now see our British father preparing to march out of the garrison.

"Father!—You have got the arms and ammunition which our great father sent for his red children. If you have an idea of going away, give them to us, and you may go and welcome. Our lives are in the hands of the Great Spirit. We are determined to defend our lands, and if it be his will, we wish to leave our bones upon them."

The battle of the Thames, October 5, 1813, with its disastrous ending, followed. A military critic has observed: "If Proctor had taken Tecumseh's advice and fought the Americans before retreating, the result must have been more glorious at least, if not entirely favorable to British arms!" Proctor's lines broke at the first assault, save where Tecumseh and his warriors held the ground. He wore a white plume like that which graced the helmet of Navarre. It was seen waving everywhere along the right wing until the mass of American troops nearly enfolded it. Then it vanished and when the field was scanned Tecumseh was among the dead. No man knows who actually slew him, but Colonel Richard M. Johnson, of Kentucky, claimed the laurel and this made him vice-president of the United States.

Tippecanoe elected Harrison to the presidency, which he was destined to fill but a single month, dying April 4, 1841.

To all white men with whom he came in contact, Tecumseh appealed strongly as a man and a patriot. A great admirer was Charles R. Sherman, who, coming from Connecticut, had settled in Lancaster, Ohio. He named his youngest son William Tecumseh, but the lad was not formally christened until he was nine years old, and after the death of his father. The clergyman demurred at what he called the "heathen name," but the boy replied stoutly: "My father called me Tecumseh and Tecumseh I will be whether you like it or not." And Tecumseh he remained. So the name of one great warrior thus became perpetuated in that of another.

CHAPTER XIV

ETHAN ALLEN—LIBERATOR OF VERMONT

ETHAN ALLEN, of Vermont, was the first person to proclaim the authority of the Continental Congress, and he did it six hours before that august assemblage called itself together at Philadelphia, early on the morning of May 10, 1775. Lexington had been fought; Bunker Hill was yet to come, when Allen, with two hundred and seventy volunteers, laid plans to take Ticonderoga, the key to Canada by way of Lake Champlain. This and Crown Point, a few miles up the lake, had been the French strongholds in the Seven Years' War and Crown Point had been strengthened by Britain at the cost of millions of pounds. Allen and his lieutenant, Seth Warner, had assembled their force of Vermonters at Castleton, fourteen miles from Whitehall, and laid plans for the descent as arranged by the zealous General Assembly of Connecticut, which had initiated the enterprise, and had sent Edward Mott and Noah Phelps to solicit the services of Allen and his Green Mountain Boys.

A New Haven druggist had marched a company to Cambridge, and while awaiting events, had suggested to the Massachusetts Committee of Safety a move on Ticonderoga. When told to go ahead, he made some effort to enlist men for the expedition, but hearing of Allen's proposed attempt, he hurried to Castleton and claimed command. As he brought no one with him but a valet the borderers said him nay, and he remained as a gentleman volunteer. His name was Benedict Arnold.

Ticonderoga was held by a small garrison, some forty-eight men, under Major Delaplace, whom Allen knew well. The assaulting party of eighty men reached the fort at dawn, after Allen had again successfully disputed Arnold's leadership, and kept the command. The single sentinel pulled the trigger of his flintlock as he saw the party enter the sally-port and ran to give an alarm, while Allen rapped smartly upon the entrance with his sword hilt. Delaplace, half dressed, opened the door and demanded to know by what authority he was so rudely disturbed.

"In the name of the great Jehovah and the Continental Congress," was the thunderous reply. He, with his troopers, was soon on the march for Hartford as prisoners of war. Ticonderoga was well armed and more than one hundred excellent cannon were carted across country to Boston, where they performed important service in persuading the British to evacuate the city, forming a formidable factor in General George Washington's equipment during the siege.

The way to Canada being thus unbarred the next step was to make use of the opportunity. Allen, with Seth Warner, went to Philadelphia and appeared before the Congress, whose might had been so lustily proclaimed, and asked for men to take the domain to the North. Congress was too helpless to do anything and referred the heroes to the New York convention. Now it chanced that there was a price on the heads of both Allen and Warner, growing out of the celebrated Hampshire grants, which Governor Tryon had held belonged to New York and from which he sought to exclude Vermonters by force. The uprising of the Green Mountain Boys was the result, and the New York settlers were themselves expelled. Not only was a price set by the New York Assembly, but the pair was outlawed and under sentence to be hanged if caught. Things had changed, however. The Assembly was dissolved and Tryon put to flight. So Allen and Warner boldly presented themselves to the Convention. There was some hesitation about recognizing the "outlaws," but Isaac Sears, head of the Sons of Liberty, became their sponsor and the pair was given the privilege of the floor.

The final outcome was the organization of General Montgomery's expedition, which ended in ill fate at Quebec, where Arnold won deserved fame by an extraordinary winter march through the forests of Maine. Vermont was asked to raise a regiment and did so, with the thought that Allen would be made colonel. Warner became lieutenant-

colonel, but a hitch arose as to the first in rank.
Philip Schuyler was to be head of the troops with
whom the Vermonters were to serve. Now York's
jealousy of Allen asserted itself in the alleged fear
that he would not be a good subordinate. Allen
then joined as a gentleman volunteer and Schuyler
made use of him to enlist Canadian support, but
little or none of this materialized, though a few
hundred followed Allen to camp. Schuyler became ill and Montgomery took command. Allen
was now asked to attempt to take Montreal by surprise, with the help of eighty of his Canadians and
about forty Americans. The attempt was made
on the dark night of September twenty-fourth.
Major Brown was to have cooperated, but failed to
appear. Montreal declined to give three cheers and
join the new republic. Instead, an armed force
greatly outnumbering Allen's, surrounded him.
His Canadians deserted and the Americans, after
a desperate stand, with considerable loss, surrendered.

Taken before Prescott, the British commander-
in-chief, Allen was called a rebel and threatened
with death on Tyburn Tree, while Prescott, bran-
dishing his cane, seemed about to administer corporal punishment then and there. "I told him,"
says Allen in the published narrative of his captivity, "that he would do well not to cane me, as I
was not accustomed to it." He also met the bran-
dished cane by shaking his fist in Prescott's face
and warning him that it would be his last hour if

he dared to strike. Prescott retaliated by having
the prisoner bound hand and foot and placed on
board the schooner of war, *Gaspe*. Here he wore
heavy shackles on arms and legs, linked to a bar
eight feet long—like the wire in a dog kennel. For
five weeks Allen and his men endured this brutal
captivity. He had neither bed nor chair, but a
sailor, with some feeling, lent him a chest to sit on.

In the interim Montgomery took St. Johns and
Chambly, an exploit in which Seth Warner and
Allen's Vermonters had a share. This caused the
transfer of the prisoners to Quebec, where they
were sent aboard another vessel and were used
decently. Their irons were removed and Captain
Littlejohn, Allen's new custodian, treated him as
a gentleman. The approach of Arnold's expedition to Quebec now caused a hasty transfer of the
prisoners to the *Adamant,* which at once set sail for
England. On board their lot again became severe.
Guy Johnson and a group of refugee Tories from
the Mohawk Valley kept them uncomfortable company. It was a grilling, unpleasant voyage in winter weather. The Vermonters were in irons and
under hatches all the way across. Landing at
Portsmouth they were confined in Pendennis Castle. Here Allen, though still in irons, was well
treated by Hamilton, the governor, who fed him
from his own table, and gave him an occasional
bottle of wine. The gentry in the neighborhood
were interested in the doughty captor of Ticonderoga and often sent him food, so he fared well dur-

ing his stay at Pendennis. Yet it was undoubtedly
the purpose of His Majesty's government to carry
out Prescott's threat and hang the captive on Tyburn Tree. Quite aware of this Allen put on a
bold front, despite the shackles on his arms and
legs. He asked permission to address a note to
Congress. This was given under the impression that he would send something urging submission. The letter, when written, was quite the
contrary. It breathed defiance, setting forth the
outrageous treatment he and his fellows had received. It contained one hint: That Congress
should not retaliate until it learned his final fate.
This missive, "To the Illustrious Continental Congress," went instead to Lord North and gave him
exactly the information Allen intended should
reach that worthy. "This," Allen wrote in his account, "gave me intense satisfaction, though I carefully concealed it with pretended resentment; for I
found I had come the Yankee over them, and that
the letter had gone to the identical person I had designed it for."

His Majesty's Opposition used the facts with
telling effect in Parliament and the Ministry yielding to the clamor and the fear that Washington
might hang a few high officers, who were in his
hands, consented to treat Allen and his comrades
as prisoners of war and not as traitors. Allen was
now shipped to Halifax in the *Solebay* frigate.
Her captain, a cad named Symonds, ordered him
to stay below and not show his face on deck, as

that was reserved for "gentlemen." After a couple
of days between decks Allen made a careful toilet
and appeared on the forbidden planks. Symonds
was a bit dazed when told that his guest expected
to be considered a gentleman, as he was "Colonel
Allen" and of that class. The matter was compro-
mised by giving him one side of the deck for a
promenade, while the officers paraded on the other.
The ship put in at Cork, where sundry merchants
fitted Allen out with fine clothing and sent him a
supply of luxuries, which Symonds confiscated as
the gift of Irish traitors to an American one. The
Solebay was much buffeted by storms and instead
of reaching Halifax, made the Cape Fear River.
Here Allen was transferred to the *Mercury,* to be
taken to Halifax. His high manner and the good
clothes procured in Cork, had softened Symonds,
but Montague, the master of the *Mercury,* treated
him badly. The ship's surgeon was not permitted
to aid the Americans, and Allen's protest was met
with the reply that it did not matter if they lived or
died; the living would all be hanged when they
reached Halifax, while Washington and the Continental Congress were due for the same fate.
"You will die of old age," cautioned Allen, "if you
wait for that event."

The *Mercury* paused at Sandy Hook, where
Lord Admiral Howe's fleet was anchored. Washington was in control of New York, and Tryon,
Allen's ancient foe of the Hampshire grant dispute, was on the flagship, together with the Royal

Attorney General Kemp. The pair visited the
Mercury. Both knew Allen, but declined to recognize him. "Tryon," he writes in his account,
"viewed me with a stern countenance as I was
walking on the leeward side of the deck with the
midshipman. What passed between the officers
and these visitors I know not; but this I know, that
my treatment from them was more severe afterward."

Reaching Halifax in mid-June the Vermonters
were transferred to an old sloop anchored in the
harbor where Montague again became their jailor
and handled them with his customary brutality.
The persistent Allen contrived to send word to
Governor Arbuthnot, who was a gentleman, and
as a result they were taken from the sloop to the
city jail. Scurvy sent some of them to the hos-
pital; others were set to work on the streets, like
convicts. At the end of August only thirteen of
his companions on the Montreal raid were left in
his company. He found a distinguished companion in toils, James Lowell, of Boston, a leading patriot, afterward an eminent member of the Continental Congress. His friends joined those of
Allen in trying to effect their release. Finally
word came to send them to New York and they
sailed thither on the frigate *Lark,* Captain Smith.
"When I came on deck," Allen records, "he met
me with his hand, welcomed me to his ship, invited
me to dine with him that day, and assured me I
should be treated as a gentleman." Allen was

quite overcome by the kindness and his stout heart relaxing, he gave himself up to tears. "This is a mutable world," remarked the captain in excusing his decent conduct, "and one gentleman never knows but it may be in his power to help another."

This thought was soon to be put to the test. There was a large cartel of American prisoners on board, who plotted a mutiny and would have succeeded, perhaps, had not Allen sternly forbade it. They arrived at New York late in October. Lowell was exchanged and Allen given the freedom of the city on parole, which was much better than being held between decks. With his customary boldness, Allen upheld his cause and in a spirited moment set out to chastise James Rivington, the king's printer, for sundry reflections on the Continental cause printed in his *Gazette*. Rivington, aware of his coming and knowing him by sight, was quite prepared to receive his visitor when he saw him at the door. He has left an amusing account of the interview:

"There was no retreat. I was certain the hour of reckoning had come. He entered the store and asked of the clerk 'Does James Rivington live here?' He answered 'Yes, sir.' 'Is he at home?' He said he would see and went up to my room to inquire what should be done. I had made up my mind. I looked at the bottle of Madeira—possibly took a glass. There was a fearful moment of suspense. I heard him on the stairs. In he stalked. 'Is your name James Rivington?' 'It is, sir, and no one could be more happy than I am to see Colonel Ethan Allen.' 'Sir, I have come—' 'Not another word, my dear Colonel, until you have taken a seat and a glass of old Madeira.' 'But, sir, I don't think it proper—' 'Not another word, Colonel. Taste this wine. I have had it in glass for ten years. Old wine, you know, unless it is originally sound does not improve with age.' He took the glass, swallowed the wine, smacked his lips and shook his head approvingly. 'Sir, I have come—' 'Not another word until you have taken another glass; and then, my dear Colonel, we will talk of old affairs; and I have some droll events to detail.' In short, we finished two bottles of Madeira and parted as good friends as if we never had cause to be otherwise."

The prisons of the city were crowded with prisoners from the Battle of Brooklyn, and the lot of some was hard, notably those confined in the old sugar house, owned by the Rhinelanders on Monkey Hill, where they were badly crowded and wretchedly used. Allen exerted himself on their behalf. He was out of cash and an effort was made to tempt him to turn traitor, with the offer of a regiment, money and land. He told the tempter "that if by faithfulness I had recommended myself to General Howe, I should be loath by unfaithfulness to lose the general's good opinion; besides that, I vowed the offer of land to be similar to that which the devil offered to Jesus Christ, to give him all the kingdom of the world if he would fall down and

worship him; when at the same time the damned
soul had not a foot of land upon earth. This
closed the conversation." His point was well
made, for the land in question was to be the spoil
from the conquered Yankees. The result of the
Battle of Trenton improved the lot of the prisoners
somewhat. Washington could retaliate. The lim-
its of Allen's parole were extended in January to
Long Island and he sojourned there until August,
then, accused falsely of violating his parole he was
brought to New York and locked up in the old
Provost prison, the gray stone building that stood
until a few decades ago in City Hall Park, under
the brute called Cunningham, who was provost
marshal. For three days he was deprived of food
and was kept in duress, under lock and key, until
May, 1778. On the third of that month he was
exchanged for Colonel Alexander Campbell. Incidentally, the beaten Burgoyne had surrendered
and the "rebels" enjoyed an improved status. The
news came to Allen while in prison, who hurrahed
through the bars of his cell and informed some
passing soldiers that "Burgoyne had marched to
Boston to the tune of *Yankee Doodle.*"

Campbell was brought to New York by Elias
Boudinot, Exchange Commissioner for the Con-
tinentals. He greeted Allen cordially, saying he
"was never so glad to see a gentleman in his life."
"I gave him to understand," says Allen, "that I
was equally glad to see him and was apprehensive
it was from the same motive." Allen had indeed

cause for rejoicing, having endured a rigorous captivity for thirty-one months. Immediately upon his release he proceeded to Valley Forge, where Washington had his headquarters, and reported to the commander-in-chief. Leave was granted him to return home and recuperate, with full pay as lieutenant-colonel from the date of his capture. May thirty-first, he arrived at Bennington, to the surprise and delight of the community. Cannon were fired in celebration. He found that the New Hampshire grants had thrown off all bondage, and had become the sovereign state of Vermont, preserving in its nomenclature, the memory due Allen and his Green Mountain Boys. Thus an independence had been declared that might mean conflict with both New York and New Hampshire. Allen, in this juncture, was appointed commander-in-chief of the new state's forces and took high ground in arranging its freedom in perpetuity. The British saw in this situation some hope of coaxing the territory back under their flag. Governor Crittenden was not above using this feeling to advance the interests of his people. A truce was offered in the warfare so far as Vermont was concerned, and accepted. A threatened invasion from Canada was abandoned and Vermont disbanded its militia. This proceeding caused Washington an anxiety that was not relieved by the state's attitude after the war, when it refused for two years to accept the Constitution of the United States.

The justification of her course lay in the situation between the claims of New York and New Hampshire. Allen summed it up very concisely in a letter to Congress, which thus concluded: "I am as resolutely determined to defend the independence of Vermont as Congress are that of the United States, and, rather than fail, I will retire with hardy Green Mountain Boys, into the desolate caverns of the mountains and wage war with human nature at large."

For the rest of the war the British kept away from Vermont and cherished the hope that her people would abandon the patriot cause as a result of their concern for their own. Allen and his brother Ira were in constant communication with General Haldimand, the commander-in-chief in Canada. Ira even paid him a visit. It was the plainest sort of double-dealing, but it kept the English out of the state and so relieved Congress of the responsibility for its defense, meanwhile leaving Vermont in a position to act should Congress fail to recognize the full independence she had created for herself. Naturally, the Allens do not stand high in Revolutionary annals, but they do in Vermont, where Ethan remains the titular hero. He was given a commission as colonel in the Continental Army, but never entered the service. After some shifting about he settled for life on the Onion River, taking up a large section of land. He died at Burlington, February 13, 1789. He was born in Litchfield, Connecticut, January 10, 1737, so he was still young.

Resolute, daring and outspoken, he feared neither men nor their opinions, publishing at Bennington, in 1784, *Reason, the Only Oracle of Man; or, a Compendious System of Natural Religion.* He did not abandon the great Jehovah, whom he invoked at Ticonderoga, but was pretty severe on the New England orthodoxy of the day and antedated by some years Thomas Paine's *Age of Reason,* though sharing a part of the obloquy earned by the latter. By strange anomaly, one of his daughters became a nun and spent her life in a Canadian convent.

Colonel Allen was always independent in his actions and much of a law unto himself. He was in financial difficulties and a Connecticut official sought to arrest him in a civil action while in that state. He seized the bridle of Allen's horse, whereon the colonel drew his sword and cried out: "You little woodchuck! Go back to your burrow, or I'll cut your head off!" He was on a military errand and the officious one prudently decided to keep his head on his shoulders.

Ethan Allen left his stamp on Vermont. It remains ineffaceable.

CHAPTER XV

THOUGH electing to spend and end his life abroad, James Abbott McNeil Whistler was essentially an American. While he permitted the impression to prevail that he had been born in Russia, he really saw the light in Lowell, Massachusetts, July 10, 1834. He came of a military line and might have remained in it, had he not expedited his departure from West Point by failing to remember that silicon was a substance, not a gas. His grandfather, John Whistler, was a soldier in General John Burgoyne's army and was made a prisoner at the Battle of Saratoga. Paroled, he returned to England, but having a scent of the New World in his nostrils he came back to America and enlisted in our small regular army, serving as orderly to General Arthur St. Clair at his defeat by the Northwestern Confederacy of Indian tribes in the Maumee Country, November 4, 1796.

Under a rule of the day that permitted promotion for successful recruiting, John Whistler was soon captain and at last major. In this latter capacity he built Fort Dearborn and so became responsible for the birth of Chicago. He had no horses; his soldiers cut and hauled the logs, and constructed the stockade. It was said he could attract more men to the colors and get more out of them when in the ranks, than any other officer in the service.

His son, George W. Whistler, James' father, also became a major in the Engineer Corps, being lured therefrom to serve under Czar Nicholas in building the Russian railroads laid out by that powerful potentate.

Through this shift in scene young Whistler saw much of St. Petersburg and created the tradition of his birth beside the Neva.

Art was in his soul. At West Point he was an artist of quality, as his early sketches show. Debarred from a commission he took a turn as draftsman in the Coast Survey and his earliest etching is a map of Anacapa Island, the plate of which, still preserved in the department, bears some neat remarques bitten in its edge.

He did not fit into a department so mechanical and in due season found himself an art student in Paris, breaking in on his studies but once and then to make a voyage around the Horn to Valparaiso, Chile. He lived the life of an art student to the full measure, continuing his etching, begun on the map plates in the Hydrographic office. Here he was to win immortality. He studied in Paris, etched in Venice and finally installed himself in London, there to become a figure of note and a center of controversy for the rest of his years.

The delivery of Mr. Whistler's exordium on art, *Ten O'clock,* in London at that hour on the evening of February 20, 1885, marked his entrance into the higher realm. He spoke at the instance of Mrs. R. D'Oyley Carte to a select and invited few, who perhaps for the first time in their lives, listened to a true and lofty note. *Ten O'clock* is a threnody, a great chant that might be sung by a chorus of male voices in a Greek stadium. It is worthy of the atmosphere of the Acropolis.

The success of *Ten O'clock* led to the idea that Whistler might visit his native land and repeat the lecture. He half prepared to go and encouraged the gossip with the remark: "This is no time for hesitation—one can not continually disappoint a continent." But in the end he failed to come, and never recrossed the sea.

Besides being a master of the brush, pencil and etching needle, and pretty handy with his pen, Mr. Whistler was a master of the great art of attracting attention which is given to a carefully selected few of the earth's millions, by some well-planned scheme that accurately gages the amount the universe can stand. This art he cultivated and practised ardently. From the West Point day, when he neglected to recall that silicon was not a gas, to his last hour, he made himself the center of interest in whatever circle he cared to affect, until the world was his stage.

Theatrical, eccentric and quarrelsome according to the common view, he had, on the other hand, a nice idea of the requirements of advertising, and quite upset the ethics of his profession by his assiduity in keeping himself before the public until his merits as an artist were so clearly recognized as no longer to need what might be called the "playing up" of his personality.

Whatever hardships may have attended his long career, they were the results of temperament rather than obscurity. His was no attic genius shivering in the shade. He lived as he pleased, liked and hated as he pleased, through the many-hued years of the last two-thirds of the nineteenth century, and stood long enough on the threshold of the twentieth to be remembered as one of the great figures clustered about its dawn.

The numerous conflicts carried on in the London press, the art societies, and the courts were summed up for all time in *The Gentle Art of Making Enemies,* issued in 1890. Neither the idea nor the title was Whistler's, but the material was, and the book is the true starting point in Whistler literature.

This combination of pertness and pasquinade, with clear sense in art, had its origin in the ingenious mind of Mr. Sheridan Ford, a talented American journalist, poet and critic. While in London writing for the Irving Bacheller Syndicate in the late 'eighties, he formed the acquaintance of Whistler, and the fortunes of both being at a low ebb, it occurred to Mr. Ford that the letters and talks of the artist might be put together in an inter-

esting book, to their mutual advantage. The
inevitable break did not come until Whistler, in
going over the completed book, ordered a letter
from Oscar Wilde, which replied to the artist's
charge of plagiarism January 9, 1890, page 118,
(Ford Edition), omitted. It accused the artist in
plain terms of lying. Mr. Ford thought it unfair
to omit the letter, and Whistler's sharp refusal to
permit its retention led to a violent quarrel, with
threatened fisticuffs, which ended in Mr. Ford's
departing with the copy, determined to issue it on
his own responsibility, though then and there forbidden to do so. It was put into type by Messrs.
Field & Tuer, of the Leadenhall Press, and plates
were made, but no impressions had been taken,
when learning of Whistler's objections, they declined to proceed with its publication. As it was
not legally feasible to publish it in London, Mr.
Ford took the book in hasty flight to Antwerp.
Originally it had borne the commonplace title of
The Correspondence of James McNeil Whistler.
The printer, with a keen eye to the merit of the
work, objected to so poor a name and was invited
by the compiler to pick a better one if he could.
This he very promptly did. Pointing to a par-
agraph in the introduction, written by Mr. Ford,
reading: "This collection of letters and miscel-
lany covers something over a quarter of a century,
from 1862 to the present year. It illustrates the
gentle art of making enemies, and is in part the
record of some unpleasantness between the Brush

and Pen"—he said: "There's your title. Don't use this other thing." And "there" it was.

Put into type once more, two thousand copies were printed, when the irate and pursuing artist, with the help of the *Procureur du Roi* and Sir George Lewis, caused the confiscation of type forms and printed sheets.

Determined not to be thwarted, and burning to defeat his adversary, Mr. Ford retreated to Ghent, where he found another English printer who agreed to compose and print the book in three days. The one thousand francs capital brought from London to Antwerp had been exhausted, but Mr. Ford's watch and jewelry remained, and a friendly *mont-de-piété* furnished five hundred francs, funds enough to insure the printer, so that the book came out on time and eluded "Jimmy." It bore this on its title page: "The Gentle Art of Making Enemies. Edited by Sheridan Ford. Paris: Delabrosse & Cie, 1890." It carried this dedication: "To all good comrades who like a fair field and no quarter these pages are peacefully inscribed."

Mr. Ford was quite fair in his introductory note, saying amiably: "As custom would sanction, in a work of this character, a complacent boast touching the sometime soulful intimacy between Mr. Whistler and myself, I may point out that nothing of the kind existed. The reader might otherwise be pardoned a casual inference that we were on terms of commonplace amity and acquiescence. I commend the book to Mr. Whistler's

JAMES A. McNEILL WHISTLER

enemies, with the soothing assurance that should each of them purchase a copy the edition will be exhausted in a week."

The little 12mo of two hundred and fifty text pages included also a two-page advertisement of "Art: A Commodity. By Sheridan Ford." It was bound in gray-green paper, with the title but not the imprint on the front cover. Butterflies in silhouette mark the Whistler notes. I have seen but one copy—my own—and have noted but two in the sales. Although four thousand copies were printed, few reached the book stalls. A supply of sheets bearing the New York imprint of "Frederick Stokes & Brothers" was shipped to the United States. The binding was similar to that of the Delabrosse edition, but the cover title was imprinted in red. When a few copies had been sold, the rest of the edition was destroyed by a fire in the Messrs. Stokes' establishment. It is a true rarity.

Whistler's life, if not always pleasant, was never dull. Elevated to the head of the British Society of Artists the controversies engendered finally led to his departure from that body, or, as he put it neatly: "The artists retired; the British remained." Rich sitters were rudely treated and he wore out their patience. Painting a portrait of Lady Leyland, he was not satisfied with the setting provided by the room where it was to hang. Taking possession he decorated it to suit his fancy. Thus it was transferred from a quadrangle of drab leather into the gorgeous "Peacock Room" that now adorns the Freer collection owned by the Government at Washington. He fell out with Leyland—with almost every one except Richard A. Canfield, the eminent American gambler whose portrait he painted and with gentle irony dubbed *His Reverence.* Canfield was anything but that, save in sleekness and suavity. The gambler greatly enjoyed his experience. "In spite of all that has been said of him," he observed afterward, "I know that James McNeil Whistler was one of the intensest Americans who ever lived. He was not what you would call an enthusiastic man, but when he reverted to the old days at the military academy, his enthusiasm was infectious. I think he was really prouder of the years he spent there—three I think they were—than any other years of his life, and he often said to me that the American army officer trained at West Point was the finest specimen of manhood and honor in the world."

Only one person ever really got the best of him. That was Mark Twain. Visiting the studio he put on an air of almost total stupidity and approaching a nearly finished painting, observed:

"Not at all bad, Mr. Whistler; not at all bad. Only here in this corner," he added reflectively, with a motion as if to rub the paint, "I'd do away with that cloud."

"Gad, sir," cried the painter. "Do be careful there! Don't you see the paint is not yet dry?"

"Oh, don't mind that," said Mark sweetly. "I'm wearing gloves, you see."

They got on after that.

He made his own points usually with such consummate skill as to be unassailable. A certain sitter posed with a cat in her arms. The animal was nervous and yowled continuously. "Madame," queried the artist, "will you have the cat in the foreground or in the back yard?"

His quips survive in legions. One of the best was his reply to a languishing lady who greeted him with: "I know only two painters in the world—yourself and Velasquez."

"Why," answered Whistler in dulcet tones, "why drag in Velasquez?"

William M. Chase once asked him if he said this seriously. "Of course not," he replied. "You don't suppose I couple myself with Velasquez? I only wanted to take her down."

The incident which lingers most prominently in the artist's career was his clash with Ruskin that ended in a very celebrated libel suit. The critic had written in *Fors Clavigera,* reviewing the opening of the Grosvenor Gallery in 1877: "The ill-educated conceit of the artist nearly approached the aspect of wilful ·imposture. I have seen and heard much of cockney impudence before now, but never expected to hear a coxcomb ask two hundred guineas for flinging a pot of paint in the public's face."

For this Whistler brought Ruskin to trial in November, 1878. After an amusing contest the jury gave the aggrieved artist a farthing in damages. Whistler made much of the resulting advertising and wore the farthing afterward as an ornament to his watch chain.

He could be cruelly caustic. Dante Gabriel Rossetti had painted a picture which Whistler had commended in an early state, and inquiring later how it was progressing, Rossetti replied, "All right. I've ordered a stunning frame for it." When Whistler next saw the painting it was beautifully framed.

"You've done nothing to it since I saw it, have you?" he asked.

"No-o," responded Rossetti, "but I've written a sonnet on the subject, if you'd like to hear it."

He read the lines. They were beautiful and tender.

"Take out the picture," said Whistler, "and frame the sonnet."

He could write with infinite grace and point. The considerable interchange with Oscar Wilde affords some of the best examples, while the latter's replies were classic. Both were accomplished poseurs, but both possessed talent to the nth degree. That Wilde became degenerate and an outcast is one of the great tragedies in the high realm of merit. They bickered with each other privately and in public, to the huge entertainment of both. When Whistler began to lecture on Art, Oscar set a danger signal: "There were two painters, called Benjamin West and Paul Delaroche, who lectured upon Art. As of their works nothing at all remains, I conclude that they explained themselves away. Be warned in time, James; and remain as I do, incomprehensible. To be great is to be misunderstood."

Whistler said something especially bright. "I wish I had said that," ejaculated Wilde.

"You will, Oscar, you will," was the acid reply.

After a long and very Bohemian bachelorhood Whistler married the widow of Godwin, the architect, who made his last years happy. His fame was secure and his commissions brought in high returns. His etchings grew to be precious; one New York collection in time sold for two hundred and fifty thousand dollars. Strong American friends like Howard Mansfield and Charles L. Freer came to his support. But as threescore and ten came nigh his strength left him; invalidism prevented much exertion and nipped the point of his pen. Now and then a flash of the old spirit showed as in a letter to the *London Morning Post,* August 6, 1902. The paper had made an error in alluding to the "rejection" of the *Little White Girl* by the Paris Salon, but coupled the mistake with some kind words. Whistler, after correcting the slip, added: "I ask you again to contradict it, and appeal to your own sense of kind sympathy, when I tell you that I have lurking in London still a friend, though for the life of me I can not remember his name."

Whistler's accomplishments in art remain supreme; his dictums unshaken. Combining the methods of Velasquez with those of the Japanese, he produced paintings supreme in color and delightful in composition. Call them "nocturnes" or what you will, they remain unique and imperishable as achievements, while as an etcher he continues unsurpassed. Probably he was wise in remaining abroad. The best artists America has produced have had to "find" themselves across the sea, from Benjamin West and Copley to Whistler and John Singer Sargent.

He died at No. 74 Cheyne Walk, Chelsea, July 17, 1903. They buried him in Chiswick Churchyard, with Hogarth and Joe Miller the jester, as comrades in his sleep.

CHAPTER XVI

EDMUND FANNING—PATHFINDER OF THE PACIFIC

ON THE eastern shore of Long Island Sound, near the point where Connecticut meets Rhode Island, is the ancient town of Stonington, now asleep, but once very active as the home of adventurous seamen, two of whom at least made names for themselves, Edmund and Nathaniel Fanning. Both were sons of Gilbert Fanning, who, with his brother, Phineas, was an ardent patriot in the Revolution. Two uncles, Thomas and Edmund, fought on England's side, Edmund becoming a general. There were six other and younger Fannings, all of whom became men of the sea. Two, Gilbert and Thomas, were taken from a captured privateer, the *Weasel,* and Gilbert died in misery on the prison ship *Jersey,* after a valiant effort to escape. Thomas was rescued from a like fate by his uncle, the general.

Nathaniel served under John Paul Jones in the fight between the *Bon Homme Richard* and *Serapis,* September 23, 1779. Stationed on the main yard he threw the hand grenades that exploded enough loose powder on the Briton to force her surrender. It is recorded in the log of the *Alliance,* to which the youngster was transferred after giving the prize over to France, that Mr. Midshipman Fanning had the distinction of being kicked by the commodore and ordered below. He died as commandant of the Charleston, South Carolina, Navy Yard, September 30, 1805.

Of his brother, Edmund, there is a longer story to tell. He was a man of vision, who foresaw that in time the Pacific would become an American problem and by precept and example, sought to make his country realize its interest in the South Sea. A pioneer in the China trade, his ships often breasted the Pacific after battling their way around the Horn, and he left, to his credit, the single discovery of an archipelago due to the enterprise of an American. The Fanning group now bears his name and the main island forms the relay station for our trans-Pacific cable system.

He began his adventuring in 1797 by a bold and hazardous enterprise, an assault on the seal rookeries of South Georgia, in the Antarctic. Here seals flocked in large numbers. Their oil was valuable, but more so their skins, which were in great demand in China. So Fanning opened the way for an industry that bred great profits, as long as the seals lasted. He sold the skins in China and brought back tea, silk and Chinese notions, which he sold at a great profit in New York.

When Fanning began casting his far-seeing eyes over the waters that lead to Asia, the west coast was Mexican, British and Russian. Canada reached the Pacific and the czar had seized Alaska from the near vantage of the Siberian shore at Bering Straits. Oregon and Washington, though on the map of the United States, were unoutlined and unclaimed, save for the contention of rival trappers and fur-trading companies. The distance by sea was enormous and the journey by land dangerous. As to the ocean itself, it was too vast and vague to stir the imagination of Americans—of all save Edmund Fanning.

Fanning, as a merchant navigator, owned part interest in several ships sailing out of New York and went on trading trips with them, sometimes as director and again as captain. One of these voyages, undertaken in 1806-1807, was in the ship *Hope,* Reuben Brumley, Captain. This was a venturesome voyage, through the little known South Sea islands to Australia and China; taking in the Fiji Islands on the way. This proved a severe experience. The ship's water supply became exhausted and the crew suffered from scurvy. An ingenious cook rigged up a still, with a gun barrel for a worm, and distilled fifteen gallons of fresh water from salt every twenty-four hours. They finally made Tonga, and thence, Fiji. Here they traded with the natives and entertained a cannibal king who, in return, presented Fanning with a large fat boar hog. The ship had a thrilling adventure in getting criss-crossed with savage warfare, the rebels from another island surrounding her with a great fleet of canoes filled with armed men.

The *Hope* was well equipped with cannon and cleared for action, as the chief·laid his large canoe across her prows. She was under way and Fanning yawed off, thus avoiding a collision and a fight. The fleet sheered off and the *Hope* went on her way to a safe harbor, where she obtained her objective—the first cargo of sandalwood ever collected by an American for the China trade. Brown, the first officer of the *Hope,* made a hit with the king, the result of which was the perfecting of a trade treaty, the first of its kind with a South Sea potentate, by which he agreed to collect sandalwood to load a return ship. Fanning had the carpenter build the king a great chest, with separate compartments, and taught him the use of keys and padlocks, to the huge delight of His Majesty. A holdful of the precious wood was secured in exchange for about nine hundred dollars' worth of beads and trinkets brought from New York. It sold in Canton for thirty cents a pound and an additional profit was secured by purchasing silks and Chinese wares with the money. The *Hope's* trial trading trip was a great success. En route for Canton a new island was discovered and charted, being given the name of *Hope.*

The experiment was so successful that Fanning and his associates purchased a fine new vessel, double-decked and pierced for twenty-two guns, called the *Tonquin,* which was destined to meet with a tragic end. She sailed for the South Sea and more sandalwood, May 26, 1807, with

Fanning himself as captain. Reaching Macao, Fanning ran into an international difficulty of the first dimensions, one of the incidents that led up to the War of 1812. A British brig of war had undertaken to impress some seamen from an armed American schooner, hailing out of Baltimore. She was probably a sealer, which, after loading with skins at South Georgia, was marketing them in China, this being then a great source of trade. The bold seamen on the schooner resisted and she was cornered, with some loss of life on both sides, the upshot leaving a smirch on English "honor." Reaching Macao roads the *Tonquin* found a British squadron at anchor, commanded by Commodore Pellew, son of Lord Exmouth, whose title is now held by an American college professor—from Baltimore! Passing the fleet and proceeding to Whampoa, the anchorage for Canton, the *Tonquin* was boarded by a British lieutenant and trouble began. There were a number of American ships in port and their officers were aroused over the affair of the schooner and the arrogant airs of the English. They formed an association and resolved to defend themselves. In all they were eleven sail, well-manned, with ample supply of cannon and muskets. Pellew was reported to have made threats against their safety and the situation became tense. Fanning had met the elder Exmouth in England and a pleasant acquaintance had followed. He relied upon this, should an extremity arise, but joined the others in their purpose. This was fixed and definite. If Pellew wanted war they resolved to give him plenty of it. A commodore and vice-commodore were selected from the captains. Two of the strongest ships were chosen to guard the channel. Fitted with extra crews and ordnance, they dropped down-stream to await the next move of His Majesty's squadron. A state of war was thus established. Meanwhile the *Tonquin,* with several other vessels, had stowed its cargo and was ready to sail. The others did not like to risk a move, but Fanning determined to leave. Hoisting the American flag and under jib and foresail, the *Tonquin* swept slowly downstream, direct for the British blockaders. Soon a gun was fired across her bow and two barges and five cutters loaded with men were alongside and aboard. Something like two hundred seamen and marines swarmed the decks, and First Officer Mackay was ordered to 'bout ship and run her under the stern of the commodore's frigate. This he declined to do. The lieutenant commanding ordered a seaman to take the wheel. At this Fanning formally surrendered the *Tonquin* and hauled down his flag, observing that they were under the guns of the frigate, which were cleared for action. The lieutenant made a wry face at this, but leaving a prize crew on board, took all the seamen and the junior officers away as prisoners.

Fanning remained with the ship awaiting events. He knew he held the keys of war. He had sent word to the American merchant fleet by the

Chinese pilot. What might have happened had Pellew persisted is problematic, but it is more than likely that he would have had a battle on his hands with by no means certain victory on his side. He called a council of the other commanders, the result of which was that the captured sailors were restored. Pellew apologized and the *Tonquin* went on her way, all hands rejoicing. Later, the other ships were allowed to pass unmolested. The conflict between the two nations was thus postponed for five years.

The *Tonquin* returned to New York and found the celebrated Jeffersonian embargo in force, by which American ships were forbidden to sail to foreign lands. The thought that the king in Fiji was piling up sandalwood only to have it decay, while he himself formed a poor opinion of white men, nerved Fanning to apply to President Madison for a special permit. As China goods paid a thirty per cent. duty, Albert Gallatin, Secretary of the Treasury, added his weight to the plea and it was granted. The *Tonquin* sailed again, this time with Reuben Brumley as captain, and Fanning acting as director. Brown was first officer. In due time they reached Fiji and found His Majesty had the sandalwood ready. He was very glad to see them and came on board in state. He embraced Brown as his son and wept tears of joy. They were treated royally and loaded with fresh stores, as well as the sandalwood, much to the chagrin of several British traders lying in the harbor, who had

tried hard to persuade the king to part with the
wood, but he resolutely kept his "treaty" with the
Americans. The enormity of the "embargo" does
not call for discussion here, but its enforcement in
the case of the *Tonquin* would have added another
chapter to our ill-considered course in the Pacific
then and thereafter.

The spirit of adventure and exploration was
strong in Fanning and he sailed for Canton by a
new route, during the course of which a number
of uncharted isles were discovered, the chief of
which now bears his name. A safe and profitable
voyage was the result, besides adding much to the
geographic knowledge of the South Sea.

The tragic story of the *Tonquin* now follows.
The fine ship was sold to John Jacob Astor, who
was establishing himself in the fur trade, at the
mouth of the Columbia River in Oregon. While
lying off the river she was boarded by a swarm of
Indians and a general massacre followed. Captain
Thorn was wounded; Lewis, supercargo's clerk,
was unhurt, as were four seamen who took refuge
in the rigging, from which they escaped and made
shore during the night. The next day Lewis en-
ticed the savages back to the ship with promises of
opening trade, and when the decks were crowded
with them he and Thorn blew her up, with tremen-
dous slaughter. The details of this dreadful episode will be found in Irving's *Astoria*.

The inspiration that came to Fanning as the
result of his South Sea voyages, with incidental

discoveries, caused him to petition Congress, under date of November 7, 1831, that it should "in its wisdom" be "pleased to grant an appropriation with power for a competent National Exploring and Discovery Expedition to the South Sea, Pacific, &c., &c." He cited in support of this, the contention "that by the trial and result" he had learned that "no private exploring expedition could ever produce or obtain . . . the desired national benefits to commerce, navigation and trade."

This plea producing no result, he filed a petition with the Senate, December 18, 1833, pressing his point, remarking: "In 1797, your memoralist sailed on his voyages in the capacity of commander, supercargo and director, to prosecute commercial trade and seal fishery, to the South Seas, Pacific Ocean, China, and around the world. This new and enterprising voyage opened the gate to his fellow-citizens to their South Pacific and China commercial trade; by which, and thereafter, under his command and agency, were taken from these regions to China on American account, the first cargoes of sandalwood, seals, fur, bêche-de-mer, bird's nest, mother of pearl, shark's fins, turtle shell, &c., being the productions of those South Sea and Pacific regions; which on being exchanged in Canton for China goods, and these brought home into our ports of the United States, not only enriched his brother citizens, the adventurers, but poured streams by duties on the same, of hundreds of thousands, aye, millions of dollars, into the treasury, thus enriching our country in the aggregate, and which in the course of some few years, therefore, caused this commercial traffic and fishery to increase upwards of twenty sail per annum, out of the ports of the United States, and has now got dwindled down to a very limited number."

He cites further his discoveries: Fanning's Islands, Palmyrie Island, Washington Island, Border's Island, and Palmer's Land on the Antarctic continent; also the relocation of Crozett's Islands, the South Antipodes and the fact that he was the first American to reach the Fiji group, and the South Shetlands. Further, he asked the conscript fathers pertinently: "Do not these discoveries and their effects, with the millions of wealth which this trade and fishery have heretofore brought into our country, by its enterprising citizens, and also to its national treasury, have a parental claim on government for a competent exploring and discovering expedition, to endeavor now to revive trade again?"

The reluctant outcome of this was the celebrated expedition under Captain Charles Wilkes, which, after many delays, got off, badly equipped, and made a notable cruise to the regions mentioned. The nation, however, failed to seize any advantages from the results, hence we to-day have our Pacific problem. Had Fanning's advice been followed it would not exist. The South Sea would be an American lake, in which we would be strongly posted, with no fear of a "yellow peril," while the commercial advantages do not need enumeration. Fanning led, but had no followers.

CHAPTER XVII

JOHN LEDYARD was the son of a sea captain in the West India trade, who died young, leaving his family destitute. The three sons and a daughter were brought up by their mother, a superior woman. She finally remarried and sent her eldest son John—born in 1751—to Hartford where he lived with his grandmother. and attended a grammar school. Here he showed an eager spirit for knowledge that does not lie in books. Thomas Seymour, a learned lawyer, took him into his office. He found the statutes dry reading and soon gave up the attempt to become an attorney. Thus, at the age of nineteen, with small resources, he cast about for his next step. Two years before, Doctor Eleazer Wheelock had founded a school for Indians, at Lebanon, Connecticut, which had now been removed to Hanover, New Hampshire, to become Dartmouth College. The crop of Indians proved small, though one of these, an Iroquois, called Thayendanegea, otherwise Joseph Brant, was destined to be heard from, and the good doctor sought for white students. He had been a friend of Ledyard's grandfather and persuaded the boy

231

to come to Hanover that he might be educated for
missionary work among the warriors. Samuel
Occum, about the last of the Mohicans, who won
some fame as a preacher, was a fellow-pupil. Ledyard had no great desire to fill a pulpit, but he liked
Indians and soon picked up much savage lore.
He had taken with him to school several bolts of
calico, planning to use it in fitting up a theater at
Dartmouth, which he did and so became the pioneer of countless college "shows." He set up his
stage and the students enacted a number of plays.
He found little trouble with his studies, but his
mind moved too fast for their routine. Dartmouth
had no bell, and classes were called by the doleful
hooting of a conch shell horn, blown in turn by
freshmen. Ledyard, tradition tells us, revolted at
this service and blew a very wheezy note.

Four months at college was all he could stand,
then he slipped away in the night, answering a
wanderlust that was to call him through all his life.
Three and a half months later he turned up and
again tackled his books. He had spent the time
with the Indians, to his vast enjoyment, picking up
an Algonquin vocabulary and learning much of
savage ways. He had also acquired the conviction that he was better fitted to become an Indian
than a missionary.

College soon again palled on him, the ad-
monitions of his professors not tending to make
it more popular. Planning flight, he cut down
a large pine tree that shaded the bank of the

broad Connecticut and out of its trunk fashioned a canoe fifty feet in length and three of beam. With a bearskin for covering and a scant supply of food he slipped away in the night to voyage down the stream, whose perils were quite unknown and very considerable. Drowsily drifting, he was caught in the current of the narrowing stream above Bellows Falls, but he acted in the nick of time and succeeded in rounding to his clumsy craft just in time to avoid disaster. The few witnesses regarded his escape with wonder, and commandeered enough oxen to haul the canoe to the lower level of the river, where he resumed his voyage, floating finally and triumphantly into port at Hartford, greatly astonishing that growing community. He was asleep under his bearskin, when boatmen from the shore captured his craft and rudely pulled off the cover disclosing him to some of his much amazed relatives, who had gathered with the crowd and who thought him safely absorbing scripture at Hanover. They insisted that he continue the study of theology. The effort was short-lived, however. When examined by a council of local Congregational clergymen, his replies were such as to make them refuse him a license.

He was now free to follow his irresistible inclinations and a sympathetic sea captain named Deshon took him along on a voyage to Gibraltar, where he skipped the ship and enlisted in the British garrison. Captain Deshon found him in his scarlet coat and coaxed him back again. They came home by way of the Barbary coast and the West Indies. The journey took a year and Ledyard returned with empty pockets. Labor did not appeal to him as a means of filling them, and gaining some hint of rich relations in England who might be of service, he worked a passage from New York to London to seek them out. He traced the connection, but as they had never heard of their American kinsfolk his reception was frosty and in affronted pride he turned away from the door and never again sought to open it.

London was astir over the preparations being made by Captain James Cook to start on his third and, as it proved, fatal voyage to the Pacific. This made a powerful appeal to the young adventurer. Here was something worth while. He sought out the captain, joined the *Resolution,* which, with the *Discovery,* carried the expedition and soon by his zeal and intelligence became Corporal of Marines. A petty officer fills a large place on shipboard and Ledyard made his presence felt. They sailed from London on July 12, 1776, not knowing that the American colonies had declared their independence eight days before, touched at Teneriffe and made way to the Pacific by rounding the Cape of Good Hope, where they added to the domestic stock animals brought from England, greatly to the astonishment of the natives, who took kindly only to pigs, as an antidote for cannibalism, and allowed cattle, horses, sheep and the like to perish from neglect. At Van Dieman's Land Ledyard saw the

Tasmanians, now long extinct. His journal describes them as the lowest and most wretched of mankind, wearing no clothes and having as weapons only sharpened sticks. Their habitations were sheets of bark laid on branches. They threw bread away and would not eat fish.

New Zealand came next with its handsome men and women and impressive scenery. One seaman was lured away by a Maori siren, tattooed and secreted. Cook had him hunted down and brought aboard ship. The maiden was distracted, but the *Resolution* carried her lover away, while the amiable captain forgave the escapade. Heading for Otahite, they were baffled by contrary winds and suffered much, putting in at last at the Tongas, where Omai, a native who had voyaged home with Cook, met some Otahitians who had been blown thither in a gale and had been unable to return, a hint as to the way the Pacific Islands were populated.

Otahite, Ledyard found to be a paradise where the voyagers were received agreeably by the very prepossessing inhabitants. After a short stay, a long leap brought them to Nootka Sound, on the Oregon coast, and here Ledyard stood once more on his native soil. At Bering Strait they heard of white men, discovered traces of their presence, and Ledyard was sent with a party to seek them out. He found some thirty Russians trading for furs on Unalaska Island, the advance guard of the nation that was to seize Alaska and keep it until sold to

the United States in 1866. Cook complimented
Ledyard highly on his services. The Sandwich
Islands were the next call and here Cook lost his
life, but not until Ledyard had been the first white
man to climb the lofty sides of Mauna-Loa, the
greatest of the volcanoes, though failing to reach
the top because of ice and snow. It appears in
Ledyard's journal that Cook's death grew out of
trouble caused by commandeering natives to help
set a rudder that had fallen out of gear. Their
lack of mechanical knowledge made them seem
stupid and they resented the resulting abuse.
Wishing wood, Cook demanded a fence that
guarded a native morai, cemetery, which was sacred, and broke it down when the Kanakas refused
its sale. They sailed in search of good water, but
a storm drove them back and Cook, imprudently
landing, was involved in a resulting mêlée and
so lost his valuable life.

The ships returned to England in season, and
Ledyard remained in the naval service, not being
stirred by the independence of America, though declining to serve against his country by transfer to
the Halifax squadron. With the design of getting
home in 1782, he came over on a war-ship and, securing a furlough, landed on Long Island, where
he found and astonished his mother. He did not
return to the frigate, but visited Hartford and there
wrote his journal of Cook's voyage. Hartford
soon becoming dull, he conceived the plan of a
commercial voyage to the northwest coast and

sought to interest sundry New York and Philadelphia merchants. None could see any merit in the idea. Finally, Robert Morris agreed to outfit an argosy. Failure to find a suitable ship caused Morris to relinquish his share in the design. Ledyard tried to enlist his old captain, Deshon of New London, but he feared the risk. The adventurer then turned his face again to Europe, sailing to Cadiz; hence he made his way to L'Orient in France. Here a commercial company agreed to back him, but fixed a delayed date for sailing, during which time he was paid a salary and led an easy life. The plan fell through, however, and he left the port for Paris, where he made himself known to Thomas Jefferson, then American minister, who was sympathetic and promised help. He also met Commodore John Paul Jones, who agreed to find the needed means. This he did not do, and after three months of vain waiting, tempered by the society of Jefferson and Lafayette, Ledyard conceived the idea of making his way to the northwest by way of Europe, crossing Siberia to Bering Strait. He applied for a passport to enter Russia and while awaiting it, a London company offered to send out a ship. He bought an outfit and went aboard. The vessel was recalled as she reached the Downs and Ledyard gave way to despair. "Fortitude, adieu," he wrote in his diary.

After a breath, he determined to attempt the land journey. Another venturesome American, Major Langhorn, quite as eccentric as Ledyard, was in Europe, traveling in the same state as Ledyard—largely on his "face." Learning of his presence in Copenhagen, Ledyard managed to join him, reaching the Danish city with ten guineas in his pocket, only to find Langhorn penniless and in deep distress. He shared his slender purse, but Langhorn refused to follow his lead. "No," he said in declining, "much as I esteem you, I can not travel with you. I can travel with no man on earth."

So the indefatigable Yankee went on alone, a draft on a London friend providing scanty means. He proceeded to Stockholm and thence with much hardship, for winter had come, tramped twelve hundred miles to St. Petersburg at the rate of two hundred miles a week.

No passport could be had unless signed by the Empress Catherine, who was absent at Odessa, where she was to spend the winter. The document had to be forwarded. It came back in mid-May. In company with one Brown, a British doctor who had a commission of some sort from Catherine, he set out at last for his goal. They parted a little beyond Tobolsk and Ledyard pushed on to Tomsk and then to Irkutsk, the capital of Siberia. Awaiting mail, he explored Lake Baikal, after which he rode on to the Lena with a Swedish officer for company and floated toward the Arctic in an open boat for fourteen hundred miles, reaching Yakutsk on the seventeenth of September, 1788. He now found it too late to cover the six hundred-mile trip to Okotsk, the port from which vessels sailed to Kamchatka, and while lingering, Captain Billings, who had been assistant astronomer on the voyage with Cook, arrived from an exploring expedition to the river called Kolyma. Billings invited him to return to Irkutsk and await the spring. They made the journey by sleds on the frozen Lena. At Irkutsk, to his amazement, he was arrested by order of Catherine, charged with being a spy of France and, guarded by two soldiers, was hurried across the frozen wastes to Moscow, whence he was speedily deported to Poland, still a kingdom. No true motive for the move was ever learned, though it might be well suspected that the Russian-American Fur Company had a hand in the affair, not wishing its rich Alaskan preserves to be sought out by competitors.

Somehow, low in purse and health, Ledyard got to London, after being absent five months more than a year.

During his several sojourns in England he had formed a pleasant acquaintance with Sir Joseph Banks. Interest in Africa was rising and Sir Joseph commended Ledyard to the African association as an enterprising spirit, who could be trusted to balk at nothing. He was asked when he could start. "To-morrow morning," was the prompt reply. Like the sailor, when his hat was on his family was with him. June 30, 1789, he left London for Cairo, saying to the secretary of the association: "I am accustomed to hardships.

I have known both hunger and nakedness to the utmost extremity of human suffering. I have known what it is to have food given me as charity to a madman; and I have at times been obliged to shelter myself under the miseries of that character, to avoid a heavier calamity. My distresses have been greater than I have ever owned, or ever will own to any man. Such evils are terrible to bear; but they never yet had power to turn me from my purpose. If I live, I will faithfully perform, in its utmost extent, my engagement to the society; and if I perish in the attempt, my honor will still be safe, for death cancels all bonds."

He arrived at Cairo on August nineteenth, and prepared to make his way to the interior by caravan, to Sennaar, when, seized by a sudden illness, he failed to rally and died November 17, 1789.

"To those who have never seen Mr. Ledyard," wrote one who knew him, "it may not, perhaps, be uninteresting to know that his person, though scarcely exceeding the middle size, was remarkably expressive of activity and strength; and that his manners, though unpolished, were neither uncivil nor unpleasing. Little attentive to difference of rank, he seemed to consider all men as his equals, and as such he respected them. His genius, though uncultivated and irregular, was original and comprehensive. Ardent in his wishes, yet calm in his deliberation; daring in his purposes, but guarded in his measures; impatient of control, yet capable of strong endurance; adventurous beyond the conception of ordinary men, yet wary and considerate, and attentive to all precautions—he appeared to be formed by nature for achicvements of hardihood and peril."

CHAPTER XVIII

HINTON ROWAN HELPER—VOICE IN THE WILDERNESS

IT HAS usually taken the United States about a generation to deal with an obvious wrong, and not very wisely then. The War of 1812 was thirty years in brewing. It was thirty years from the time when Andrew Jackson defied the slave-owning power of the South, until it threw itself upon the sword. It was thirty years from the outbreak of the first Cuban revolt, until we stepped in and freed the oppressed island.

None of these problems really required war for their settlement, but they failed to interest the multitude until too acute to be wisely adjusted by diplomacy.

It would have been supposed that in thirty years enough sanity could have been developed to have dealt peacefully with slavery. Jackson's stern: "The Union. It must and shall be preserved," penetrated no further than the surface. Beneath, the problem boiled. Those who sought to free the blacks in the North were "fanatics": those who dared to think ill of the institution in the South were menaced into silence, just as in the

242

North the men who oppose a protective tariff in mill towns have a hard time.

To the student it would appear that the non-slaveholders in the South should have perceived the evils that sapped their own progress and kept them ignorant and poor.   They did not.   Only one voice was lifted in their behalf.   In 1857, Hinton Rowan Helper "of North Carolina," as he boldly inscribed it upon his title page, wrote an extraordinary book: *The Impending Crisis of the South; How to Meet It.*   It was issued in New York by A. B. Burdick, at 145 Nassau Street, in a 12mo volume of four hundred and thirteen pages.

"Yankee wives," Helper said in his introduction, "have written the most popular anti-slavery literature of the day.   Against this I have nothing to say; it is all well enough for women to give the fictions of slavery; men should give the facts."   In this he was aiming mainly at Harriet Beecher Stowe, who seven years before with a child on her arm, in the midst of household duties at Brunswick, Maine, had written *Uncle Tom's Cabin*, a book that set an enormous wave of anti-slavery sentiment in motion in the North, and excited almost equally active resentment in the South It became the "best seller" of the day until Helper's book appeared. He was correct as to the value of facts. His volume rivaled Mrs. Stowe's in its sales. But where she roused the North, his failed, despite its purpose, to awaken the non-slaveholders of the Southern States to a sense of their true interests.   The political power of the oligarchy was so great, the means of securing publicity so small, that he could not reach the people he aimed at.   So the North bought the book, and the southern powers drove its author into exile. Probably no one reads it now save researchers, or the very curious. Yet he wrote with a pen of fire against conditions below Mason and Dixon's line that have not wholly been remedied by the abolition of slavery. It remains an invaluable aid to political and ecomonic study.

By the use of official figures, he proved clearly that slavery was heading the South toward economic destruction, that it earned barely one per cent. profit upon its agricultural output, which, with all the so-called advantage of slave labor, had a value, in round figures, of $60,000,000 less than that of the North, based on the census of 1850, while the value of farms and stock in the North was $2,233,058,619, against a southern total of $1,183,-995,274. This did not, of course, include the value of slaves.   The southern claim for agricultural supremacy vanished before these facts.   The entire estimated wealth of the Northern States was $4,102,172,108; that of the Southern States was $2,936,090,737, including slaves, a difference in favor of the former of $1,166,081,371.   He placed the estimated value of the slaves at $1,600,000,000, thus reducing the "true wealth" of the South to $1,336,090,737. Yet the "fruitful" South possessed 544,926,720 acres of land at that day, the "sterile" North but 392,062,082.

Besides these economic sockdolagers, Helper took up the cudgel for the "poor whites," who, even to this day, have not been educated or emancipated. "The lords of the lash," he wrote with a burning pen, "are not only absolute masters of the blacks . . . but they are also the oracles and arbiters of all non-slaveholding whites, whose freedom is merely nominal, and whose unparalleled illiteracy and degradation is purposely and fiendishly, perpetuated. How little the poor white trash, the great majority of the Southern people, know of the real conditions of the country, is, indeed, sadly astonishing. . . . They know nothing of public measures, and little of private affairs, except what their imperious masters, the slavedrivers, condescend to tell, and that is but precious little. . . . There is no legislation except for the benefit of slavery and slaveholders. As a general rule, poor white persons are regarded with less esteem and attention than negroes, and though the condition of the latter is wretched beyond description, vast numbers of the former are infinitely worse off. A cunningly devised mockery of freedom is guaranteed them, and that is all. To all intents and purposes they are disfranchised and outlawed, and the only privilege extended to them, is a shallow and circumscribed participation in the political movements that usher slaveholders into office."

He had "breathed away seven and twenty years in the South" when he wrote this indictment.

"Poor whites," he went on, "may hear with fear and trembling, but not speak. . . . They may thirst for knowledge, but there is no Moses among them to smite it out of the rocks of Horeb."

With fact and logic, he spoke clearly in the common interest against class distinctions, pointing out that, with the first census, that of 1790, the South was far in the lead. Cotton was not king; slavery was a subject, not a master. It also prevailed in the North. Virginia had 748,308 inhabitants; New York 340,120, or less than one half. Sixty years later, New York, long without slaves, had a population of 3,097,394; Virginia 1,421,661, so completely had progress turned the tables, while in money-making output, New York, in 1850 produced values to the extent of $237,597,-249; Virginia but $29,705,387. The value of Virginia's real and personal property, including slaves, was $391,646,348; that of New York $1,-080,309,216. Farm values in New York footed up $576,631,568; those of Virginia $223,423,315. It was as Helper wrote "a humiliating comparison." North Carolina made an equally beggarly showing when compared with Massachusetts, while Pennsylvania—and this was before her great mining development—served in like contrast with South Carolina. Transportation by rail and canal made even a worse showing.

In one respect, however, the South had not lost ground—that was in political power. Of eighteen presidential elections, twelve had selected southern

slaveholders for the highest office in the land. Six
only had been carried by northerners—two from
Massachusetts, one from Ohio, one from New
York, one from New Hampshire and one from
Pennsylvania. Of twenty-two secretaries of
state, fourteen had been from Slave States, eight
from Free. From 1809 to 1857, all but two presi-
dents pro tem of the Senate had been from the
South, and twenty-one out of twenty-three speakers of the House. Seventeen out of twenty-eight
judges of the United States Supreme Court came
from below the line, and fourteen out of nineteen
attorney-generals. So the "solid South," that still
prevails, was equally "solid" then.

While pointing out the inhumanity of slavery,
and calling its practitioners harshly to account,
Helper's real aim was the emancipation of the poor
whites. This, he established, could not be done
without destroying slavery. He did not call on
the nation at large to perform this gigantic task,
but urged it upon the white people of the states,
who were the sufferers. "Within its pestilential
atmosphere," he wrote, "nothing succeeds; progress and prosperity are unknown; inanition and
slothfulness ensue; everything becomes dull, dismal and unprofitable; wretchedness and desolation
run riot throughout the land; an aspect of most
melancholy inactivity and dilapidation broods over
every city and town; ignorance and prejudice sit
enthroned over minds of people; usurping despots
wield the sceptre of power; everywhere and in ev-

erything, between Delaware Bay and the Gulf of Mexico, are the multitudinous evils of slavery apparent."

This charge was well substantiated about the same time, by Frederick Law Olmstead, later the eminent landscape architect, who took extended journeys through the byways of the South, from Virginia to the Rio Grande, with no other object than to learn the exact conditions. He made the same report in letters to the *New York Times*, which were enlarged into three of the most intelligent and interesting volumes ever written about the South.

Helper proposed to exterminate the curse by a boycotting program, nearly thirty years before the Irish captain unwillingly gave his name to the process. There were in bondage at the time 3,200,364 blacks, against a white population of 6,184,477, of whom but 347,525 owned slaves— about half of them, less than five. They were overwhelmingly outnumbered by the non-owners, to whom Helper made his appeal. This was his plan:

1st. Thorough Organization and Independent Political Action on the part of the Non-slaveholding whites of the South.

2nd. Ineligibility of Slaveholders—Never another vote to the Trafficker in Human Flesh.

3rd. No Co-Operation with Slaveholders in Politics—No Fellowship with them in Religion— No Affiliation with them in Society.

4th. No Patronage to Slaveholding Merchants—No Guestship in Slave-waiting Hotels—No fees to Slaveholding Lawyers—No Employment of Slaveholding Physicians—No Audience to Slaveholding Parsons.

5th. No Recognition of Pro-slavery Men, except as Ruffians, Outlaws, and Criminals.

6th. Abrupt Discontinuance of Subscription to Pro-slavery Newspapers.

7th. The Greatest Possible Encouragement to Free White Labor.

8th. No more Hiring of Slaves by Non-slaveholders.

9th. Immediate Proscription of its Advocates during the Period of its Existence.

10th. A Tax of Sixty Dollars on every Slaveholder for each and every Negro in his Possession at the present time, or at any intermediate time between now and the 4th of July, 1863—said Money to be Applied to the Transportation of the Blacks to Liberia, to their Colonization in Central or South America, or to their Comfortable Settlement within the Boundaries of the United States.

11th. An additional Tax of Forty Dollars per annum to be levied annually, on every Slaveholder for each and every Negro found in his possession after the 4th of July, 1863—said Money to be paid into the hands of the Negroes so held in Slavery, or, in cases of death, to their next of kin, and to be used by them at their own option.

It is difficult now to visualize the storm raised

by the volume. Southern legislatures passed laws forbidding its possession or sale. Three men were hanged in Arkansas for owning copies. The Reverend Daniel Worth, member of an eminent North Carolina family, was indicted at Greensboro in 1860 as a "malicious and seditious person, of wicked and depraved mind" for circulating and believing in the book. He was convicted in the Guilford County court. On appeal the verdict was affirmed. Released on bail, he escaped with the connivance of his sureties. Later he was again indicted in Randolph County, and convicted. He had in the meantime made his way to Indiana and safety. Under the law he would have received thirty-nine lashes and a year in jail, with death overhanging, should he offend again. Three other preachers, Messrs. Crooks, McBride and Bacon, who upheld Helper, were driven out of Guilford and Randolph Counties by mobs.

The volume became a campaign document for the new Republican Party, which had formed under John C. Frémont, a year before. John Sherman, of Ohio, then a rising young congressman, indorsed it, pending his own candidacy for speaker of the House of Representatives in 1859. The indorsement was, as he later wrote, "a thoughtless, foolish, unfortunate act," as it cost him the place, but the stir aroused by the contest gave great impetus to the sale of the book. The Congress met December fifth, on the heels of the excitement caused by John Brown's raid on Harper's Ferry, for which the extremists from the South were inclined to give Helper's book much credit.   It was closely divided politically, but the one hundred and one Democrats were outclassed by one hundred and nine Republicans, while twenty-seven called themselves "Americans," whatever that might have meant.   The Republicans were thus powerfully visible for the first time, presaging what was to come in another year.

Thomas S. Bocock, of Virginia, Democrat, received eighty-six votes; Sherman sixty-six.   The rest scattered.   Then John B. Clark, of Missouri, offered the following, aimed at Sherman:

"Whereas certain Members of this House, now in nomination for Speaker, did endorse and recommend the book hereinafter mentioned.

"Resolved, That the doctrine and sentiments of a certain book called 'The Impending Crisis of the South—How to Meet It,' purporting to have been written by one Hinton R. Helper, are insurrectionary and hostile to the domestic peace and tranquillity of the country, and that no Member of this House who has indorsed and recommended it, or the compound from it, is fit to be Speaker of this House."

There was no cloture rule and Clark talked for two days in denunciation of Sherman, and Helper's book.   John A. Gilmer, of North Carolina, moved as a substitute:

"That, fully indorsing these national sentiments, it is the duty of every good citizen of this

Union to resist all attempts at renewing, in Congress or out of it, the slavery agitation, under whatever shape and color the attempt may be made."

A motion to table both resolutions met with a tie—one hundred and sixty-six to one hundred and sixty-six.   The House worked itself into a frenzy and many of its members threatened secession. Frank P. Blair, then a resident of Maryland, had been charged with approval of the book, and with purposing to compress it into pamphlet form for wider circulation.   He was even more bitterly denounced than Sherman, who, querying him on his stand, received the following reply:

"Washington City, December 6, 1859.
"Dear Sir:—I perceive that a debate has arisen in Congress in which Mr. Helper's book, the 'Impending Crisis,' is brought up as an exponent of Republican principles.   As the names of many leading Republicans are presented as recommending a compendium of the volume, it is proper that I should explain how those names were obtained in advance of the publication.   Mr. Helper brought his book to me at Silver Spring to examine and recommend, if I thought well of it, as a work to be encouraged by Republicans.   I had never seen it before.   After its perusal, I either wrote to Mr. Helper, or told him that it was objectionable in many particulars, to which I adverted; and he promised me, in writing, that he would obviate the objections by omitting entirely or altering the

matter objected to. I understand that it was in consequence of his assurance to me that the obnoxious matter in the original publication would be expurgated, that Members of Congress and other influential men among the Republicans were induced to give their countenance to the circulation of the edition so to be expurgated.

"F. P. Blair

"Silver Spring.

"Hon. John Sherman."

The full report of the John Brown raid, given to the Senate, added fuel to the flame. Roger A. Pryor, of Richmond, a member of the House, declared that Helper's book rioted in "rebellion, treason and insurrection," and was written in the spirit that had inspired the tragedy at Harper's Ferry. The contest raged until February first, when Sherman withdrew and William Pennington, a New Jersey Republican, was elected by one hundred and seventeen votes. Francis E. Spinner, of New York, he of the serpentine signature, refused to change from Sherman. Thaddeus Stevens swore to stand by until "the crack of doom." He did not. When reminded of the promise he said he "thought he heard it cracking." It took forty-one ballots to reach the result.

Helper's own story is briefly told, though his life was long. He was born at Mocksville, North Carolina, December 27, 1829, of pure American stock. The family owned a little land, and enough slaves to demonstrate their industrial worthlessness.   In 1851, he felt the call of California, like thousands of other American youths, and essayed to reach the El Dorado by a voyage around the Horn.   The ship was overwhelmed in a terrible storm and dismasted, but managed to make Valparaiso, in Chile, for repairs.   Subsequently, she reached San Francisco.   He was not one of the lucky prospectors, but had some interesting experiences, which were chronicled in a volume called *The Land of Gold.*

He had written in *The Impending Crisis* that expressions such as he had uttered meant martyrdom or exile.   The former fate would have been his had he come within lynching distance—more than likely at the hands of the very class in whose behalf he spoke.   He preferred exile and kept above Mason and Dixon's line, the great sales of the book making him prosperous.   In 1862, President Lincoln appointed him consul to Buenos Ayres.   He held the position for four years, returning home in 1866, having wedded Miss Maria Louisa Rodrieguez during his stay.   This was his last appearance in public life.   His several experiences in South America bred in his mind a great project—a railway line that should unite the three Americas, running from the United States, through Mexico and Central America to the Southern Continent and down to Punta Arenas, on the Strait of Magellan.   On this project he labored the rest of his days without result, though he lived to see the iron horse penetrate far into Mexico. Capital, however, was never forthcoming.

In 1899 his wife was stricken with blindness, and his fortunes having fallen low in pursuit of his idea, she returned to Buenos Ayres. Helper lived much of his time in New York, pursuing capitalists, who were ever shy. His was a distinguished personality—tall, white-bearded and dignified—a true gentleman of the South.

His last years were spent in Washington. Here, on the ninth of March, 1909, he was found dead in an obscure lodging-house, having ended his life—a suicide. A note in his pocketbook said he had expended seventy thousand dollars on the tri-America schemes. This included five thousand dollars given in 1880 in prizes for essays on the subject. In all one hundred and forty-four editions of *The Impending Crisis* were published.

CHAPTER XIX

IN THE Capitoline Museum at Rome is a bust
of Socrates, that bears a most extraordinary resemblance to Henry George, whose *Progress and
Poverty; An Inquiry into the Cause of Industrial
Depressions, and of Increase of Want with Increase of Wealth* caused a stir in the early 'eighties
and made its author an international figure to be
respected by economists the world over.

Thus in the endless struggle for economic
equality—a much overlooked phase of liberty—his
name must live, even though with lesser fame,
along with Adam Smith and John Stuart Mill.
These two were master logicians; George an ex-
pounder and inventor.   He evolved a theory of
taxation that has taken root, and in part at least,
finds favor to-day in many communities.   The
single tax which he urged, was really a discrimi-
native one, based on the theory that control of the
soil meant economic rule.   It was well expressed
in a speech made during a tour through Australia
in 1899, at the Town Hall, in Melbourne:

"I am a free trader—a free trader absolutely.
I should abolish all revenue tariffs.   I should make

trade absolutely free between Victoria and all other countries. I should go further than that; I should abolish all taxes that fall upon labor and capital— all taxes that fall upon the products of human industry, or any of the modes of human industry. How then should I raise needed revenues? I should raise them by a tax upon land values, irrespective of improvements—a tax that would fall upon the holder of a vacant plot of land near the city as heavily as upon like land upon which a hundred cottages stood."

Before consecrating his life to the advocacy of this doctrine, he had an eventful and truly American career. He was born in Philadelphia, September 2, 1839, a son of Richard Samuel George and Catherine Pratt Vallance, a second wife. The elder George, in partnership with Thomas Latimer, a brother-in-law, published religious works for the Episcopal church. The business becoming unprofitable, he retired to a clerkship in the Philadelphia Custom House. There were ten children in the family, six being girls. Henry was the eldest of the four sons. The father was a strong churchman, and the children had their fill of litany and catechism, at St. Paul's, of which the Reverend Doctor Richard Newton was pastor. Two of the rector's sons were in Henry's Sunday-school class. One of them, R. Heber Newton, became much celebrated later in New York, where he was to renew his relations with his boyhood friend.

The boy enjoyed good schooling, but the Customs House salary of eight hundred dollars, stretched thinly over the household needs. When Henry reached the mature age of fourteen, he felt the call to do something, and like most lads of the day, his desire turned to the sea. But several minor employments kept him ashore, the last, much to his liking, in a marine insurance office. The command of an East India bark, the *Hindoo*, a seasoned vessel, twenty-five years old, had come to Captain Samuel W. Miller, whose years were the same as his ship's, and at the instance of one of the Latimers, he invited the boy to sail on the next voyage. He had shown some rebelliousness of spirit at home, for which the sea was then considered a remedy, so his father, after a promise from Captain Miller to bear down on the son's discipline, consented to the venture. On April 2, 1855, armed with a Bible and a copy of *James' Anxious Inquirer*, he departed for New York to join the ship. He signed the articles at six dollars per month receiving twelve dollars "advance," and on the tenth, the *Hindoo* put to sea.

Unlike the usual tale of such voyages, the 'prentice did not have a hard time. The ship, with her crew of twenty, was manned by decent men, and the captain made the boy something of a companion. He soon learned the ropes and climbed about like a young simian. In ninety-seven days they were at the Cape of Good Hope, and in forty more reached Australia. Making port at Mel-

bourne, the crew became crazed with the gold fever
and refusing duties demanded discharge. The
American consul had the mutineers removed to
jail by the harbor police, but thirty days in that
democratic institution failed to cure them. They
were released and the *Hindoo* made for Calcutta
with a new outfit. There she loaded with one
thousand, two hundred tons of rice. June 16,
1856, Henry was home again, after an absence of
one year and sixty-five days, bringing with him
fifty dollars and a tame monkey.

He was now eighteen, and restless. The orderly restraints of home irked him. Some idea of
going again to sea was snuffed out by Captain Miller, who told him he would be wasting his life. He
was then tactfully steered into the printing office
of King & Baird, there to learn the art of typeset-
ting, which was to lead him to his eminent career.
His father was a Democrat, but Henry took to the
anti-slavery side, which brought domestic clashes,
though the breach was soon healed. He received
only two dollars a week, and very little instruction,
at King & Baird's. Resenting the foreman's
tyranny, he left. Chance—a strike—gave him a
week's work on the *Daily Evening Argus,* a long-
dead Philadelphia newspaper, where he got his
first sniff of journalism. The strike was settled
and he was again out of a job, but had earned nine
dollars and fifty cents. He was making progress
and could "set up" five thousand ems of solid matter a day. Hearing of high wages in Oregon,

where he thought he could make twenty-five dollars a week, he half planned to go to the Pacific coast. A situation on the *Weekly Democrat* delayed his departure, but it was not permanent. He made a voyage to Boston on a coal schooner, earning the pay of an able seaman. The call to California now became insistent. Through the friendly help of Congressman Thomas B. Florence he secured the berth of steward on the lighthouse steamer, *Shubrick*, Commander John De Camp, bound for San Francisco. He signed up for one year and on December 22, 1857, sailed for the Golden Gate.

Phrenology was a budding science at the time, and young George, curious about himself, secured a chart of his cranial bumps. It showed: large assertiveness, adhesiveness, combativeness, destructiveness, self-esteem, conscientiousness and individuality, but small acquisitiveness and mirthfulness —a pretty accurate intellectual diagnosis.

Thus equipped mentally, he reached San Francisco May 27, 1858, after a perilous voyage of one hundred and fifty-five days, during which the *Shubrick* had several narrow escapes from foundering and shipwreck. A cousin, James George, made him welcome. He could not be given a legal discharge from the *Shubrick*, but Commander De Camp did not hunt for him when he failed to return, and did not write him down on the record as a deserter, though he had more than half a year to serve. Failing to find work as a compositor, a gold strike on the Fraser River sent him to British Columbia as a sailor on a schooner. Cousin James had preceded him to Victoria and opened a miner's supply store, where on his arrival Henry became a clerk, but he did not fit and was soon adrift, without his cousin's friendship. The "diggings" were unpromising. In poverty, without a coat he could call his own, he managed to borrow one and some money, and so got back to San Francisco. Here he found David Bond, who had worked with him in King & Baird's, and through him, secured a place in Frank Eastman's job office. He now worked and studied, his mind shaping itself to serious things. The lure of the mines, however, was ever present and he made for Placerville, only to meet with failure. He tramped about for two months, doing farm work and having a pretty hard time. Bond again came to his rescue and placed him in the *Home Journal* shop, at twelve dollars a week—boy's pay. He was not yet of age and could not claim journeyman's wages. He worked steadily, joined the Methodist church, fell in love with Annie Corsina Fox, then seventeen, and cast his first vote for Abraham Lincoln—all this in 1860.

Joseph C. Duncan, owner of the *Home Journal*, sold out and George was set adrift. He worked as a substitute on the dailies, and then, in June, joined with five other printers, James J. Knowlton, Abel Gee, John G. Smith, Freeman A. Camp and Anson C. Benham, in producing the *Evening Journal*.

The telegraph had not reached the coast. News came part way by wire, then by stage or a fast riding "pony express." It was eagerly sought by the exiles, and 'Frisco was heavily newspapered, for a town of its size. Henry put in one hundred dollars, and the paper got under way just before word that Fort Sumter had been fired upon reached the coast. Soon the telegraph was completed to the city and the stronger papers could outbid the six printers, so three of them, including George, sold out to the other three. Without money, without work and without prospects, he now married Miss Fox, December 3, 1861. She was an orphan, dependent on an uncle, and no better off than her husband.

"Subbing" at the "case" kept him a-going, until he found regular work in the office of the *Sacramento Union.* Incidentally, he "took tickets" at the door when Mark Twain first lectured in the town. He worked on the *Union* until January 26, 1864, when a dispute with the foreman cost him his place. Henry George, Jr., had arrived November 3, 1862, and with his mother, joined the senior in San Francisco, whither he journeyed again, seeking work. He tried selling patent clothes wringers and soliciting subscribers to the *Journal,* but with poor success. Then he went back to the "case," landing finally on the *Bulletin,* where the situation was solid and the pay good. Later he shifted to the *American Flag,* a change that proved a mistake. The frequent dis-

HENRY GEORGE

agreements with the foreman ended the "sit." He next went into a printing partnership with Isaac Trump, a shipmate on the *Shubrick,* but the enterprise did not pay and the partners were soon in deep distress. The George cupboard was often empty, and a second child, Richard, came, to find the father penniless and the mother suffering for food. George held up a chance stranger on the street, asking for five dollars. The man gave it to him and prevented a suicide. He surrendered his share in the shop to Trump, in exchange for a promise to pay. Then odd jobs kept his head above water, while his wife paid the rent by sewing for the landlady.

Hunger had stirred his brain. It is the best known stimulant to intellectual effort. The poor printer began to write. He slipped a fervid piece of patriotic composition, following the death of Lincoln, in the editor's box of the *Alta-California,* where he did some subbing. It was printed, with a foot-note of praise, and led to his engagement as a special writer. One of his first assignments was to join a bunch of filibusters, organized to aid Juarez in his fight to expel Maximillian from Mexico. It got no further than the dock, the government seizing the bark *Brontes,* in which it was booked to sail. After some months of reporting, a place opened in the State Printer's plant at Sacramento, and this he took. The job lasted a year. During this stay in the state capital, he became connected with a debating society, and a discussion of free trade roused his interest in that phase of economics. He also kept on writing, with some success. The first issue of the *San Francisco Times,* November 5, 1866, took him back to that city, where he began work as a compositor on the new sheet. James McClatchy was the editor. He knew George, and encouraged him to write. McClatchy only lasted three weeks and was succeeded by Noah Brooks, a man of parts. Brooks took George on the staff, first as reporter, then as editorial writer. Brooks fell out with the owners and George became his successor as managing editor in June, 1867, keeping the place until August 12, 1868.

Charles De Young then took him on as managing editor of the *Chronicle,* but their ideas were too far apart for the relationship to endure. James Nugent now revived the *San Francisco Herald* and sent George east to secure an Associated Press service. This was refused by the directors of that institution, so George, with John Hasson, opened an office in Philadelphia to serve the *Herald.* The Associated Press invoked the power of the Western Union Telegraph Company to suppress this puny rivalry. The company promptly raised the *Herald's* rates, and reduced those of the A. P. Mr. George protested in person, without avail, but made as much of a row as he could secure publicity for, then retired to the coast. He found work for the moment on the *Oakland Transcript,* and wrote for eastern journals. An article on the Chinese question, then beginning to rise (1869-70), printed in the *New York Tribune,* brought him to the notice of John Stuart Mill and attracted wide attention. He was at last beginning to find himself. The Western Union adventure had jarred him; the poverty of New York at the period had appalled him, and the vast acreage held by great estates in California had pressed him to believe that men were being deprived of their just heritage. This produced *Progress and Poverty,* and with it, lasting fame.

Henry H. Haight, Governor of California, had begun the long warfare against the Pacific railway plutocrats, headed by Collis P. Huntington, and selected George to edit the *Sacramento Reporter* in his interest. The job lasted through a winter, and included a vigorous renewal of the A. P.-Western Union fight. In the spring he retired to San Francisco to become a pamphleteer on behalf of Haight and his cause. He next ventured further in discussing *Our Land and Land Policy, National and State,* having in mind the huge subsidies in soil granted the Transcontinental railroads. Land, he held, was not wealth—that could come only from human labor. It was, instead, the storehouse from which man must draw the material for labor by means of which he could satisfy his desires. Soundly he remarked: "The wealth of a community depends upon the product of the community," while "the production powers of land are precisely the same, whether its price is low or high." Further, he pointed out: "In a new coun-

try the value of labor is at its maximum, the value
of land at its minimum." This, however, is an
obiter dictum that does not always prove true.
Labor being scarce, and land plenty, each is reg-
ulated in value by the principle of competition.
The fear in his mind was that as monopolies grew,
land would become the property of a few who
could hold it against the needs of others and extort
high rental for its use, or high prices for its purchase. Thus he proposed to tax land heavily and
show mercy to improvements. This land "monopoly" has not appeared. More men are land
poor than land rich, while transportation and
improved methods of farming steadily make the
need of soil-tilling less imperative as to the numbers engaged in it. The full play of the theory
would ruin many landholders who are free from
monopolies. Yet the separate taxing of land and
improvements has come about to a considerable
extent, so that the owner at least knows where he
stands. George was certain that:

"Land taxation does not bear at all upon production; it adds nothing to prices, and does not
affect the cost of living. As it does not add to
prices, it costs the people nothing in addition to
what it yields the Government; while as land cannot be hid or moved, this tax can be collected with
more ease and certainty, and with less expense
than any other tax; and the land-owner cannot
shift it to any one else.

"A tax upon the value of land is the most equal of all taxes, because the value of land is something that belongs to all, and in taxing land values we are merely taking for the use of the community something which belongs to the community. By the value of land is meant the value of the land itself, not the value of any improvement which has been made upon it—what is sometimes called in England the *unearned* value.

"The mere holder would be called on to pay just as much taxes as the user of the land. The owner of a vacant lot would have to pay as much as his neighbor who is using his. The monopolizer of agricultural land would be taxed as much as though his land were covered with improvements, with crops and with stock.

"Land prices would fall; land speculation would receive its death-blow; land monopolization would no longer pay. Millions and millions of acres from which settlers are now shut out, would be abandoned by their present owners, or sold to settlers on nominal terms.

"The whole weight of taxation would be lifted from productive industry. The million dollar manufactory and needle of the seamstress, the mechanic's cottage and the grand hotel, the farmer's plow and the ocean steamship, would be alike untaxed. All would be free to buy or sell, to make or save, unannoyed by the tax-gatherer."

In 1871, William M. Hinton, a successful

printer, induced Mr. George to join him in establishing the one cent *Evening Post*. The cent was not a common coin in the land of gold, and a quantity had to be imported to secure the sale of the paper. This was done, and along with George's editorials, made the paper go. He put in no money, and was soon glad to join his partners in selling the property to H. W. Thompson. The editor got two thousand and seven hundred dollars for his share. Thompson could not supply moral vigor and the paper drooped. Hinton, George and Frank Mahan bought it back at a discount. The paper supported Horace Greeley in the campaign of 1872, but could not keep its penny price. The coins were too unpopular—so it went to five cents with the others. This did not stop its growth, but a mistake was made in accepting an offer from Senator John P. Jones, of Nevada, to buy them a perfecting press, which done, the partners set up a morning edition called the *Ledger*. Competing with themselves proved poor policy. Jones called his loans, and on November 27, 1875, four years after the beginning, the property was handed over to him and the editor departed without a cent for his well-earned interest. Governor William S. Irwin gave him the office of state inspector of gas meters, a somewhat nebulous task. It left him plenty of time to think and talk. He did much of both. The fees of office shrank, and he bethought it time to produce something for profit. A "Land Reform League" was estab-

lished to push the ideas in his pamphlet, and he
went forth to lecture in its interest. Some people
came to hear, but not enough to pay. The concentration however, crystallized his thoughts and
he sat himself down to write *Progress and Poverty*.
Henry, Jr., learned stenography and became a
valuable aid.

March 22, 1879, the completed manuscript was
forwarded to D. Appleton and Company in New
York. They found the work "very aggressive" and
not likely to sell. It was therefore declined. Harper
Brothers rejected it as "revolutionary." Scribner's
sniffed at it suspiciously and refused to undertake
the publication. So the masterpiece came back,
like the traditional cat. Hinton, George's partner,
still ran a job office, and agreed to get the book out
and trust to luck. George went to the office and
"set up" the first two stickfuls of type himself. He
revised the work with care and occasionally
dropped in to set a little more type. Edward L.
Taylor, a warm friend, also helped out at the case.
Five hundred copies were printed as an "author's"
edition, and enough were sold at three dollars each
to take some care of their cost. Incidentally, he
sent an unbound copy to Appleton's. It looked
better to them in type, and they offered to issue a
regular edition. This came out in time to coincide
with the loss of his gas job, when George C. Per-
kins, taking office as governor in 1880, gave the
position to a Republican. Mr. George had been a
steadfast Democrat after the Greeley campaign.

A page review of the book in the *New York Sun,* written by that matchless dissector, Mayo W. Hazeltine, gave it a great lift and it soon met with wide popular favor at two dollars a copy. Later, a one dollar edition appeared that sold all over the world, although the publishers had not protected the author's foreign rights.

In mid-August Mr. George went east. William Swinton, the historian; John Swinton of the *Sun,* his brother; Charles Nordhoff, then on the *New York Herald,* and John Russell Young, were his sole acquaintances. This list was soon enlarged by the addition of William C. DeWitt, a brilliant Brooklyn lawyer, Thomas Kinsella, the powerful editor of the *Brooklyn Daily Eagle* and his associate, Andrew McLean. These gentlemen were engaged in a fight with the Democratic machine ruled by Hugh McLaughlin. The movement was styled "Jefferson Hall," after its meeting-place, corner of Adams and Willoughby Streets, where Henry George first made himself heard in the East. Hancock's defeat for the presidency, which Mr. George believed due to dodging the tariff, followed; and political hopes, if any, were gone. Abram S. Hewitt, then a member of Congress, had read *Progress and Poverty* with appreciation. He engaged its author to write a labor report, at fifty dollars a week. George drew one hundred dollars and when he asked for more, Hewitt thought "it was costing too much." The engagement then ended. *Progress and Poverty,* however, had begun to move, though pirated editions in England and Germany did better than at home. He was able, with the aid of some small borrowing, to bring his family on to New York. Through Andrew McLean he lectured in Brooklyn. The venture paid, as did others that followed. Appleton's printed a pamphlet on the Irish land question, then a burning one, that added to his repute. Thomas G. Shearman, a rich and able Brooklyn lawyer, became his friend. Tariff reform was a live question. Its friends got behind George. His lecture dates grew in number, and he was able to set up a residence in Brooklyn. Francis Gould Shaw, father of Robert Gould Shaw who was killed leading his black regiment at Fort Wagner and who had been "buried with his niggers," bought one thousand copies of *Progress and Poverty*. So support became considerable. He accumulated many friends of high quality, and always kept them.

The Irish land-leaguers called him to Europe in October, 1881, and his stay was a triumph. He fell in with the leaders in the cause, including Parnell and Gladstone, had a famous controversy with the able Duke of Argyle and came home internationally famous. While in England he got out a six penny edition of *Progress and Poverty,* that had an enormous sale. Several subsequent trips were made to England, each adding to his reputation.

In 1884, he was active in the Cleveland campaign, and his son, Henry, Jr., joined the staff of

the *Brooklyn Eagle,* where I met him and became
a sort of counselor and friend in the rough office.
He was much like his father, with less bodily force
but a fine mentality. He disliked reporting and
soon left to join the *North American Review,* then
owned by Allen Thorndike Rice, as secretary to
the interesting James Redpath, who was managing
editor. Thus I became acquainted with his father
and the very agreeable family. A little later the
household left Brooklyn for a home on Pleasant
Avenue, in Harlem.

In 1886, Henry George's following in New
York among laborites and intellectuals, was so
great that it nominated him for mayor. Abram S.
Hewitt, who had flunked as his employer, was the
Democratic candidate, and Theodore Roosevelt, a
delicate youngster, home for a season from his Dakota ranch, the Republican. Hewitt won with
90,552 votes; George received 68,110 and Roosevelt 60,435. The campaign was one of extraordinary vigor on the part of the George following.
Orators spouted from truck-ends and at street corners. The town was in a fury of excitement. Fear
of his ideas caused a concentration on Hewitt. Yet
of the three, George was far the noblest character.
Hewitt was able, but cunning. Of Roosevelt,
nothing need now be said.

A weekly paper, the *Standard,* edited in company with W. T. Croasdale, then engaged George's
attention. It was fairly supported by the single
tax following and those interested in economic dis-

cussion. In 1890, George made his second journey
to Australia on a lecture tour, and was received
with much acclaim. He paused at San Francisco
en route and gave two talks, both to full houses.
He came back around the world.

The journey was a strain on his strength, and
he returned ill. He had suffered a stroke of apha-
sia on the trip and was never again well. Chance
had made him acquainted with Tom L. Johnson,
who was to become famous as a single-taxer,
mayor of Cleveland, and a street railway promoter. The Georges had been living in Nineteenth Street, New York, when Johnson induced
them to take possession of a house at Fort Hamilton, looking toward the Narrows. The *Hindoo*
had sailed past it forty years before, but it was still
fine and comfortable. Into this they moved in
1895. It was his last home. Added prosperity
came in the form of legacies from admirers, and his
books sold. On Johnson's advice he withdrew from
the *Standard,* which did not long survive his departure.

Comfortably circumstanced, he now devoted
himself to study and casual work, putting *The Science of Political Economy* into manuscript form.
It was published posthumously.

When President Cleveland's Venezuela message disturbed the country, Mr. George took the
side of peace and endorsed the *New York World*
in its efforts to allay the storm, writing to its owner
and editor, Joseph Pulitzer, in these terms:

Dec 19/95

Dear Mr. Pulitzer:

I so much appreciate the true Democratic position taken by the World on the Guyer message of the President, that I should like personally to thank you. The common sense of our people as soon as they come to fully understand the question must ultimately endorse you.

Yours sincerely
Henry George

Henry George's life closed in 1897, as the result of a tragic effort to perform a public service. Greater New York was preparing to elect its first mayor, to take over the rule of the consolidated communities, January 1, 1898. Tammany had nominated Robert A. Van Wyck, who represented that organization in its worst phase. The Independents of the community had selected Seth Low to lead them, while the Republicans, failing to endorse Mr. Low, named General B. F. Tracy, Thomas C. Platt, then boss, believing he could win in a three-cornered fight. In general protest the remnants of Henry George's following of a decade before, insisted that he run. Though far from well, he consented, and at once began a vigorous campaign. The strain soon told on him. Some days before election the writer met him on the stairs of the Brooklyn Bridge, leading to Park Row. His step was feeble and uncertain. He was headed for his office on Ann Street. I steered him through the crowd and never saw him again. The flesh around his spinal chord had shrunken, a certain sign of coming collapse. That same day his son, Henry, Jr., called on me. I told him they were killing his father. He laughed at my fears. Two days later Henry George was dead. He had gone to rest over night, after a campaign effort, at the Union Square Hotel, when at five o'clock in the morning of October thirtieth, a stroke of apoplexy ended his life. He was buried in Greenwood, where a bust by his son, Richard, marks the grave.

Consternation followed among his followers, who concluded to replace his name on the ticket with that of Henry, Jr. The result of the election gave victory to Van Wyck, and the city, a bad administrator.

The charming family was short-lived. Jennie, the eldest daughter, died first, having married William J. Atkinson of Baltimore. Richard, the second son, and a sculptor of merit, followed, and Henry, Jr., after serving several terms in Congress with great credit, from a New York district, and writing an extended biography of his father, succumbed November 14, 1916. Anna, the youngest, became Mrs. William C. De Mille, and the sole survivor.

Henry George's theory of the single tax survives. Such wealthy men as Joseph Fels and Robert Schalkenback have endowed the cause richly, so that an able propaganda, carried on by enthusiastic believers, is kept alive.

CHAPTER XX

To ESTABLISH a new cult among the many forms of religious belief, and in the face of modern knowledge and scientific skepticism, is an achievement of high order. When this gathers to itself people of considerable culture and means, the achievement becomes all the more remarkable. This is the case of Mary Baker Glover Eddy, the New England woman who created the Church of Christ, Scientist, and wrote a book called *Science and Health,* first editions of which are now valued at one thousand dollars a copy.

It would be idle to analyze the "Science," or to disparage the "Health" in this volume. We are here to deal with the woman, and not her doctrines.

To begin with, she was not young when she began her inspirations, nor especially attractive personally. She was a widow, with a grown son who had wandered west to become an unprogressive Dakota farmer. She had tried several husbands, without success, and was adrift, middle-aged and poor. It is difficult to imagine a harder lot than that of a New England widow thus circumstanced.

Faith cures have flourished ever since Christ

276

laid hands on the lame and halt and the leper lost his sores. There have been many varieties and forms. They exist in substantial fashion at St. Anne de Beaupré, in Canada, near the city of Quebec, and at the dripping Grotto of Lourdes, in the foot-hills of the Pyrenees, while faith doctors have been numerous.

Mrs. Eddy was born at Bow, New Hampshire, about five miles from Concord, July 16, 1821, of good New England stock, descending from John Baker, who was a yeoman in Charlestown as early as 1634, one of the first Puritans to arrive in the vicinage of Shawmut, and a daughter of Captain John Lovewell, famous in the early Indian wars of New England. Her mother was Abigail Ambrose, who came from a line of Scotch McNeills. A sister of Abigail became the grandmother of Governor Hoke Smith, of Georgia, later a United States senator. There were six children in the Baker family, three of them girls. Mary was the youngest—a frail child, deemed too delicate to go to school. She was kept at home and taught by her elders, while a brother gave her some insight into Latin.

The religious complex developed early in the child. Alone much of the time, with little to read, she took to the Bible. Her father was an orthodox deacon, and the family discipline was sternly pious. Learning that the prophet Samuel prayed seven times a day, the little girl followed the fashion. So, self-wrought up, she "saw things" and had perhaps more than her share of the weird imaginings that come to solitary children in such surroundings. When she was twelve she thought very much for herself and repulsed Mark Baker, her father, who wished her to join the church. The conflict of opinion was spirited, the parent being worsted. He is quoted as saying that "if Mary Magdalen had seven devils, our Mary has ten."

The next year the Bakers removed from Bow, to Tilton, New Hampshire, where, when seventeen, Mary joined the Congregational church, coming considerably under the influence of its pastor, the Reverend Enoch Corser. Up to this time her health had suffered from the family friction. She was nervously upset most of the time. This tendency now disappeared, due, as she claimed long after, to her evolving and using the doctrine upon which she built her great achievement. She is described as then being "slender and graceful, with a shower of chestnut curls, delicate and refined features and great blue eyes, that on occasions of unwonted interest became almost black." She also knew how to garb herself, wearing "a fashionable mantle over her silk gown," and the bonnet of the period, which came round her face, relieved with a delicate ruching of white from under which her curls escaped, while it shaded "cheeks so glowing that they rivaled the rose."

Her brother, Samuel, had some years before been in partnership with George Washington Glover. The firm dissolved and Glover estab-

lished himself as a contractor at Charleston, South
Carolina. Prospering modestly, he kept up his
acquaintance with the Bakers. Mary's brown
curls enmeshed him and they were married at Tilton in 1843. He took his bride to Charleston,
where her outspoken views against slavery soon
made her an undesirable. Indeed, her husband
feared she might be physically assailed. In this
mood he took her to Wilmington the following
summer, where he fell victim to yellow fever, leaving her a widow after a bare year of married life.
She returned to Charleston, freed his slaves and
came north—to Tilton, where a son was born and
named George Washington Glover. Too frail,
and possibly too poor to provide for the infant,
he was taken in by various kindly friends and
passed along from family to family, and almost
out of her knowledge.

More or less an invalid, she taught off and on
in Professor Sanford Dyer's school, living by turns
with her father and married sister. This went on
for five years. She wrote a few articles on slavery,
growing out of her adventures, for the New
Hampshire *Patriot*. Her mother was dead; after
two years her father married again, and she went
to live all of the time with her sister. Here her
anti-slavery views caused a clash that finally sent
her alone into the world.

The celebrated Fox sisters had invented spiritualism, and in this the neurotic young widow took
a deep interest. "Magnetism" became a fad and

she adopted that. About this time spinal trouble developed and she became almost wholly an invalid. Daniel Patterson, a dentist, who was related to Mary's stepmother, became interested in the fast-fading cheeks and married her. For three years they lived in the near-by town of Franklin. This was in 1853. Patterson was a "traveling" tooth-puller and much on the road. So she was alone, and fed her mind with books dealing with mesmerism, spiritualism and the queer psychics of the day. She made some effort to secure her son, but he was kept away by whoever had him in hand and finally drifted west, to remain out of sight until he was grown up, and a veteran of the Civil War.

Her invalidism was of the sort to make her mentally subjective to imaginative influences, and learning of the "cures" wrought in Portland, Maine, by Phineas P. Quimby, a "mystic" healer of note, she overruled her family's opposition and paid him a visit. This was the beginning of her "scientific" development. Quimby had won a great repute. His name is a familiar one in Maine, and he had a large number of patrons. The frail lady appealed to him and he found in her a persistent patient. He was the son of a clockmaker, and had been a blacksmith until he discovered the power that came of "laying on hands."

Mrs. Patterson found him in a large suite of rooms at the International Hotel, doing a thriving business. He was a follower of Charles Poyen, the French mesmerist, and beyond doubt possessed hypnotic powers.

Whatever merit there may have been in Quimby's theory, it worked in the case of his visitor. She went home "cured" and became a warm advocate of the method, writing testimonials for the doctor and giving him much vocal praise. The War between the States was now on and Doctor Patterson entered the army medical service. He was taken captive and kept in Libby Prison. She journeyed to Washington and secured his release by exchange. The pair set up a residence in Lynn, Massachusetts, and the lady there began to practise a compound of faith and Quimby's "science." Here she had a "fall" that jarred the troublesome spine. The regular physician who was called in, expressed little hope for her recovery, but in three days she pulled herself together and walked downstairs. This was in 1866. She has written of the event: "In the year 1866 I discovered the Christ Science, or divine laws of life and named it Christian Science."

Quimby was dead, but his influence had become the most powerful factor in her life. She had written soon after the accident to a former Quimby patient in Portland, who, she thought, had some inside knowledge of the secret of his "power," appealing for aid. This the ex-patient declined to give. Apparently the future Mother of the Church then evolved an idea of his system and made it her own. Patterson proved to be an unreliable husband. He ran away with another woman, and while he returned repentent, she declined more of his society. She now took care of herself for a number of years, boarding around in various households and practising "faith cure" upon those whom she could interest. This led to some unpleasant experiences where men showed more faith in the healer than their wives thought proper. In one instance there was an explosion because of her undue influence over a daughter. By 1870, she had secured two disciples, Richard Kennedy and Sarah Bagley, and had written a pamphlet, *The Science of Man,* printed several years later, a prelude to the greater work. In 1873 she procured a divorce from Doctor Patterson, with four hundred dollars a year alimony, which he appears to have paid until she became the more prosperous of the two, and remitted the obligation. In company with Kennedy she opened a school in Lynn, where for several years she taught faith-healing. Money came in from tuition fees, but the pupils did not succeed in the practise, so the enterprise was precarious and some refused to pay. These she sued.

Meanwhile she had been writing *Science and Health.* It was first issued in 1875. With money obtained by teaching and preaching, she bought the house at No. 8 Broad Street, Lynn, for five thousand six hundred and fifty dollars, and hung out a sign, "Christian Science Home." The book sold slowly, though pushed by friendly pupils, and she had a hard time paying the printer. Fixing three hundred dollars as a fee for a three weeks' course in "Science and Health," she found enough people willing to pay it to keep the movement going. Daniel H. Spofford and seven other pupils organized the first church and the "healing" took on the aspect of a religious cult. The eight, on June 6, 1875, pledged ten dollars a week to pay for the use of a hall on a Sunday, and here gathered the first Christian Science congregation. There were early dissensions, but things went well until a new student upset the school, in the person of Asa Gilbert Eddy.

Eddy soon became a star pupil, and the favor shown him by the high priestess angered the others. She married him January 1, 1877, put him in charge of the sale of a second edition of *Science and Health* and he became a potent figure in the "Home." Spofford, who had first come to her support, was now disgruntled, and George Barry, who had previously been sales manager, left in revolt. He sued her for two thousand seven hundred dollars on account of unrequited toil. The court gave him three hundred and fifty dollars. Spofford accused her of bad business methods, and of influencing the minds of others against himself and Barry. This was the first public appearance of Malicious Animal Magnetism. Stormy days followed. Spofford charged that M. A. M. was being used against himself and Barry. To top it all, Miss Lucretia L. S. Brown, of Ipswich, sued Spofford for mentally interrupting the treatment given her by Dorcas Brown, an Eddy pupil, charging him with being a mesmerist, who injured the minds and bodies of others. One Edward J. Arens argued the case for Miss Brown. Soon after, Spofford disappeared. A body was identified as his and the grand jury in Boston indicted Eddy and Arens for murder. Fortunately, Spofford turned up before their trial and the case was nolled, in January, 1879.

By this time Mrs. Eddy was well along in her fifties and she transferred her activities to Boston, speaking in the Shawmut Avenue Baptist Church, and later in the Parker Fraternity building. Gaining a following, she removed the school from Lynn and set up shop in the center of culture. August 23, 1879, the first Christian Science Church was incorporated, with twenty-six members, an organization having been effected at the home of Mrs. Margaret Dunshee, in Charlestown.

Mrs. Eddy had reached the "Mother" stage. Her appearance at the time is thus described: "A graceful figure in a violet colored house gown, finished with lace at the throat and wrists. Her hands were small and expressive, her hair rippled about her face and was dressed high at the back of her well-shaped head. Her cheeks glowed with color and her eyes were clear, unwavering, like wells of light."

The congregation listened to her teachings at private houses until 1883, when Hawthorne Hall, in Oak Street, became the church center. Malicious Animal Magnestism continued to persist. Numbers of the congregation rebelled at the "Mother's" autocratic methods, but she was strong enough to maintain herself against their protests and the recalcitrants lost out. Accused of undue love of power and money, as well as bad temper, she held her ground and prospered, sending out teachers to spread the doctrine. Arens became a source of annoyance and interfered with her income by publishing a science and health volume of his own editing, which drew heavily upon the parent book. She enjoined him and won the suit.

Eddy fell ill and Doctor Rufus K. Noyes diagnosed the disease as "valvular of the heart." Mrs. Eddy pitted all her "faith" against this, but he died June 3, 1882. The post mortem showed that Doctor Noyes was correct. Mrs. Eddy insisted that he had been killed by "mesmeric poison"— whatever that may be. He had been much excited over the Arens row, and the widow's animus centered on the latter as the malicious mesmerist.

She next established the *Journal of Christian Science,* with the aid of a young follower, Arthur True Briswell. The cult was now under great headway. Edition followed edition of *Science and Health*—the fifteenth coming in 1885. She traveled and lectured much, forming congregations over the country, chiefly in cities where people of means took kindliest to the call. The book was much revised, Reverend James H. Wiggin spending five years in clearing up its incoherencies. Its sale has been enormous. Some one hundred and sixty editions had been issued up to the time of its author's death. She produced other books; or at least they bore her name: *Unity of Good and Unreality of Evil, Christian Healing, People's Idea of Good, Christian Science, No and Yes, Mind Healing, an Historical Sketch and Rudiments and Rules of a Divine Science.*

In 1888 she established herself in a palatial residence just outside of Boston and adopted Doctor Ebenezer Johnson Foster as her son. He called himself Foster-Eddy and was made publisher of her works. Her own son had paid her a visit. He was a dull, middle-aged Dakota farmer, and was sent back to the bad lands. Foster-Eddy was forty years old.

Concord, New Hampshire, was now selected as a new abiding place, echoing perhaps her early days at near-by Bow. Here she put two large properties together, built a fine house and named it "Pleasant View." On leaving Boston for Concord she gave the Boston congregation a lot where a magnificent "Mother Church" was built, costing two hundred and fifty thousand dollars, contributed by followers from all over the land. It ranks as one of the finest edifices in the country.

Mrs. Eddy made her home at Pleasant View from 1892 until 1908, growing each year in wealth and power. In 1907 she was annoyed by the reappearance of her farmer son, George W. Glover,

MARY BAKER G. EDDY

of South Dakota, now sixty-five years old and poor, who came east on a money hunt. He secured counsel, assailed his mother's estate, claiming that she was under undue restraint, making Calvin A. Frye and Alfred Farquhar the chief defendants, and involving also the officers of the Mother Church. Ably advised, Mrs. Eddy made a trust of her estate, placing it in the hands of Archibald McLellan, Joseph Furnald and Adam H. Dickey. The suit failed to develop anything and was dropped, Glover receiving compensation that ended his desire for litigation.

Venerable now in years, and weak in body, Mrs. Eddy was entirely in the hands of her trustees. Concord being conspicuous, the Lawrence mansion on Beacon Street, Chestnut Hill, Brookline, Massachusetts, was purchased, and remodeled, in 1907. To this house she was removed, with the utmost secrecy, in January of the following year. Here she lived amid much elegance, but in strict retirement—until ten-forty-five on the evening of December 4, 1910, when her life closed. She had entered her ninetieth year, and certainly testified by her own longevity, the efficacy of her faith. "God is my life," were her last written words. Pneumonia, added to the weight of age, was the immediate cause of her death. Her body was interred in Mount Auburn Cemetery, where the elect of Boston lie, encased in an enormous tomb of solid cement. There was no sermon at the funeral, only a few carefully chosen words that

skilfully ignored the presence of death. Long-
fellow, Holmes, Lowell, Charles Sumner, Rufus
Choate and Charlotte Cushman are neighbors at
Mount Auburn.

Mrs. Eddy had brought Christ and Science
together, much as the essayist in *Pickwick Papers*
wrote his celebrated thesis on Chinese metaphysics,
by ingeniously combining the articles on "China"
and "Metaphysics" in the Encyclopedia, yet at her
death she had a following of over two hundred
thousand, which has now grown to more than two
hundred and fifty thousand, and shows no signs of
weakness, though there have been schisms over
leadership. A daily newspaper of extraordinary
merit, the *Christian Science Monitor,* has long
been successfully maintained in Boston, and the
church's publishing house is a flourishing concern.
Unlike the Mormons, whose numbers they probably exceed, the members of the Church of Christ,
Scientist, underwent no hardships, suffered no
persecution, cherished no martyrs. It is a faith of
purple and fine linen. Briefly stated, these are
its tenets, as set forth by the founder:

"When apparently near the confines of mortal
existence, standing already within the shadow of
the death valley, I learned these truths in Divine
Science; that all real Being is in the Divine Mind
and idea; that Life, Truth and Love are all-
powerful and ever-present; that the opposite of
Truth—called error, sin, sickness, disease, death—

is the false testimony of false material sense; that this false sense evolves, in belief, a subjective state of mortal mind, which this same mind calls *matter,* thereby shutting out the true sense of Spirit.

"My discovery that erring, mortal, misnamed *mind* produces all the organism and action of the mortal body, set my thoughts to work in new channels, and led up to my demonstration of the proposition that Mind is All, and matter is nought, as the leading factor in Mind Science.

"Christian Science reveals incontrovertibly that Mind is All-in-all, that the only realities are the Divine Mind and idea. The great fact is not, however, seen to be supported by sensible evidence, until its Principle is demonstrated by healing the sick, and thus proved absolute and divine. This proof once seen, no other conclusion can be reached.

"God is the principle of Christian Science. . . . The fundamental propositions of Christian Science in the four following, to me *self-evident* propositions. . . . God is all in all; (2) God is good; Good is Mind; (3) God, spirit, being all, nothing is matter; (4) Life, God, omnipotent Good, deny death, evil, sin, disease—disease, sin, evil, death deny good, omnipotent God Life. . . . Man is God's universal idea, individual, perfect, eternal."

The style of her writings is turgid and obscure, yet it seems clear enough to her followers. When the first number of her *Journal of Christian*

Science appeared, April 14, 1883, the opening
sentence of the prospectus read: "The ancient
Greek looked longingly for the Olympiad, the
Chaldean watched for the appearing of a star; to
him no higher destiny dawned upon the dome of
being than that foreshadowed by the signs of the
heavens." The rest was equally vague—a potter-
ing of words. Critical comment lost itself in trying to explain the inexplicable in her writings.
Mark Twain wasted a volume in a futile assault.
She was invulnerable.

Materially, the woman ranked at her death high
among the richest. Her estate totaled three million five hundred thousand dollars. It became an
endowment for the church.

CHAPTER XXI

EDWIN FORREST—WHOSE HISS BRED A RIOT

TWENTIETH-CENTURY Americans do not take their opinions seriously. Elections are sporting events, forgotten after the bets are paid. Prohibition is passed with a mighty show of virtue, and becomes a jest in all but the poorest circles. We have elevated our standards of immorality to such a height, that divorces do not shock, nor scandals ostracize. Rape is quite frequently punished with a trifling fine. Arson is the concern of the insurance companies, not of the public. Criticism must be jazzed to be read. In the matter of the theater, people go to see the play and are indifferent to the actors. More than ever fill the seats at the show, but few can give the names of the performers.

In the stern days of yore, all this was different. Opinions were faced with granite. Elections were almost civil wars. A divorce or freedom in love meant social outlawry. Men were hanged for rape and arson. The drunkard was an outcast. Actors filled the stage. The play was of no account. Auditors thrilled at the thunders of Edwin Forrest, and shivered at the shrill shrieks of Charlotte Cushman. When they were displeased they hissed,

291

not politely, but with the venomous meaning of a
serpent. One such hiss brought on a great tragedy, of which this is the story.

In the middle of the glorious 'forties, Edwin
Forrest had become the theatrical idol of our ex-
panding nation. Born in Philadelphia, March 9,
1806, at twenty he was a tragedian with a big T,
who soon brooked no rivalry and demanded reverence. A thick-set personage, with the face of a
Bowery boy of the period, wearing love-locks
meeting narrow sideboards, and a spit whisker
under his lower lip, he stalked the stage like a lion
and roared at the gallery gods. These adored him.
Macbeth, the Gladiator and Metamora were his
pet parts. Metamora was a noble Indian chief.
I remember, as a very small boy, a ruined dock at
Nyack-on-the-Hudson called after Metamora, because a river steamer of that name used to land
there. She had been named after the fustian
warrior.

As a preliminary, it must be parenthetically
observed, that at this period, we did not extend
our hands across the sea very warmly. We visited
back and forth a little, with displeasing results.
Our free and independent people had smarted for
more than a decade under the accurate observations
of Mrs. Trollope and Captain Basil Hall, when
Charles Dickens poured salt into their wounds.
They hated England with the fire of second-
growth patriots, and now they extended their
resentment to include the London stage.

William C. Macready was the bright particular star of Britain. In 1827 when things were pretty crude he attempted to extend his triumphs to America and succeeded in antedating Mrs. Trollope and Captain Hall. Playing *William Tell* in the cultivated community still called Baltimore, the property man failed to provide an arrow to be broken as part of the by-play, and the tragedian had to break one of those used in shooting the apple off the head of his sacrificial son. Wrathfully reproving the negligent wight, he observed with petulance: "I can't get such an arrow in your country, sir." The intelligent press of the day garbled this into "I can't get wood to make such an arrow in your country." This was considered an insult to the land of boundless opportunity, and popular feeling rose high. Macready was in danger of being mobbed, until he gave out a correct version of his remarks. This allayed the excitement, but his popularity was permanently impaired. Forrest had well risen over the horizon, and toured the country in rivalry with Macready, who was a veteran—Forrest a youth of twenty-four. The Englishman appears to have taken on a kind and encouraging attitude toward the youngster, and by the late 'thirties, Forrest's fame was secure. He made a tour in England and took the Britons by storm, Macready generously added to the acclaim. Returning home, his native city of Philadelphia gave him a banquet; more practical New York, his adopted home, offered him a seat in Congress, via the Democratic ticket, which he tactfully declined and kept to the stage, with great profit.

In 1844, Macready again came to America. Forrest met him with a friendly greeting, but rival managers played one against the other. The older man was losing fire, and where he encountered Forrest, the full house greeted the younger man. Macready's tour was a semi-failure. Forrest was billed as the American tragedian. The public mind harked back to the arrow incident, and the sly managers played upon patriotism. Macready went home sour. His following there resented his treatment, and when Forrest visited England soon after, they opened fire. Newspapers took flings at him and he received a dose of displeasure that left the London seats empty. Only in the provinces could he make headway. John Bull knew how to retaliate, and did it.

It is quite certain that Macready, who was a gentleman, had no part in the procedure. Indeed, he deprecated it and did all he could to still the storm. Forrest, a man of temper, and with a greatly enlarged head, insisted on fastening the quarrel upon his rival. Chancing to be in Edinburgh one night, he attended a performance of *Hamlet* with Macready in the leading part. As a bit of local coloring, he interpolated a Highland fling. Sitting in a box, Forrest had the bad taste to hiss this novelty, in what is described as "the most marked and offensive manner." The result was to complete the ruin of Forrest's tour. He was attacked unmercifully for his lack of manners, and it became unsafe for him to appear in public. The criticism penetrated his rather tough hide, and he sought to palliate his offense in this lame letter to the *London Times*:

"Sir—Having seen in your journal of the 12th instant, an article headed '*Professional Jealousy,*' a part of which originally appeared in the *Scotsman* published in Edinburgh, I beg leave, through the medium of your columns, to state, that at the time of its publication, I addressed a letter to the editor of the *Scotsman* upon the subject, which, as I then was in Dumfries, I sent to a friend in Edinburgh, requesting him to obtain its insertion; but as I was informed, the *Scotsman* refused to receive any communication upon the subject. I need say nothing of the injustice of this refusal. Here then I was disposed to let the matter rest, as upon more mature reflection, I did not deem it worth further attention; but now, as the matter has assumed 'a questionable shape' by the appearance of the article in your journal, I feel called upon, although reluctantly, to answer it.

"There are two legitimate modes of evincing approbation and disapprobation in the theatre— one expressive of approbation, by the clapping of hands, and the other by hisses to mark dissent; and as well timed and high applause is the just need of the actor who deserves well, so also is hissing,

a salutary and wholesome corrective of the abuses
of the stage; and it was against one of these abuses
that my dissent was expressed, and not, as was
stated, 'with a view of expressing his (my) disapproval of the manner in which Mr. Macready
gave effect to a particular passage.' The truth is,
Mr. Macready thought fit to introduce a fancy
dance into his performance of Hamlet, which I
thought, and still think, a desecration of the scene,
and at which I evinced that disapprobation, for
which the pseudo-critic is pleased to term me an
'offender,' and this was the only time during the
performance that I did so, although the writer evidently seeks, in the article alluded to, to convey a
different impression. It must be observed also,
that I was by no means 'solitary' in this expression
of opinion.

"That a man may manifest his pleasure or displeasure after the recognized mode, according to
the best of his judgment, actuated by proper motives, and for justifiable ends, is a right, which,
until now, I have never once heard questioned, and
I contend, that right extends equally to an actor,
in his capacity as a spectator, as to any other man;
besides, from the nature of his studies, he is much
more competent to judge of a theatrical performance than any *soidisant* critic, who has never himself been an actor. The writer of the article in
the *Scotsman,* who has most unwarrantably singled
me out for public animadversion, has carefully
omitted to notice the fact, that I warmly ap-

plauded several points of Mr. Macready's performance; and more than once I regretted that the audience did not second me in so doing. As to the pitiful charge of professional jealousy preferred against me, I dismiss it with the contempt it merits, confidently relying upon all those of the profession with whom I have been associated, for a refutation of this slander.

"Yours respectfully, Edwin Forrest."

This was published on April fourth. Britain refused to be soothed, and Forrest, much chagrined, came home. The Eagle screamed over the affair, which made a great stir on both sides of the sea. Previous to his retreat, Forrest tried to secure an engagement in Paris. The prudent French would have none of him. This he laid to the influence of Macready, who was in the city at the time, and it increased his grievance, following, incidentally, the iron rule that no man can forgive one he has wronged.

In October, 1848, Macready had the temerity to return to America, apparently failing to realize how thoroughly the feeling against him had been worked up by Forrest's partizans. He opened in New York and mistakenly, on the ill advice of some friends, replied rather contemptuously to an attack made on him by the *Boston Evening Mail.* Proceeding to the Hub, he met with this vitriolic welcome from the *Mail*:

"Mr. Macready has at length arrived, and next to the grand water celebration, will create such excitement, as will emphatically mark the present epoch in time's calendar. He plays this evening at the Howard Athenæum, and refuses to show himself for less than one dollar a ticket. This was his price in New York, and with the exception of the first night, resulted in a 'beggarly account of empty boxes.' We repeat what we said in a former article, that Mr. Pelby, the enterprising manager of the National Theatre, deserves immortal honors for not acceding to the dictatorial terms of this actor autocrat. Although Macready saw fit on his opening night in New York, on being called out by some friends, to slur a 'certain penny paper' that had 'dared' to express an opinion regarding his talents and conduct, we shall not by any means give him the retort churlish; we only pity his ignorance of the institutions of this country, and hope for his own credit's sake that he will not, when he gets home, write a black book about American manners, &c, à la Trollope and others, but if he does, that he will spare us in the production of his brain. The reader will no doubt ask, what fault we find with Mr. Macready. Has he not the same right as other men have, to do as he pleases? We answer yes. He has a right to come to this country in the exercise of his profession; he has a right to demand a dollar from every person who witnesses his acting, and if managers of theatres are willing to accede to his arbitrary proposals, he has certainly a right to make them. We complain not of any of these. Our charges against Macready are based on more important grounds. It is his conduct in his own country in relation to Mr. Forrest, that we are about investigating; his inhospitality, his crushing influence, his vindictive opposition, and his steadfast determination to ruin the prospects of that gentleman in England, that we bring to his door. Let him deny them if he can. Every true American takes a pride in that which represents his country's interests, industry, and enterprise, and from the smallest commodity gathered from his soil to the loftiest labors of his genius, his ambition goes with it, and the strong arm of his power will protect it in every clime. Mr. Edwin Forrest is titled the American Tragedian—he is justly entitled to this honor—he has acquired it by his own labors; from a poor boy in a circus, he has arisen to be a man of fame and wealth, all of which he has lastingly gained by enterprise and talent, and secured both by economy and temperance.

"Every American-born man is willing that Mr. Forrest should wear this title, and when he visited England they were anxiously interested in his success. Macready had previously been in this country, and played engagements in every city, and made a fortune. He was extolled by the press, and treated as a gentleman by the citizens of every place he visited. But instead of returning this kindness, he acted openly towards Mr. Forrest as his determined foe. We speak by card, and write

upon the very best information, viz, the highest
authority. In Paris Mr. Macready and Mr. Forrest met. The latter was anxious to appear on the
French boards; but Macready threw obstacles in
the way, and this was the first time that the two
parties were enemies. Mr. Mitchell, the enterprising lessee of St. James Theatre in London, took
an English company of actors to the French capital, with Mr. Macready at the head of the list.
Macready was to be the hero—the great attraction
of Paris. He failed, however, to draw money to
the treasury, and Mr. Mitchell lost a large sum
by the speculation, or rather would have lost it,
if Louis Philippe had not made him most liberal
presents. Mr. Forrest had letters of introduction
to Mr. Mitchell from his friends in London, but
Macready was jealous, lest Forrest should prove
to be *the* great star, and he cautioned Mitchell not
to allow Forrest to appear. The result was that
Mr. Mitchell refused to see Mr. Forrest.

"The parties returned to London. The hypocrisy of Macready is apparent in his note of invitation to Mr. Forrest to dine with him. The latter,
knowing the intrigue that had been carried on in
Paris by Macready and Mitchell, refused, as every
high-minded man should, to dine with him. This
is a very different version to that recently given
by some of Macready's friends—if friends he have
—that Forrest was offended because he was not
invited to dine; as if such a man as Mr. Forrest
could take offense at such a trifle, when at the

same time he was invited to dine with many of the leading nobility of England, but especially of Scotland, where he passed several months as their guest.

"The next mean act towards Forrest, brought about through the influence of Macready, was when Mr. F. appeared at the Princess's Theatre in London. Mac had been endeavoring for a long time to effect an engagement with some London manager, but was unsuccessful. The success of Forrest stung him, and he resolved to 'put him down.' It was said at the time that he or his friends actually hired men to visit the theatre, and hiss Forrest off the stage, and Forrest was consequently received with a shower of hisses before he was heard. This mean conduct was followed up by the press, by which Forrest was most outrageously assailed, and not Forrest alone, but his country, which is proud to own him as one of her sons.

"Forrest and Macready next met in Edinburgh, and from this city were sent forth the grossest calumnies against Forrest. Macready was playing at the Theatre Royal in *Hamlet*—Forrest was present. During the beginning of the piece Mr. Forrest applauded several times, and, as we are informed by an eye witness, he started the applause when some brilliant effect had been given to a passage, so that the whole house followed him. But now comes Forrest's great sin—that giant sin which Mac will never forgive—the sin of hissing Macready for dancing and throwing up his handkerchief across the stage in the *Pas de Mouchoir*.

"Mr. F. not only hissed, but the whole house hissed, and yet Macready dared to write to London, that Forrest had singly and alone attempted to hiss him from the stage.

"To show that Mr. Forrest was not alone in this matter, we are able to state that two weeks afterwards *Hamlet* was repeated, when the whole house again hissed Macready's dance across the stage.

"Out of this simple incident Macready contrived to create a great deal of sympathy for himself. He is, or was, part proprietor of the London *Examiner*; or if not sole owner, he possesses the body and soul of its theatrical critic, Forster, who does all kinds of dirty work for his master. Macready gave the cue to Forster, and Forrest was denounced by the *Examiner* and other papers, in which Forster or Mac had any influence. A false coloring was put on this affair, and Mac appeared to the world as a persecuted man, whereas Forrest was the man who met with persecution at every corner—in Paris, in London, in Edinburgh, and in London a second time.

"But Macready's persecution did not stop here. Forrest wished to appear in London, in Bulwer's *Lady of Lyons* and *Richelieu.* To do this, permission must be obtained of the author. Forrest addressed a note to Bulwer, asking his terms for the plays. After a long delay, Bulwer replied, that he should charge Forrest £2 per night for the use of them, and he must play forty nights! Such terms for plays, that had in a great measure lost their interest, compelled Forrest to reject them. It was ascertained that Macready and Bulwer had been much together, and that the former had prevailed on the latter not to allow Forrest the use of his compositions.

"Forrest could not entertain any jealous feelings towards Mac, for he drew crowded houses during his engagement at the Princess's Theatre, whereas Macready had very slim audiences; and on one occasion we know that our own charming actress, Mrs. Barrett, on one of the off-nights, at the time Mac was playing, actually drew more money to the treasury than Macready.

"We have now given a plain statement of facts, and such as cannot be controverted. It proves that actors, like Macready, Anderson, and others, find it very hard scratching in their own country, and much better pickings here. It is to be hoped, however, that we Americans will finally become awakened to the mercenary motives of such artistes, and when we have any surplus of dollars to spend, that we will be generous and just to our own home genius."

This article in a general way covers all of the anti-Macready propaganda. Nothing worse than poor audiences—that bane of the actor—resulted. Returning to New York, Macready appeared at the Astor Place Opera House, while Forrest opened at the Broadway Theater. The press agents of the day used the rivalry for all it was worth, but there was no disturbance, and the rival stars removed their august persons to Philadelphia. Forrest was paraded in his native city as having come out of retirement to vindicate the superiority of American dramatic art. He had become rich, and planted a large slice of his fortune in a great stone castle near Yonkers, on the Hudson River, which still stands as part of the plant of a Catholic school. This "vindication" roused Macready, who attributed it to Forrest in a footlight speech charging the latter with being ungenerous. This spurred Forrest to issue a card to the public, in which he said:

"Mr. Macready, in his speech, last night, to the audience assembled at the Arch Street Theater, made allusion, I understand, to 'an American actor' who had the temerity, on one occasion, 'openly to hiss him.' This is true, and by the way, the only truth which I have been enabled to gather from the whole scope of his address. But why say 'an American actor'? Why not openly charge me with the act? for I did it, and publicly avowed it in the *Times* newspaper of London, and at the same time asserted my right to do so.

"On the occasion alluded to, Mr. Macready introduced a fancy dance into his performance of *Hamlet*, which I designated as a *pas de mouchoir*, and which I hissed, for I thought it a desecration of the scene, and the audience thought so too, for in a few nights afterwards, when Mr. Macready repeated the part of Hamlet with the same 'tomfoolery,' the intelligent audience of Edinburgh greeted it with a universal hiss.

"Mr. Macready is stated to have said last night, that up to the time of this act, on my part, he had 'never entertained towards me a feeling of unkindness.' I unhesitatingly pronounce this to be a wilful and unblushing falsehood. I most solemnly aver, and do believe, that Mr. Macready, instigated by his narrow envious mind, and his selfish fears, did secretly—not openly—suborn several writers for the English press, to write me down. Among them was one Forster, a 'toady' of the eminent gentleman—one who is ever ready to do his dirty work; and this Forster, at the bidding of his patron, attacked me in print even before I appeared on the London boards, and continued his abuse at every opportunity afterwards.

"I assert, also, and solemnly believe, that Mr. Macready connived when his friends went to the theatre in London to hiss me, and did hiss me, with the purpose of driving me from the stage—and all this happened many months before the affair at Edinburgh, to which Mr. Macready refers, and in relation to which he jesuitically remarks, that 'until that act, he never entertained towards me a feeling of unkindness.' Bah! Mr. Macready has no feeling of kindness for any actor who is likely, by his talent, to stand in his way. His whole course as manager and actor proves this—there is nothing

in him but self—self—self—and his own countrymen, the English actors, know this well. Mr. Macready has a very lively imagination, and often
draws upon it for his facts. He said in a speech
at New York, that there, also, there was an 'organized opposition' to him, which is likewise false.
There was no opposition manifested towards him
there—for I was in the city at the time, and was
careful to watch every movement with regard to
such a matter. Many of my friends called upon
me when Mr. Macready was announced to perform, and proposed to drive him from the stage
for his conduct towards me in London. My advice
was, do nothing—let the superannuated driveller
alone—to oppose him would be but to make him
of some importance. My friends agreed with me
it was, at least, the most dignified course to pursue,
and it was immediately adopted. With regard to
'an organized opposition to him' in Boston, this is,
I believe, equally false, but perhaps in charity to
the poor old man, I should impute these 'chimeras
dire,' rather to the disturbed state of his guilty
conscience, than to any desire on his part wilfully
to misrepresent."

The vicious epistle could not pass without notice, and Macready countered thus:

"In a card published in the *Public Ledger* and
other morning papers of this day, Mr. Forrest
having avowed himself the author of the statement,

which Mr. Macready has solemnly pledged his honor to be without the least foundation, Mr. Macready cannot be wanting in self-respect so far as to bandy words upon the subject, but as the circulation of such statements is manifestly calculated to prejudice Mr. Macready in the opinion of the American public, and affect both his professional interests and his estimation in society, Mr. Macready respectfully requests the public to suspend their judgment upon the question, until the decision of a Legal Tribunal, before which he will immediately take measures to bring it, and before which he will prove his veracity, hitherto unquestioned, shall place the truth beyond doubt.

"Reluctant as he is to notice further Mr. Forrest's Card, Mr. Macready has to observe, that when Mr. Forrest appeared at the Princess's Theatre in London, he himself was absent some hundred miles from that city and was ignorant of his engagement until after it had begun; that not one single notice on Mr. Forrest's acting appeared in the *Examiner* during that engagement (as its files will prove,) Mr. Forster, the distinguished editor, whom Mr. Macready had the honor to call his friend, having been confined to his bed with a rheumatic fever during the whole period, and some weeks before and after.

"For the other aspersions upon Mr. Macready, published in the *Boston Mail*, and now, as it is understood, avowed by Mr. Forrest, Mr. Macready will without delay appeal for legal redress."

He accordingly engaged Messrs. Reed & Mere-
dith to institute an action for libel, but the sensible
legal gentlemen persuaded him to drop it. Macready then went south, and was warmly greeted in
New Orleans, so much so that he took heart and
again went at Forrest with a pamphlet that detailed the origin of the row in England, and put
the American in an evil light. Macready now arrived for a final engagement in New York. The
pamphlet fired Forrest's supporters, and they resolved to prevent the Englishman's appearance.
The feeling spread to all English actors, and one,
Mr. Anderson, was rudely treated in Philadelphia. "American actors for Americans" became
the order of the day.

When the sale of tickets opened at the Astor
Place Opera House, Captain Isaiah Rynders, a
notorious ruffian, leader of the "Boys" in the tough
politics of the day, bought fifty tickets and came
with a gang to break up the performance. Some
Americans in the cast were received "with obstreperous applause," but when Macready began to de-
liver his lines as "Macbeth," his voice was drowned
in cat-calls and other forms of discordant vocalism.
Amid indescribable uproar he contrived to keep on,
but all in dumb show. He could not make himself
heard above the howls. This failing to drive him
from the stage, rotten eggs and minor missiles,
such as the big copper pennies then in use, were
hurled at him. Enthusiasts in the gallery tore up
chairs and threw them at the stage, to the peril of

their compatriots below. To protect the ladies in
the audience the curtain was then rung down.

Quite naturally, Macready felt that he should
not risk himself or others again, but James H.
Hackett, his manager, who hated Forrest, insisted
on his going on. A committee of fifty worthy
citizens headed by Washington Irving and Charles
King, indignant at the outrage, requested him to
continue, and pledged support. This only made
a bad matter worse. The will of "the people" was
now being defied by a combination of aristocrats.
Feeling rose to a pitch of fury. The mayor and
magistrates were called upon to close the theater.
They requested Hackett and William Niblo, his
partner, to yield in the interest of public safety.
Both were obdurate and demanded the protection
due them under the law that licensed the house.
C. S. Woodhull was mayor and he promised to
take measures. *Macbeth* was announced for Thursday evening, May tenth. Tickets were freely dis-
tributed to friends of the actor, to fill the house,
while his foes posted inflammatory hand-bills calling on the people to rise and prevent this defiance
of the popular mandate. The entire police force
consisted of but nine hundred men. George W.
Matsell, their chief, informed the mayor that he
could not provide a sufficient guard to handle the
situation, and called for military support. This
was the great mistake. Woodhull asked Major-
General Sandford, commanding the local militia,
to provide a supply of soldiers. He made matters

worse by ordering out the aristocratic Seventh
Regiment. Two hundred police were detailed inside the house, a few within reach outside, while
the control of the streets was given over to the
militia. The police utterly failed to act. No ring-
leaders were arrested and a great crowd was allowed to collect in and around Astor Place. There
had never been a public disturbance in New York,
save some patriotic splutters in colonial days, and
the authorities refused to believe one was now due.
For motive there was more than Macready. The
"people" had arranged themselves against the
fifty, and determined to read a lesson to the
"aristocrats."

The opera-house was full long before the hour
for the performance. Only seven women braved
the risk. The theater was barricaded, and the
audience being mainly picked, gave Macready a
loud greeting that drowned the minority of ob-
jectors who had managed to get in. The noisiest
of these were arrested by the police, and stored in
the basement. *Macbeth* then murdered sleep in
comparative quiet.

Outside things were not so calm. Something
like fifteen thousand people surged in the square,
on whom the few police could make no impression.
They howled and cheered by turn, but did nothing
until word reached them that the play was proceeding, and that their representatives had been
silenced. Repairs on a sewer were under way and
a liberal supply of paving stones was stacked in

the gutters. These were turned into ammunition, and used to bombard the building. Windows were broken and barricades smashed by the heavy blocks. As was the custom, a farce followed the tragedy. It was not completed. The sounds of volley-firing without brought down the curtain. A greater tragedy than *Macbeth* had been enacted. A company of light artillery had attempted to head off the mob in the Bowery, and had been assailed with a shower of stones, but it cleared the ground, causing the crowd to devote its attention to the infantry. The soldiers under Colonel Abram Duryea attempted to divide the throng, forcing one part to Broadway, the other to the Bowery, in an effort to clear Astor Place. They were resisted with stones and brick-bats. The colonel then ordered a bayonet charge, but the crowd pressed so close that this proved futile and the sheriff commanded the mob to disperse or the soldiers would fire. He was hooted down and more stones thrown, injuring some of the men. A volley was then fired over the heads of the crowd. As no one fell, the leaders cried out: "They have only blank cartridges. Give it to them again!" Brigadier-General Hall then gave the order to fire low. This was done. The mob broke, but made a stand in Lafayette Place and was again fired on. Men fell in all directions and resistance ceased. The audience left the theater by the Eighth Street entrance, and Macready, disguised in a policeman's uniform, mounted a battery horse and escaped.

He was escorted to the suburbs by a group of friends, and left the next day for Boston, whence he soon sailed for Europe. It was an amazing experience and more than trying for a man of threescore and ten.

New York took account of stock the next day. Twenty-three persons, some of them innocent passers-by, were killed or mortally wounded, and fifty reported their injuries. Public opinion was in part ashamed, in part resentful. The resentment manifested itself in a mass meeting, which passed resolutions denouncing the affair as "the most wanton and murderous outrage ever perpetrated in this civilized world" and demanded the indictment of the mayor, recorder and sheriff. Edward Strahan, Michael Walsh and Isaiah Rynders, the chief inciters, were speakers. The militia was kept on guard and at night word was passed that a crowd was coming to raze the offending opera-house. The crowd came, but this time the police were ready. Arrests were made and the gathering dispersed. One bloc raised a barricade on Ninth Street, but this was stormed and taken without bloodshed. By midnight the neighborhood was in order. Thus ended the most amazing incident in the history of the drama in America. Forrest survived until December 12, 1872, when he left this life in the city of his birth.

CHAPTER XXII

DAVID CROCKETT—WHO DIED FOR TEXAS

IN MID-TENNESSEE lies a rough region, less remote from urban contacts than the mountains of the state's western part, but producing a people no less independent and unique, chief of whom in tradition and repute was Colonel David Crockett. The legends about him are many; the facts so far as they can be gathered are romantic, humorous and tragic. Crockett gained his first fame by rough wit—his last by heroism.

"Fashion," he wrote in his autobiography, "is a thing I care mighty little about, except when it happens to run just according to my own notion." With this as a guiding thought he created a fashion of his own by coming into public life clad in a hunting shirt and bearing a rifle, in the use of which he was an adept. Andrew Jackson had put Tennessee very much upon the map of the United States, and Crockett loomed up in some ways as a rude rival. He got into politics as the successful outcome of a squirrel hunt in Heckman County, which was part of a campaign for a seat in the Legislature. Let him tell it: "About this time there was a great squirrel hunt on Duck River, which

313

was among my people. They were to hunt two days; then to meet and count the scalps, and have a big barbecue, and what might be called a tip-top country frolic. The dinner and a general treat was all to be paid for by the party having taken the fewest scalps. I joined one side, taking the place of one of the hunters, and got a gun ready for the hunt. I killed a great many squirrels, and when we counted scalps my party was victorious."

Being a candidate he was called upon to make a speech at the barbecue, something he had never done, though he could play a fiddle and dance a jig. "I got up," he recounts, "and told the people I reckoned they knowed what I had come for, but if not, I could tell them I had come for their votes, and if they didn't watch mighty close, I'd get them too. But the worst of all was that I couldn't tell them anything about government. I tried to speak about something and I cared very little what, until I choked up as bad as if my mouth had been jammed and crammed chock full of dry mush. At last I told them that I was like a fellow I had heard of not long before. He was beating on the head of an empty barrel near the roadside, when a traveller who was passing along, asked him what he was doing that for. The fellow replied that there was some cider in that barrel a few days before, and he was trying to see if there was any there then, but if there was he couldn't get at it. So there had been a little bit of speech in me a while ago, but I believed I couldn't get it out."

The crowd "roared mightily" at this, and Crockett soon became voluble enough in stump-speaking, aided by frequent "horns" of corn whisky, the popular beverage. He beat his competitor with "double the number of votes and nine over."

Thus he started in politics and on the road to fame. He had begun low down in the scale of both living and intelligence. His father was John Crockett, of Scotch-Irish descent; his mother, Rebecca Hawkins, Maryland born. He himself first saw the light, August 17, 1786, on a poor farm at the mouth of Limestone on the Nola-chuc River. There were other children—David the only one heard from. They lived on the high road from the Farther West to Baltimore over the Cumberlands. Drovers and wagoners were always passing by with great herds of cattle or heavy loads of wheat and flour. One of the drovers hired David from his father for six dollars, to help escort four hundred cattle to the sea. He managed to get back after sundry adventures and was sent to school. A fight with another boy on the third day of attendance ended this effort. Fearing punishment, he evaded school for three days, when his father, finding out his truancy, started after him with a hickory rod. David, being the better runner and "winding" his parent, found the high road, and took a job with a drover. He was gone three years, coming back a stalwart lad, with plenty of experience but no other knowledge. "It will be a source of astonishment," he wrote in 1834, "to many who reflect that I am now a member of the American Congress, the most enlightened body of men in the world, that at so advanced an age, the age of fifteen, I did not know the first letter in the book."

The father forgave him and he did penance by working out a paternal debt of thirty-six dollars due a neighbor. This took six months of arduous toil. The next six months were spent working out another of his father's obligations, a forty dollar note held by John Kennedy, a Quaker. So for a year he toiled without reward, save as he enjoyed the smiles of the Quaker's niece. She was engaged to another, and this spoiled his romance. His love was so hot "it mighty nigh to burst my boilers."

Discerning that his ignorance made him unattractive to the fair sex, he went to work for the Quaker's son, putting in four days of schooling and doing chores, and three days' work a week to pay for it. In six months he could read the primer and write his name—slow progress. Then his "schooling" stopped for life. He had fallen in love again—with a rifle and a pretty girl. She wouldn't have him, but like all warm lovers, he tried again with another, was accepted and married. The mother-in-law gave the couple some stock, and David began his struggles to get a living on a rented farm. It did not pay. He migrated from one county to another, settling at last

in Franklin. When the Creek War broke he volunteered to fight Indians. He made the campaign
but escaped any special distinction, and hired a
substitute to finish out his time. His wife died,
leaving three children, and he soon wedded a widow who had lost her poorer half in the War of
1812. Then after some exploring of new lands he
settled at Shoal Creek. There was no law in the
neighborhood and he became a home-made magistrate. His section was then added to Giles County by the Legislature, and David began to be
heard from. "My judgments," he remarks, "were
never appealed from, and if they had been they
would have stuck like wax, as I gave my decisions
on the principles of common justice and honesty
between man and man, and relied on natural born
sense, and not on law learning to guide me; for
I had never read a page of a law book in all my
life."

Before getting into the Legislature he had
been elected colonel of the local militia regiment,
and so came properly by the title he ever after
wore, even though the regiment "mustered" but
once a year, and was then hardly sober enough to
drill. He was prominent in the Legislature despite
his ignorance and became a coming man.

Financial ill luck spoiled his political success.
A freshet swept away a powder mill and distillery
he had erected on borrowed money. This left him
pretty blue. He had the right sort of wife, however, who said: "Just pay up, as long as you have

a bit's worth in the world; and then everybody will
be satisfied and we will scuffle for more." On
this he comments: "This was just such a talk as
I wanted to hear, for a man's wife can hold him
devilish uneasy, if she begins to scold, and fret,
and perplex him, at a time when he has a full load
for a rail car on his mind already. I therefore gave
up all I had and took a bran-fire new start."

This determined him to make another move
and he picked out land on the Obion, seven miles
from the nearest house. Here he "slapped up"
a cabin, and provisioning it with four barrels of
meal, one of salt and ten gallons of whisky, began
life over again. He killed six buck elk in one day
and was provided with meat for a long pull. Land
was cleared, corn planted and after the crops were
gathered he hunted for winter stores—bear and
deer. This was in 1822.

He again stood for the Legislature in a new
district and beat two opponents in the running.
His first antagonism to Jackson followed when
he voted against him for member of the United
States Senate. "I let the people know early as
then," he said, "that I wouldn't take a collar
around my neck with the letters engraved on it
'My dog, Andrew Jackson.'" This attitude led
to the colonel's "standing" for Congress against
Colonel Adam R. Alexander. Cotton was twenty-
five cents a pound and Alexander laid it to a tariff
which he had supported. This Crockett could not
gainsay, though he was beaten by only two votes.

I am happy to acknowledge this to be
the only correct likeness that has been
Taken of me.
David Crockett

Taking a back seat for two years Crockett operated flatboats, farmed and hunted bears, killing forty-seven in one season. When the next election came around cotton had dropped to six and eight cents a pound. He decided to tackle Alexander again, and did. General William Arnold was a third candidate. In the three-cornered fight Crockett won. This was in 1827. Though opposed to Jackson in Congress he won another term in 1829. His antagonism to the president grew during the second term, and when he ran for a third, the administration forces were concentrated against him, supporting William Fitzgerald. As Crockett put it, he "was hunted like a wild varmint," and defeated. He survived this setback and came back strong, making good use of the dog collar and winning a seat in the Twenty-third Congress by three thousand five hundred majority. The victory made him a more than conspicuous figure, while his sayings and doings were everywhere quoted, especially this couplet, to which his memory still clings:

"I leave this rule for others when I'm dead,
Be always sure you're right—then go ahead!"

With all of his lack of education, Colonel Crockett became rather facile with his pen. His picturesque vocabulary stood him in great stead as an orator, while humor and homespun stories illuminated his speech. He was able to transfer much of this to the printed page and writing his autobiography in 1834, it attained a large sale; indeed, was often reprinted, earning the distinction of a London edition. Martin Van Buren was in line as Jackson's successor in the presidency, with that stern statesman's collar firmly riveted around his neck. Crockett wrote a scurrilous "life" of the Kinderhook fox which was popular, but did not serve to defeat him.

During the Van Buren campaign the colonel made his celebrated "tour" through the East, being received with great acclaim by the anti-Jacksonians of Philadelphia, New York and Boston. He wrote an account of it that, with its backwoods observations on men and things, pleased the public. So wide became the fame of the bear-hunter that Ben Hardin published a Crockett Almanac in Nashville, which survived annually for many years after the demise of its namesake.

Quite naturally these diversions kept him away from his district. He banked upon his majority to keep him in Congress as long as he wished to stay, but miscounted human fickleness and the political power of Jackson, who was something of a hunter himself, but with men, not bears, as game. Adam Huntsman opposed Crockett and won by two hundred and thirty majority. The despised Van Buren also got in. The pearly gates of politics shut themselves suddenly in Crockett's face. He was filled with bitterness and despair. Life had been very agreeable for him in Washington. He was the center of admiring groups and the foes of Jackson had made much of him. As he expressed his feelings: "My appetite for politics was at one time just about as sharp set as a saw mill, but late events has given me something of a surfeit—more than I could well digest." But he was "gratified at having spoken the truth" to the people of his district "regardless of consequences."

"I would not," he continued, "be compelled to bow down to the idol [Jackson] for a seat in Congress during life. I have never known what it was to sacrifice my own judgment to gratify my party, and I have no doubt of the time being close at hand when I will be rewarded for letting my tongue speak what my heart thinks. I have suffered myself to be politically sacrificed to save my country from ruin and disgrace; and if I am never again elected, I will have the gratification of knowing I have done my duty. This much I say in relation to the manner in which my downfall was effected, and in laying it before the public—I take the responsibility. I may add in the words of the man in the play: 'Crockett's occupation is gone.' "

Indeed, it was. Public life had become to him the air in which he breathed. He could not rest content in the dull country until it became again time to test the hustings. Like other statesmen he sought adventure for the two years in which he would have to lie fallow while the hated Huntsman filled his seat. He had opposed tariff and favored Biddle's Bank of the United States. Jackson had wrecked Biddle's money monopoly in the interest of the people, but had made a huge mistake. He detested the men behind the bank, who were corrupt, and had the great Daniel Webster on their pay-roll. The bank itself was needed and its destruction was a national calamity. Crockett sized it up well in discussing the "government and its succession" at a meeting of his constituents after his defeat. "I told them," he said, "to keep a sharp lookout for the depositor, for it requires an eye as insinuating as a dissecting knife to see what safety there is in placing one million of the public funds in some little country shaving shop with no more than $100,000 capital. The bank, we will just suppose, without being too particular, is in the neighborhood of some of the public lands, when speculators who have everything to gain and nothing to lose, swarm like crows about carrion. They buy United States' lands upon a large scale, get discounts from the aforesaid shaving shop, which are made upon a large scale also, upon the United States funds; they pay the whole purchase money with these discounts and get a clear title to the land; so that when the shaving shop comes to make a Flemish account of its transactions the government will discover that it has not only lost the original deposits, but a large body of the public lands to boot."

The orgy of "wildcat" banking that followed quite justified Crockett, but he was not to be alive to enjoy the vindication he deserved.

Events were astir in the great Southwest. Texas, which Aaron Burr in bitterness of heart, such as Crockett suffered, had sought to take as an empire of his own, was in revolt against Mexico. The adventurous and out-of-luck were flocking thither to support Samuel Houston, another broken-hearted Tennessean who had taken the lead for independence. The movement was one of the purest kind of filibustering, the justification being that there was more land than the backward greasers could or ever would use. Hence take it for the benefit of the enterprising!

Mexico had, however, a leader, Antonio Lopez de Santa Anna. She had also men and money. The rebels were scantily supplied with both. Their difficulties seemed insuperable and therefore all the more attractive to the daring. Many Tennesseans had joined Houston and here Crockett determined to turn his steps, undertaking the journey in this fashion: "I dressed myself in a clean hunting shirt, put on a new fox-skin cap with the tail hanging behind, took hold of my rifle Betsey, which all the world knows was presented to me by the.patriotic citizens of Philadelphia, and thus equipped, I started off with a heavy heart for Mill's Point to take a steamboat down the Mississippi, and go ahead in a new world."

He was picked up by the *Mediterranean*, one of the biggest boats on the river, and found a large company on board, many of whom he knew and not a few of whom were bound on the same wild

venture. The journey down-stream became a sort
of triumphant progress. Many stops were made,
at which the colonel was placed on exhibition. At
Vicksburg he met with a great reception, the distinguished Sargent S. Prentiss being one of the
committee that bade him welcome. At Helena,
Arkansas, leading citizens of the South came on
board and subscribed eighty thousand dollars to
help Texas, calling it the Crockett Fund. The
donors included John Slidell, famous afterward as
Captain Charles Wilkes' captive in the Mason-
Slidell affair that nearly brought on war with England; John R. Preston, S. S. Prentiss and Colonel
J. M. Estill. The money, it was specified, "to be
used for the purposes of aiding our countrymen
now in the field, and to be further used in recruiting five companies of two hundred fifty men each."
Slidell, then a lawyer in New Orleans, was made
treasurer. The full sum was paid in and used.

The Texas conflict was long drawn out and
desultory, and the patriots, as the Americans
termed themselves, were frequently defeated and
occasionally massacred by their Mexican opponents. The strategic standpoint became San Antonio de Bexar, as it was called. Houston was
in the field, more occupied with evading, than
fighting, his enemies, when Santa Anna concentrated for a drive against the little town. It was
defended by a small body of exceptional men,
numbering in all one hundred fifty-three, commanded by Colonel William B. Travis, occupy-

ing an ancient public building called the Alamo. Probably a more notable body of fighters never came together, either in personnel or leadership. The men were the cream of desperate adventurers, many of whom had come to Texas as an alternative to hell, and Travis had for lieutenants, James Bowie, inventor of the celebrated knife, and David Crockett.

News that Santa Anna was concentrating on San Antonio reached the garrison early on Washington's Birthday, February 22, 1836. The people of the place, about one thousand two hundred in all, were not in great sympathy with their defenders and Houston could afford no relief. Travis was therefore compelled to do his best alone. There was no way of protecting the town itself as it lay open to the plain. Its defenders might have taken refuge in flight, but would probably have been cut off by the numerous Mexican cavalry. They determined, however, to make a stand in the Alamo, whose heavy walls were deemed impervious to bullets, and from embrasures in which they could take toll upon their assailants, as the event proved. They had scarcely stowed themselves and their supplies in the building before Santa Anna took possession of the town. His troops carried a red flag, which was interpreted as meaning no quarter. The defenders asked none. By afternoon they were beleaguered, and on being summoned to surrender, replied with a cannon shot, answering at the same time the

Mexican warning that all would be put to the sword. Travis contrived to send word to Colonel James W. Fannin at Goliad that he was besieged and asked for help, which failed to come, but thirty men crept in from Gonzales. Thus strengthened, Travis, on February twenty-fourth, issued a proclamation, reading:

"I am besieged by a thousand Mexicans with Santa Anna at their head. On their arrival, they sent and demanded an unconditional surrender of the garrison under my command, or we would all be put to the sword indiscriminately. I answered their demand with a cannon shot. I have sustained a bombardment and heavy cannonade for the last twenty-four hours. I have not lost a man. Fellow citizens, assist me now, for the good of all; for, if they are flushed with victory, they will be much harder to conquer. I shall defend myself to the last extremity, and die as becomes a soldier. I never intend to retreat or surrender. Victory or death!"

This was no idle bombast, as the besiegers soon found to their cost. The "fellow citizens" did not respond. Santa Anna threw up earthworks to defend his rear and began a regular siege. Bowie was ill in bed and could be of no service. The strain fell on Travis and Crockett. The strong walls around the Alamo stood a heavy bombardment on February twenty-seventh. The building itself then became an object of destruction. A gun was placed to range it and Crockett killed the cannoneer as he was about to touch the match from a vantage on the roof. In swift succession he killed five men, each as he attempted to fire the piece. This silenced it for the moment. Finding it vain to reduce the stronghold by cannon, Santa Anna determined to take it by assault, and brought four thousand men to the task on the morning of Sunday, March 6, 1836. The offensive began at four A.M., or just at dawn. By six o'clock General Castrillon's division effected an entrance into the courtyard of the Alamo, and began to place scaling ladders against the building itself while their bands played the *Dequelo,* which meant death to the defenders.

Heavy barricades of sand-bags guarded the windows, and breastworks of the same lined the roof. These served to check the assault until men with ladders were under the shelter of the wall, and then forced to climb to the windows by the drawn swords of their officers. Certainly the despised greasers were no cowards on this occasion. Santa Anna himself directed the operations. It was not long before they gained the interior. Travis and those who were alive and unwounded, concentrated in the chapel, after fighting from room to room. One apartment contained fourteen wounded in beds. Upon these the Mexicans turned a shower of grape. All were killed, but from their couches they finished forty assailants. Bowie, with a last effort, rose from his cot and used his famous knife for the last time. He and his assailants died together.

Finally Travis, Crockett and four followers were the only men of the Texan force alive. General Castrillon, in person, called upon them to surrender, promising them their lives. While they stood parleying, Santa Anna issued orders that all should be ended. A volley closed this finest of fights between men.

The bodies of the Texans were carted to a field outside the town and burned to ashes. According to current accounts more than one thousand Mexican soldiers lost their lives in the assault.

A woman, wife of Lieutenant Dickinson, and an eighteen-year old Mexican servant girl escaped the carnage, but not a single defender saved his life. "Thermopylæ had its messenger of defeat," said Senator Thomas H. Benton. "The Alamo had none."

Crockett had reached his fiftieth year; Bowie was forty-six.

So the colonel's strange career ended as he would have preferred it, amid a battle against awful odds with no dog collar around his neck, and the broken barrel of "Betsey" in his hand.

THE END

C.G. Finney

Mary Baker G. Eddy

Brigham Young

Israel Putnam

Tecumseh

Martin Scott

Joseph Smith

Ethan Allen

John S. Mosby

David Crockett

Lt. General N.B. Forrest, C.S.A.